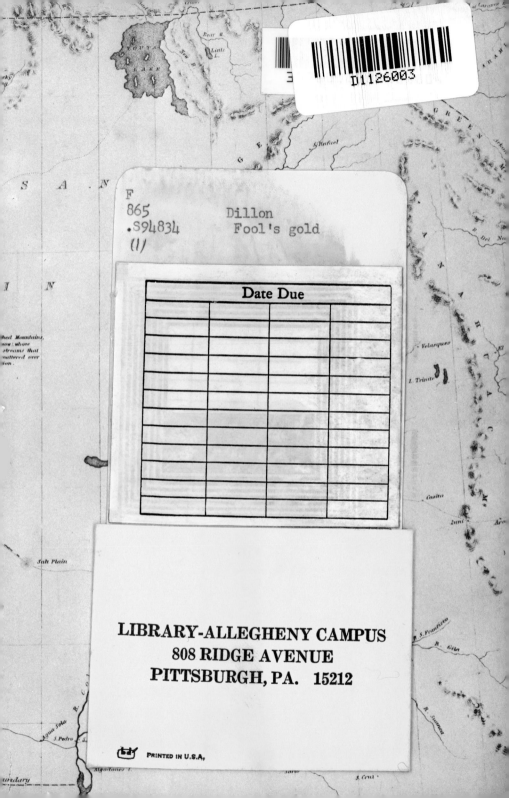

FOOL'S GOLD

Books by Richard Dillon:

The Legend of Grizzly Adams

Meriwether Lewis

Embarcadero

The Gila Trail

Shanghaiing Days

California Trail Herd

The Hatchet Men

FOOL'S GOLD

The Decline and Fall of Captain John Sutter of California

by RICHARD DILLON

Coward-McCann, Inc. NEW YORK

To
LAWRENCE CLARK POWELL
Archbibliophile of Malibu

"The history of a country is best told in a record of the lives of its people."

—MACAULAY

CONTENTS

13

CONTENTS

Illustrations follow pages 128 and 288

INTRODUCTION

CALIFORNIA—that is, American California, as distinguished from the sleepy province of Hispanic times—has been saddled with a curious and puzzling founding father, Captain John A. Sutter. His partisans have hailed him as the Saint of the Sacramento River; his detractors would have you believe he was a scoundrel. The truth, of course, lurks somewhere in between.

Certainly, Sutter was no George Washington. In fact, as state founders go, he was not even of the stature of Stephen Austin or Brigham Young, and it is no surprise to astute Californians that he is not immortalized in the marble splendor of Statuary Hall. He was a deceptively simple man—neither a genius, a hero, nor a giant. But, viewed at close range, he emerges from history as more than an ambitious Swiss adventurer in the Far West. For, in truth, Sutter was a key figure in the drama of westward expansion.

Sutter was mercurial, swinging erratically from mood to mood and altering markedly in outlook and purpose with the passing of a mere ten years. He was an ordinary man but one who did extraordinary things in a savage wilderness. Unlike his European contemporaries, he was not content to dream of the romantic American West; he remade it in his own design. Sutter came to the farthest American frontier as a bankrupt and bad debtor who had abandoned his family in his flight from a police warrant. As a colonizer, he has become a legend. Just five years after he erected a grass shack near the Sacramento River, he was master of Sutter's Fort and New Helvetia, the governor's right-hand man, and the most powerful individual in all California.

But it is as a visionary, as much as a builder, that John Sutter deserves to be remembered, and yet it is in exactly this role that historians and biographers have most neglected him. The latter have been preoccupied with the dramatic story of his fall from power, in one of the great tragedies—or, at least, ironies—of American history. Sutter's success as the preeminent colonizer of California was crowned with disaster when the Gold Rush, which he triggered, utterly destroyed him and his empire.

Before Sutter passed from the scene, he made his mark on California, a mark that can never be erased. But more, his dreams of California as a great agricultural and commercial empire, rather than as a mere source of raw minerals for the vigorously growing United States, ultimately came to pass. Yet it came too late for the empire builder who pioneered in shipping, trading, large-scale wheat growing, irrigation, lumbering, milling, mining and fur trapping, who began the state's fisheries, distilleries, factories and tanneries, and who restored cattle raising to its former greatness—when all his rivals were content merely to rip California's wealth from the mines and then move on.

RICHARD DILLON

Mill Valley
March 1967

16

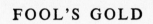

FOOL'S GOLD

CHAPTER I

———— ∿ ————

THE FUGITIVE

A CHILL wind swept down off the Sierra Nevada on New Year's Day, 1845, piercing the bright, thin, sunlight of California's Sacramento Valley and tugging at the Mexican tricolor flying over the adobe bastions of New Helvetia. The sudden, premonitory roll of a snare drum from the parade ground inside the walls of the fortress startled meadowlarks into erratic flight. Shortly, the drum roll was echoed by the skirling of a fife and the tramp of many feet through the main gate of Sutter's Fort. Onto the floodplain, flat as a billiard table, marched an army. Although small in numbers, it awed the circle of Indians who witnessed its departure. It was, in fact, the most powerful force mounted in California in all the 303 years since Juan Cabrillo claimed the frontier for His Most Catholic Majesty.

Leading the 225-odd men on a southerly course toward Mount Diablo, bulking hugely on the otherwise low-lying horizon, was a forty-two-year-old officer in the showy uniform of the Mexican Army. He looked to be a model soldier, in the very prime of life. His garb, his erect carriage, dignified bearing and military burnsides all suggested one of Napoleon's marshals. Only the closest

19

inspection would have revealed tell-tale signs of softness, a flushed complexion and a fleshiness heralding a corpulence and passivity worthy of a Bernese burgomaster.

In fact, the officer *was* Swiss, not Mexican, and in a manner of speaking he was a burgomaster, too. He was Captain John Augustus Sutter, master of the frontier settlement of New Helvetia and already a legend in his own era. Behind him paced two Negro drummers, a fifer, and an Indian boy drummer. Following them rode Sutter's shock troops, some eighty-five hard-looking men led by Capt. John Gantt. The commander of these mounted riflemen was a real soldier, although he had been ignominiously dismissed from the U.S. service for payroll frauds. Gantt's men were in the variety of costumes common to the frontier—serges, buckskins and flannels. Because of the bewildering array of nationalities mustered in Sutter's foreign legion, Gantt labeled the unit "The Heterogeneous Detachment." His lieutenants were Americans, James Hudspeth and James Coates.

Next in the order of march came Sutter's Indian troops. Capt. Ernest Rufus led ninety-seven privates, dressed neatly enough in hand-me-down Russian uniforms. The captain shouted his commands in English, Spanish and pidgin Moquelumne as well as in his native German. Keeping the redskinned grenadiers in soldierly formation were Orderly Sergeant Democrates and Ensign Homobono, both Indians, and Lieutenants Jacob Dür (alias Green), a German like Rufus, and Chief Rufino of the Moquelumne tribe.

Sutter's artillery consisted of the fine brass fieldpiece which he had obtained from the Russians at Fort Ross, as well as two of his ships' cannon, removed from the defenses of Sutter's Fort. An oxcart doubled as gun carriage and caisson for the naval artillery. The battery was served by ten artillerymen. Sutter's own staff followed on the heels of the gunners. It consisted of Dr. John Townsend and John Sinclair, aides-de-camp; Quartermaster Jasper O'Farrell; Commissary Samuel J. Hensley; and Field Secretary John Bidwell. With Sutter and his suite traveled two Indian servants and one Hawaiian, Kukui; his courier and express rider, an old associate from New Mexico days, Pablo Gutiérrez; and the prominent *ranchero* of the Sacramento Valley, Juan Vaca. The commander and his staff were escorted by a squad of nine cavalrymen commanded by Corp. Juan Elizalde.

Among the riflemen were some of the doughtiest frontiersmen ever to hit the Pacific Slope—old Caleb Greenwood, the legendary mountain man, and his two sons, John and Britton; Michel Laframboise, former leader of Hudson's Bay Company trapping parties in California; Isaac Graham, the fiery focus of an international incident of 1841 which rocked California; Ezekiel Merritt, destined to be a leader in the Bear Flag Revolt; Peter Lassen, the mountaineer; and Moses Carson, Kit Carson's brother.

Perhaps, as he rode southward from his adobe castle on the American River, Sutter mused on his career, now, although he did not know it, at its climax, and thought back to his obscure beginnings. . . .

Long before cock-crow on the morning of February 15, 1803, Johann August Sutter was born in the village of Kandern in Germany's margravate of Baden, thirteen miles north of Basel, Switzerland. His father, Johann Jakob Sutter, Jr., was the manager of the hamlet's paper mill. His mother, born Christine Wilhelmina Stober, was a pastor's daughter from Grenzach, just up the Rhine. Although Kandern was German, the mill, like the Sutter family, was Swiss.

As John Sutter grew up, Napoleon was marching and countermarching, and Austrian armies invaded Switzerland at Basel and Schaffhausen. Small wonder that, for the rest of his life, Sutter dreamed of military glory and ached for travel and adventure. But for all the hussars galloping on the dusty roads of Baden and the artillerymen thundering across the Rhine on the Basel bridge, life in Kandern remained pure tedium. It was not until Sutter was fifteen years old, sent away to school in or near Neuchâtel, that he escaped the village's galling confines. Although Neuchâtel had long been a Prussian possession, it had never lost its strong French flavor, and it turned young Sutter into an ardent Francophile.

But the small city lacked gaiety and excitement, and many times Sutter stared longingly across the lake toward Mont Blanc, the central Alps and the Bernese Oberland, wondering if he would ever travel beyond the mountains which walled in his world so narrowly.

When John Sutter left school it was not for gay *Wanderjahre;* there was no money for that. But neither did he return to Kandern. Instead, he traveled to Basel, where he became an apprentice in the printing, publishing and bookselling firm of Emanuel Thurneysen. Basel's ambience delighted Sutter's free and picaresque spirit. It straddled the busy Rhine whose waters, mingled with those of the salt sea, washed upon the beaches of the fabled New World. Like almost every other youth in Europe, Sutter was intrigued by America, its opportunities, its adventures, its wide plains and its painted savages. But when he had served out his term, Sutter found himself poorer than ever and, instead of vagabonding, he was forced to plunge back into the constricted world of trade as a mere clerk. His romantic adventuring was vicarious, and his hedonistic motto of the moment—*"Aime, bois, et chante!"*—was largely wishful thinking.

Sutter had an eye for the girls and it almost proved his undoing. He became infatuated with Annette Dübeld of Burgdorf, threw up his job and followed her to her home town, where he became a grocery clerk. When he scratched his name on a storage-room windowpane with a diamond which he could not really afford, he spelled it "Sutter" but he was already beginning to affect a French style. For a brief time, he gallicized his name to J. Auguste Soutter in order to impress the *Schweizerdeutsch*-speaking customers and, of course, Annette.

Sutter pressed his suit all too successfully. In the summer of 1826, he hurriedly petitioned the elders of his legal home, the town of Rünenberg, for permission to marry Miss Annette Dübeld. On the day after their October 24, 1826, wedding, a son

22

was born to Annette and John Sutter and named for his father. At the age of twenty-three, Sutter, the vicarious adventurer and wanderer, found himself thoroughly trapped by an impetuous love affair, a hasty marriage, and an unwanted and unforeseen family. The ring of misfortune, as he saw it, tightened inexorably as Sutter demonstrated his complete lack of business acumen. His marriage, while joining him to an old and prominent family, did little to impress the leading citizenry because of its hasty circumstances. Sutter remained an outsider, a victim not so much of scandal as of the caste system peculiar to the Alpine democracy, which left him disenfranchised and powerless to rise to the station he was convinced he deserved. Nevertheless, Sutter worked hard to make a success of himself in Burgdorf. He bought a house on the main street and gave up clerking. The upper story became a home for him and his family; the ground floor he devoted to a dry-goods and drapery shop of his own, Johann August Sutter & Company.

Perhaps to compensate for his lack of success at business and to forget his swiftly deteriorating marriage, Sutter threw himself into a parttime military career, volunteering for the reserve corps of the Canton of Berne in 1828. Soldiering, Sutter discovered, was his cup of tea. By July 15, when he completed his course of instruction, he was appointed a second under-lieutenant in the 1st Center Company of the 3d Battalion of the infantry reserve. On March 16, 1831, Sutter advanced to the rank of first under-lieutenant of the 2d Center Company of the same battalion.

While his military career prospered, Sutter's gambler's temperament led him to overextend himself in business. When bust followed boom, Johann August Sutter & Company was forced to settle with its creditors at twenty-five percent of the amount due. Next, his trusted partner, Seelhofer, took advantage of Sutter's absence on the road selling goods to run off with half the firm's stock. Sutter was forced to sell his building to his mother-in-law for 11,000 francs to pay off his more pressing debts. He continued

23

to live there with his family, as a tenant, but the humiliation rankled.

Sutter was not lazy. He worked hard to save the business, but in order not to lose face he continued to live beyond his means. He always loved stylish clothes and could not do without fine books. He paid twenty-five *livres,* which he could ill afford, for the complete works of Sir Walter Scott. In the meantime, he had fathered five children—a large family for a bankrupt with expensive tastes. Relations with his wife and her mother worsened, harsh words were exchanged, and Sutter's world began to disintegrate.

Annette Dübeld Sutter was a handsome young woman but narrow-minded and domineering where Sutter was a free and easy-going spirit, rude where he was chivalrous and charming. Photographs of Mrs. Sutter show her with a mouth like a cicatrice above a square-set jaw worthy of a Marine sergeant. She saw herself as shackled to a spendthrift, penniless, ne'erdowell. The crisis for the marriage came when her mother tired of supplying John with rent-free quarters and sold the house out from under him. For Sutter, this blow was tantamount to abject ruin. It meant not only bankruptcy but also debtor's prison. The only thing that had stood between him and his ravenous creditors was Mama Dübeld's good credit. When she withdrew it, the business crashed around his ears.

Sutter swore that he would never see the inside of a debtor's cell. His spirit had been in a jail of sorts for too long already. He chose French leave over prison. Secretly, he put together a little cash. On May 8 or 9, 1834, he abandoned his wife and children along with 51,183 francs in debts and a bare 15,000 francs in goods and credits. Giving America as his destination, he somehow secured a passport on the thirteenth of the month and vanished. Sutter may or may not have deceived his wife about his intentions. It appears that she helped him make his escape. In any case, he wrote her from Le Havre.

When the news of the bad debtor's flight spread, bankruptcy

proceedings were instituted against him and the wreckage of his firm. Sutter's chief creditors secured a warrant for his arrest on June 12, 1834, from the chief of police of Berne. After explaining Sutter's guilt and flight, the chief ended the document: "This formal request is issued and addressed to all Honorable Authorities of Police, to arrest, upon meeting him, and safely secure said fugitive Sutter, to relieve him of all drafts, cash and other valuables as he may carry on him and to notify the authorities here so that they may be able to start extradition proceedings against his person or recover his assets."

Thus, John Sutter fled by night toward the Promised Land of America. Although his mother-in-law died only six months later, his decision proved the right one. Sutter was totally out of place in the stultifying conformity of a Swiss town like Burgdorf. He was cut out for games of greater stakes in life than counterminding in a dry-goods shop. Annette Sutter's share of the Widow Dübeld's estate of 25,000 francs was, of course, confiscated as a bond against John's obligations. She and the children were forced to move to her grandparents' home where she eked out a meager existence, waiting for word from John to come and join him. For sixteen years she waited, living largely on the charity of her grandparents and her sisters, plus what little she could earn. If Sutter grieved for his family's hardship, he said little or nothing about it. He was probably so ashamed of his failure that he repressed all knowledge of their plight.

Sutter drew a veil over this period of his life. He did not choose to look back, but, from this point on, faced ever westward. The thirty-one-year-old fugitive, his head full of romantic notions of America as the vast and fertile garden of the world, sailed from Le Havre with the intention of forging a new life for himself in the Far West.

CHAPTER II

THE SANTA FE TRADER

SUTTER landed in New York in July 1834 and set out immediately for the West, determined to put as much distance as possible between himself and the Swiss authorities. He meant to lose himself in the wilderness and to find the paradise which the Swiss writer, Gottfried Duden, had described. This romantic disciple of Rousseau had extolled the parklike beauty of wilderness Missouri and celebrated the great variety of climate in the West, neglecting to mention that one often enjoyed the whole climatic gamut in a single day. As his bankruptcy record stated plainly that he took all his clothes and books with him when he fled Switzerland, it is likely that Sutter not only read the book but took it with him to America. Perhaps he whiled away the long shipboard hours between Le Havre and New York by reading Duden. The author's description of Missouri, which he compared to the fertile Nile River Valley, could not fail to fascinate the impressionable Sutter.

Sutter always flatly stated that his object in migrating to America was to become a farmer. (His natural reluctance to refer to the impetus of a police warrant can be forgiven.) There is no doubt that the paradise described by Duden was his destination. The bottom lands of the Missouri and Femme Osage rivers already were producing corn, peaches, pears, apples and wine grapes under the husbandry of German émigrés. An enterprising young man like Sutter could make his fortune there.

Sutter left New York with four new friends, two Germans and two Frenchmen. They traveled westward through Indiana to Ohio, where their paths parted. This break-up, probably at Cincinnati, was deliberate and necessary, since Sutter realized that "not one of us would learn English while we were together." After a stay of two or three months, Sutter left Ohio and headed for Missouri and its German colony. When he arrived in St. Louis, he naturally put up at the Hotel Schwyzerland on Front Street. There, he met another greenhorn, Johann August Laufkotter, from Westphalia. Laufkotter, who became Sutter's roommate, eventually acted a bitter Boswell to him as well.

About the time that Sutter and Laufkotter were welcomed into the German Club of St. Louis, a flashy stranger appeared from Prairie du Chien, Wisconsin, claiming to be an ex-colonel in the Prussian service. In fact, he hinted, he was nothing less than the former adjutant of the Crown Prince of Prussia. He cadged drinks and meals and borrowed cash from members, even nicking Sutter —who could not afford it—for $50. The "Adjutant" was finally unmasked as an impostor and jailed. According to Laufkotter, Sutter's $50 proved to be a good investment; he claimed that Sutter studied the success of the fraudulent colonel and appropriated what he thought might fit profitably into his own repertoire. Certainly, Sutter began increasingly to play the role of ex-officer and gentleman. He looked the part—slim, handsome, dapper and military, sporting a pair of soldierly sideburns. Eminently well read for the frontier, he began to concoct a more gentlemanly past than harsh history had provided him and to enrich his rather sparse military career by dipping deeply into his imagination. Sutter wore this myth like a new skin for the rest of his life. He so lived the role of Swiss officer that he came to believe it true.

Gustav Koerner, later a good friend of Abraham Lincoln and United States minister to Spain, recalled Sutter during his Missouri days. "By dint of his vivacity, his gentle and winning manners and his manly personality, he soon assembled a circle of friends about him." He lived in both St. Louis and St. Charles. In 1834 and again in 1836 he leased property, the French Tavern, on St. Charles Road, and on August 21, 1838, he formally declared before the proper authorities his intention to become a citizen of the United States. On the document he gave his correct birthplace, Baden, but did not specify the town, and he falsified his age, giving it as forty-five when he was only thirty-five years old, perhaps to throw a little dust on his already cold trail.

The Prairie du Chien impostor had sold Sutter and Laufkotter on the idea of entering the Santa Fe trade. With his unmasking, Laufkotter pulled out, but Sutter determined to go ahead with his plans. St. Charles had not turned out to be the pastoral paradise he had envisioned. "I did not like Missouri," he said later. "It was too cold in the winter and I did not think I could make anything —no market and few people there. It was the Indian frontier." Via Laufkotter and a Creole friend, Sutter got in touch with several French Santa Fe traders of St. Louis.

Sutter sold out his Missouri interests, engaged six men and joined the Frenchmen for the 1835 season. Still too poor to outfit even a single wagon properly, he sacrificed some of his wardrobe to buy trade goods. He also borrowed a little money from Laufkotter. He found cheap trinkets and pistols and German students' jackets in a St. Louis pawnshop to add to his stock of goods.

At last Sutter saw the real West. He liked what he saw. Although he fell ill on the trip to Santa Fe and spent most of his time there flat on his back, his little hockshop investment reaped him a profit and bolstered his confidence. He was back in Missouri by October 1835, brimming over with enthusiasm and optimism. He showed off his seven fine New Mexico mules and put a barrel of red El Paso wine at the service of his friends. After pasturing his little herd for several weeks on the farm of a German widow, he sold them and freely spent the profits.

Pastor Friedrich Muench, a member of Missouri's considerable German colony, claimed that Sutter was beginning to describe himself now not only as a former Swiss officer but as a veteran of the king of France's Swiss Guards who took part in the July Revolution of 1830. Laufkotter, on the other hand, was inclined to believe that the courtesy title of "Captain," by which Sutter was addressed, was due to his penchant for treating his cronies—and strangers—to drinks and regaling one and all with his adventures on the Santa Fe Trail. Laufkotter noted that local farmers thought Sutter "a capital fellow" and were willing enough to address him by the title, which appeared to fit him like a glove.

Sutter's barroom propaganda efforts were effective. He was able to borrow money from farmers, then redeem his notes by further borrowing from German friends in St. Louis and St. Charles. He had little difficulty in organizing another party to take part in the 1836 Santa Fe trade. Pastor Muench remembered, "His engaging nature and his art of persuasion soon succeeded in uniting with him a number of our German friends . . . who failed to derive satisfaction from life in the primeval wilderness." Sutter finally won the title he was affecting by being named head of the expedition. Growled Laufkotter, sourly, "We elected Sutter captain, a most generous act as he had no stake in the concern."

Sixteen men pooled their money in a common treasury. One German came all the way from New Orleans to join Sutter's company, contributing $1,300 to the pot. Sutter gambled with this sum by putting all of it into toys (a bad speculation) and purchased $14,000 worth of trade goods, using credit for about half the stock. He carefully packed the goods in the beds of four ox-drawn wagons and set the date for departure. When the day came, Sutter's partners were shocked to learn from him that there was nothing left in the treasury. The wagons and oxen had taken every remaining dollar. Sutter saved the day, however, by convincing someone of the sure profits to be made from the expedition and accepted $100 as an advance on a share of the company's stock.

The order to march was given, and the four wagons creaked and groaned their way to Marthasville, thirty-five miles from St. Charles. There, Sutter called a halt to reveal that he already had gone through the $100. He managed to wheedle another $200 through the security of a friend and, after greasing the wagon wheels and wetting the throats of his companions to bolster morale, he gave the command to get under way again. The wagons rolled into Independence in good style, where Sutter had another surprise for his companions. On April 15, before setting out from St. Charles, he had shipped a load of goods there by steamer. A big bill for freight and storage charges awaited them, which had to be paid by Sutter—who assessed each grumbling member of his company. To their further annoyance, they discovered that they were already out of meat and flour. But once more Sutter relied on his persuasive powers. Through a German friend, he secured flour from a miller and corn meal from a farmer, plus some bacon and other foodstuffs. Onward rolled the wagons, now joined by freight teams hired in Independence, at thirty-five cents per pound of cargo, to carry that which would not fit in the wagonbeds.

Sutter led his men along the time-honored route from Independence to Round Grove at the headwaters of Cedar Creek, some thirty-five miles out, then across the open prairie to the troublesome Narrows, the ridge pushing up between the Kansas and Osage rivers. For years it had borne a bad name because of its quagmires, which sucked at wagon wheels and sometimes swallowed them right up to the hubs. Sutter probably double-teamed his vehicles to get them across the bogs before heading on for the upper Osage drainage.

Quarrels, fights and even duels enlivened an otherwise routine journey. Most of the young men had been soldiers in Europe, and they practiced cavalry drill, as much for entertainment as for vigilance or training. Laufkotter, who accompanied Sutter, re-called, "When we asked Mr. Sutter to join us, he always refused, saying he never practiced such drill." Sutter's reluctance may have been inspired by concern for his lofty station as captain of the company. Or it may simply have reflected his knowledge that he was not much of a horseman. Laufkotter, jealous of the Swiss, viewed it in the worst light and sneered, "We clearly saw that our Captain was not accustomed to weapons and had probably never handled any."

One hundred and fifty miles of travel brought the company to Council Grove. Here, on the border between the true prairie and the drier, shorter-grassed plains, lay a half-mile-wide strip of timber bordering the Neosho River and Council Grove Creek. Sutter and his comrades camped under the elms, hickories and ash trees to await the arrival of other wagons. Sutter was then content to surrender his authority to a wagonmaster or caravan captain. A Captain Carr was elected for the long train, which Sutter estimated at 80 wagons and Laufkotter at 120. Sutter's party was one of the weakest segments of the train, with only four wagons for fifteen men where most traders had a wagon apiece.

Carr formed up the caravan and pushed on to a campsite at Diamond Springs, often called the Diamond of the Plains, where a fountain poured water, clear as crystal, into a handsome brook. Beyond Diamond Springs, the days began to assume an unchanging pattern. After an early breakfast, Carr would give the command "Catch up!" Sutter and the other wagoners would hurry to harness mules and to yoke the oxen. Then came Carr's crisp commands, "Stretch out!" and "Fall in!" Sutter would shout the countersign, "All's set!," and prod his beasts into a lumbering walk, as the drawn-out train began its day's march. Sutter and his men had no fear of Indians and no particular worry about making the necessary average of twelve to fifteen miles per day. So well established was the routine for travel that Sutter observed that the caravan ran like a Swiss watch. At the end of each day,

Carr formed the wagons into a circle to corral the stock, since the oxen, particularly, were capable of being badly spooked by anything—or nothing. The mere rattle of a harness could stampede them into headlong flight were it not for the wagons penning them up. Campfires were kindled outside the ring of wagons, and bedrolls, either of Mackinaw blankets or buffalo robes, were laid out for the night.

The fording of the Little Arkansas gave Sutter and his trailmates trouble. Although only a creek, five or six yards wide, it was steep-sided and mirey. This natural trap for heavily laden vehicles, plus filthy weather, caused tempers to flare and several of Sutter's Germans pulled out of the enterprise. They sold him their interests for an advance of thirty-five percent, which, according to Laufkotter, none of them ever saw. But eventually the sun came out, the Little Arkansas subsided, and the trouble blew over. Sutter led his shrinking company on to Cow Creek and the Arkansas River. Soon he saw in the distance the great landmark he had noted during the prior year, Pawnee Rock. Perhaps he explained to his companions the significance of the great red megalith looming over the buffalo plains, scratched and scarred with the names of countless travelers. The mark of an old Comanche-Pawnee battleground, it also signaled the end of American territory and the beginning of Mexico. Sutter knew well enough that ahead lay the dangerous Cimarron Desert where thirst and Indians combined to kill off some good men—men like Jedediah Smith, ambushed by Comanches just five years before Sutter's crossing.

During the passage of the Cimarron Desert, the night watch was particularly alert. Captain Carr formed his wagons into four parallel lines at the start of the day's march, for better control and defense. Sutter knew that the Comanches liked to swoop down on the tail-end stragglers of a long, single-file caravan snaking across the plains. He placed his trust in Captain Carr and followed him across fifty miles of "waterscape"—a bone-dry, sandy wasteland. It was a God-abandoned land of cactus, rattlesnakes, horned toads and lurking Comanches. Fifteen times he had to cross the dry bed of the sinuous Cimarron. But with filled water kegs, and with barrels of liquor making up much of their cargo, Sutter and his Germans weathered the desert crossing in good style.

At the Cimarron, Carr sent members of the train ahead, Sutter among them, to alert Santa Fe and to secure warehouses and salesrooms so that business could commence, *pronto*. Sutter was familiar with the route, having followed it the previous year, so he was not surprised when the plains began to hump up again between the Cimarron and Canadian rivers. He was gratified by the first sign of live water reappearing in arroyos and even of some scant grass. Soon he found himself riding through country which sustained bushes, even wild currants, plums and grape-vines. Cliffs reared up from the edge of the Oklahoma Panhandle, and the tableland that he was crossing began to be slit by deep ravines. He searched for the distinctive outline of Rabbit Ear Mounds on the horizon beyond the mirages of the rough, arid country. Behind him, his companions had to drive wooden or hoop-iron wedges between wagon-wheel rims and felloes to make a tight fit, as the latter dried out under the harsh sun and shrank away from the iron rims.

At last, Sutter began to see signs of civilization again. First, a few grazing sheep. Then an adobe house or two and the outpost of San Miguel del Vado, at the ford of the silvery Pecos River. There the road terminated its southern swing and began to loop back to the west, climbing up into a break in the New Mexican mountains toward the capital. A few miles before Sutter could see anything of Santa Fe itself, the road entered an open plain. Corn-fields came in sight, and the first of the city's adobes reminded him how much they had looked like brick kilns when he had first seen them a year before.

After making arrangements for the reception of the train and its goods at Santa Fe, Sutter and the other runners returned to San Miguel del Vado to await the caravan. Sutter brought several

Mexicans with him. According to Laufkotter, it was at this juncture that the Swiss approached him about investing in a little highly profitable, but extralegal, trading. Sutter was going to join one of his French friends in bartering with the Apaches for mules and horses. The trade was forbidden, since the Apaches were the deadly enemies of the Mexicans and since most of their stock was stolen from Mexican ranches or settlements. Because of the high profits of the forbidden trade, Sutter was willing to risk the *calabozo*. Laufkotter had already sold his share of the trading company to Sutter, so he was willing to go into the new enterprise, provided he could choose his partners. Sutter agreed. But first there was the regular trading to take care of.

As the Yankee wagons rolled into the plaza of Santa Fe, the townspeople erupted into a fiesta of welcome. *"Los Americanos! Los Carros! La entrada de la caravana!"* The wagoners responded to the cries of greeting by showing off their prowess with their whips, very much aware of dark-eyed *señoritas* admiring them. Most of the men had shaved and put on carefully hoarded clean clothing for their impressive entrance into the *Plaza Pública*. Quickly the manifests were filed and the wagons discharged at the warerooms of the customs house. The men were then free to find their various recreations after the fatiguing voyage across the plains. Seven weeks of travel had whetted their appetites for girls, drinks, *fandangos* and food. Sutter and the Germans found themselves the favorites of the Mexican girls, because of their Continental beards. Laufkotter said that all of them vied for the esteem of the ladies, especially the dashing Captain Sutter.

In the meantime, the trade goods were placed in a storeroom, rented at a high price, in charge of a clerk, whom Sutter paid what Laufkotter called an "enormous" salary. The German was increasingly critical of Sutter and his way of doing business: "Everything had to be carried on in the grandest manner. 'Make or break—and run off!' was the motto." But Sutter found trade to be dull, except in the fancy articles which he and the others gave the *señoritas* for their favors. Laufkotter said that Sutter's $1,500 worth of toys hardly netted him $20. The notorious, corrupt former governor, Manuel Armijo, was not in office again until the following year but, as a *comisario,* he managed to collect his usual surtax of bribes (*mordidas*) atop the high import duties. Sutter apparently indulged in either some smuggling or the forbidden Apache trade, and was caught. It is not clear that he was jailed, but his goods, in part, were confiscated. According to Laufkotter, it took all the influence of a powerful new friend of Sutter's, whom he identified only as Dr. M——, to get Sutter off with only the fine of a few baskets of champagne.

Some of Sutter's Germans suggested that they take their goods on to Chihuahua, since the market at Sante Fe was in such a slump. Sutter opposed the idea, and the company almost broke up into two antagonistic factions. Outsiders, with cooler heads, persuaded them to patch up their differences. But Sutter won out; the Chihuahua venture was abandoned. His opponents held their goods so long that it appeared that they would have to haul them back to St. Louis but, once again, the mysterious Dr. M—— used his influence and got Armijo to buy the lot for $2,000. This was not, unfortunately, in cash but in the shape of forty mules and a note for $1,000. Well aware of Armijo's slippery nature, the Germans were happy to sell the note at a discount of fifty percent and to get out of Santa Fe while the getting was good.

Before they left, the leaders of the caravan held a meeting to place on record the depressed conditions of the market. On August 22, 1836, they issued a joint statement which they rushed to their various Missouri backers by courier. Because of Indian trouble and the failure of some mines, trade was in a dilapidated state, they reported. They also warned the merchants of Missouri against outfitting a company during the following year or they would incur losses for two years in a row. The twentieth signature of the total of twenty-six was that of "J. A. Sutter, Capt." (The notice was published in the *Missouri Republican* and the *Anzeiger des Westens* on October 22, 1836.) They then left New Mexico precipitately, suffering terribly as a consequence, for they were ill prepared for the Cimarron Desert.

Sutter still had a chance of making a killing in his secret Apache venture. He and Laufkotter took in as partners a German and one of Sutter's new French friends. Laufkotter bought back half his trade goods at Santa Fe prices and donated the other half to the company. Sutter and his fellow conspirators waited until the main body of the caravan had started on its return to St. Louis. When asked why he was not readying himself to leave, he lied, claiming that one of his partners was sick and that they would be returning later. He then turned over his trade goods to the Frenchman, whom he designated as his guide because of his familiarity with the area. When Sutter eventually became impatient with his securing of horses, provisions and pack saddles, the man made convincing excuses. Then, one day, when the three Missouri partners were talking with the Frenchman's brother, he asked them the nature of their business. Sutter decided to let him in on the secret. To his astonishment, the man urged him to hurry to his brother's house, warning Sutter that they had probably seen the last of their trade goods. The trio rushed to the Frenchman's home to find the goods gone and the bird flown. Sutter learned that the defaulter had fallen into bad luck at gambling and lost the whole shebang. So disgusted was the new German partner that he departed at once for St. Louis.

Sutter and Laufkotter tried to find something profitable in Santa Fe but failed. They barely kept themselves alive by clerking and cooking. Sutter hated this menial work, of course, and was delighted to be rescued from it by news of a gold strike. At almost the same time, an expedition was formed to rescue some white women held captive by the Comanches. Both these adventures appealed to the romantic in Sutter, but he chose the gold rush. He learned that an Indian had exhibited a nugget in San Fernando de Taos, discovered, he claimed, on the upper reaches of the South Platte River. A gold-mining company was immediately formed by some French-Canadians of Santa Fe. Sutter and Laufkotter threw in with them and got as far as the supposed diggings before bitter weather, lack of provisions, and four feet of snow on the High Plains cooled their gold fever. Mused Laufkotter, "What risks and hardships a man will endure for 'the root of all evil.' "

Sutter and Laufkotter next tried their hands at gold mining in the old New Mexican diggings. They loaded up a jackass with provisions and prospected in the region of Real de los Dolores. Sutter soon pulled out, finding even clerking superior to grubbing for evanescent gold. Laufkotter and a new partner made just $8 in ten days of digging. More bitter than ever, Laufkotter abandoned New Mexico and joined six Americans on February 17, 1837, heading for California. He entirely blamed Sutter for his misfortunes, complaining, "Thus ended Mr. Sutter's branch expedition, and we have seen what became of his unfortunate fellows. In saying Mr. Sutter's expedition I do not intend to call him the originator, for such he never was of anything. He never made or carried out a determination, but others did and, using him as a tool, attained their object." Nevertheless, Sutter stuck it out in New Mexico and set to work to put together a modest profit by trading. He hired a Mexican, Pablo Gutiérrez, to help him drive 100 Sonora mustangs and mules on a brief run to Missouri. Many escaped on the trip, for they were all wild. Some were impossible to tame, such as the one Pastor Muench bought from him. Muench spent the entire winter trying to tame the mustang, then gave it up and had the animal shot. The Reverend harbored no hard feelings toward his friend, whom he described as "a young and sturdy man, blond and well nourished, jovial, somewhat adventurous and shrewder than one might have suspected one of his apparent cordial nature to be. He was agile to an eminent degree and full of rare spirit of enterprise. For such a one, America was the proper soil for unusual success."

At Independence, the returning Germans had been met by their most impatient creditors, who stripped them of most of their stock. Before they reached home, another group of creditors intercepted them and seized the remainder of their mules. One of the traders managed to decamp in the middle of the night with a few of the lame and crippled mules, but most were able only to heap curses on Sutter's head for wasting six months of their time and all of their investment, and leaving them saddled with $7,000 in debts. They scattered to all points of the compass to dodge their debts. One started for Europe but was arrested in St. Louis and jailed until he managed to come up with $1,000. Another, a doctor turned trader, abandoned his farm and family in order to flee to a new life unencumbered by mountainous debts.

Although Sutter had escaped with something more than his shirt, he was no longer interested in the Santa Fe trade. Nor was he eager to return permanently to St. Louis after the disastrous consequences of the venture which he had promoted so enthusiastically. Laufkotter claimed that he was actually afraid to return to St. Louis. In any case, he headed, instead, for Westport, later the site of Kansas City.

Another possible reason for Sutter's decision to move on was an apocryphal tale of his having committed a murder, which gained considerable currency in New Mexico and even hounded him to a degree when he was in California. It was picked up, passed on and given permanence by Don Benito Wilson of New Mexico and later of San Gabriel, California. Wilson told the story in a dictation, dated November 30, 1877, now in the Huntington Library. He made no mention of it in his longer dictation of December 7 of that year, *Observations on Early Days in California and New Mexico,* to historian Hubert H. Bancroft. Bancroft, for his part, kept silence on the matter except to say of Sutter, "There are reasons for not even repeating here the definite charges against him and for believing that those charges were, to a certain extent, unfounded."

Wilson had no such reservations, however. He described Sutter as having no other business in New Mexico in 1835 than peddling galvanized jewelry to Indians for mules. Then, according to Wilson, he prevailed on some unsuspecting Germans to let him take their goods down the Rio Grande to dispose of them to wealthy Mexicans of his acquaintance. He left the capital of New Mexico on August 12, 1836, and returned shortly afterward, feigning illness. Sending for the leader of the German party, a Captain Saunders, Sutter told him that he had sold the goods advantageously downriver but had been obliged to give the purchasers a few days in which to collect the money. He asked Saunders to pick it up, since he was ill. Saunders was hardly out of sight (or so the story goes) before Sutter leaped from his "sickbed" to start for Missouri via San Fernando de Taos and Bent's Fort on the Arkansas. On Saunders' arrival at the place of sale he found that every cent had already been collected by the Swiss. He hastened back to Santa Fe to find Sutter gone.

Laufkotter, though always eager to denigrate Sutter, said nothing of the Saunders affair. But he did mention an incident which, most probably, grew into the Saunders tale with constant telling and retelling around campfires. When the Frenchman gambled away the Apache trade money, Laufkotter reported, their German partner rushed for his home near St. Louis. He hired a guide, a Frenchman named Joe, although Laufkotter warned him that the man had a terrible reputation. But the German ignored his warnings and set off with his guide. They arrived at Bent's Fort, where they were joined by an American adventurer, name unknown, who was probably one of Joe's confederates. Joe and the *gringo* reached Independence safely with, in Laufkotter's own words, "everything except my partner, whom they murdered at Cottonwood, and buried in the bottom of the creek." Next summer, it was Laufkotter himself who discovered the body when passing that way, recognizing it from clothes dug up by wolves. He sent the sad news to the widow in Frankfurt, Germany, then, as he so often did, blamed Sutter. His actual words, misconstrued or only partially remembered by Don Benito Wilson, were: "This was the first victim of Mr. Sutter's great fortune-making enterprise, who came to an untimely death by the hands of Mr. Sutter's favorite Frenchman."

Sutter spent 1837 in the four-year-old town of Westport, already rivaling Independence as a fitting-out point for overland travelers. He used his mule and mustang profits to purchase a business from Lucas and Kavanaugh at Main Street and Westport Avenue. Laufkotter inevitably turned up again. He had made it only as far west as the Gila River of Arizona. On his homeward march he had met a Santa Fe trade train and learned of Sutter's supposed good fortune in Westport. Although he thoroughly doubted the rumor, thinking that not even Sutter could run 100 unbroken horses and mules into a fortune, he hurried to investigate. Once there, he accused Sutter of fraud. Unruffled by his insults and in a good humor as usual, the Swiss was his host for three weeks.

Sutter was most expansive. He told Laufkotter that he owned most of the town as well as several adjoining farms. He showed him one farm with a sawmill which, he confided, he had bought for $4,000. The farm on which he lived he had purchased, on credit, for $3,000. He convinced Laufkotter that he was the baron of Westport, although his home was so modest that he had to share his bed with his visitor. In order to enhance and extend his aura of affluence, Sutter embarked on the building of a costly and lavish hotel for the growing town. He obtained sawed logs and hired Shawnee Indians for $.75 a day; corner-men he paid $1 a day. Small wonder that Sutter got along so famously with the Shawnees. Laufkotter observed, "The most interesting feature of the contract was that, when night came on, every Indian presented himself for his pay and when asked what part of the work he was doing, he always said 'corner-man,' and consequently received his dollar without hesitation." Sutter ordered a huge sign bearing the inscription THE FAR WEST HOTEL in gold letters. Whether or not it ever arrived from St. Louis remains a mystery, but certainly Sutter never paid the $60 bill for it.

Every morning saw Sutter nervous and uneasy about coming up with enough money to pay his workmen, but somehow he always managed to replenish his purse during the day. Although

Sutter and Laufkotter boarded in town, their business headquarters was a German saloon. There Sutter spent money lav-
ishly, though neither Laufkotter nor anyone else could pry out
of him any information about its source. He was on the best of
terms with the Shawnees and Delawares and liked to treat them
to whisky which he smuggled to them in his saddlebags. Perhaps
he picked up a few dollars by this casual whisky-running. However, if Laufkotter is to be trusted, he apparently profited handsomely in a different sort of coinage, for he reported that the
girls on the Shawnee reservation found the dashing Sutter absolutely irresistible. He observed, "His attachment to the
Shawnee squaws grew stronger day by day and their visits to
town became so frequent that the ladies of Westport were forced
to petition the Common Council to have them stopped."

Once again, Sutter was unable to live within his means. He
found himself heading down a familiar trail, with all the land-
marks of bankruptcy. Briefly, he was badly depressed and even
talked of suicide to his friend, John C. McCoy, one of the town's
founders. But Sutter was hardly the suicidal type. His despond-
ency soon passed, and before long he was ready to try an alternative—California. Laufkotter was about to attempt again to reach
the Pacific Coast, this time with a party of twenty Delawares and
twenty Shawnees. Sutter agreed to join them in the Delaware
country but reneged on his promise, offering no explanation.
Laufkotter grumbled disgustedly, "I have no further confidence
in his promises."

While down in San Fernando de Taos, Sutter had become
friendly with Carlos Beaubien, whom he called "Popian," a
French-Canadian naturalized citizen of Mexico who was *alcalde*
(mayor and justice of the peace) of the town. Beaubien told
Sutter that he had traveled to California as a young man, and his
enthusiasm for the land west of the Sierra Nevada was infectious.
Sutter resolved now to make the trip with a single companion.
McCoy loaned him a little money to pay off his most pressing
debts and gave him a horse. Another friend chipped in a mount

for Sutter's companion. Sutter left McCoy many of his fine clothes and jewelry as payment, including, according to McCoy's daughter, silk vests, a gold fob, a black, satin-lined coat, and knee breeches!

According to Don Benito Wilson's story, Sutter also left behind some forged drafts, investing the ill-gotten profits in supplies for the trip west. Wilson claimed that one of the men swindled by Sutter was Dr. David Waldo, who in 1842 or 1843, hearing of Sutter's relative prosperity in California, forwarded some of the bogus paper to New Helvetia. And, Wilson maintained, Sutter paid, in order to hush up the matter, which might have affected his hard-won respectability. Whether or not this story is any more true than the Captain Saunders tale, there is little doubt that Sutter skipped out on Westport debts. His promissory note to Lucas and Kavanaugh for $1,010.54 fell due on April 1, 1838. Sutter decided to play a little April Fool's joke on them and set that date for his quiet departure for the Farther West. Not until 1850 would they recover their money. In a judgment in the Sixth District Court, Sacramento, on July 11 of that year, they were awarded $1,601.72, the principal and interest, plus $24.50 for the costs of their suit against Sutter.

John C. McCoy watched Sutter ride out of Westport on the misty morning of April 1, 1838, on an Indian pony. His sole companion should have been loyal Pablo Gutiérrez, but McCoy said that it was a man named Wetler. According to others, a man named Koch played Sancho Panza to the captain. McCoy described his departure as a "piteous procession" of two riders towing astern a sorrel packhorse, "a veritable Rosinante." But he noted that the quixotic Sutter sat erect in the saddle, eyes fixed on the far horizon, with "an air of determination about him and a gentlemanly mien that marks the aristocrat."

CHAPTER III

THE MOUNTAIN MAN

SUTTER rode no farther from Westport than the Delaware reservation across the Missouri River. He was already quite familiar with it and had many friends, of both sexes, there. He planned to make his way westward with the annual fur caravan, then split off to the Southwest and California. The reason that he could not join Laufkotter was that he had taken the German's clothes and other possessions, left with Sutter for safekeeping, to raise $150.

Meanwhile, Capt. Andrew Drips, "booshway" (*bourgeois,* or leader) of the American Fur Company's annual expedition to the Rockies, was putting the final touches on his preparations. He bought supplies, and picked his horses and mules. Finally, he selected the merchandise and supplies which would stuff his *charrettes,* or two-wheeled Red River carts, to their 800- to 900-pound capacity.

Rumor in St. Louis had it that the fur trade was on its last legs. It was not quite true. But only one more rendezvous, that of the summer of 1839, would be held in the Rockies after Drips' march to the 1838 meeting. Sutter was not concerned, of course. At the moment, he had no interest in furs. He simply planned to tag along with Drips until he could split off for the California paradise he envisioned lying west of the Rockies.

On April 22, Drips gave the signal and the long, drawn-out, caravan began to move across the prairie from the Big Muddy toward the vast stretch of blank space on the maps which Maj. Stephen H. Long, eighteen years before, had labeled the Great American Desert. When Drips' dust cloud boiled up on the reservation, Sutter and his messmates rode up to meet him. With the American Fur Company *bourgeois,* Sutter found an imposing Scotsman, William Drummond Stewart, blue-eyed, eagle-beaked, moustached and six feet tall, a veteran of the Peninsular War and Waterloo. He fell into conversation with the Scot, and, when it was over, Sutter had changed his plans. Stewart had convinced him that he would be wise to go all the way to the rendezvous with Drips in order to avoid the dangers of Sonora's Gila Trail to California. He argued that Sutter was safer with Drips' large body of men on a well-defined trail, protected by Forts Laramie, Hall and Vancouver. And from the Hudson's Bay post in Vancouver, he said, Sutter could easily drop down from Oregon into California. Sutter realized that the eccentric adventurer in the fringed buckskins knew far more about the Far West than he did, so he took his advice.

Drips' caravan was not at full strength until well into the Delaware country, where it was joined by the party of missionaries who had volunteered to reinforce Marcus Whitman in Oregon.

Sutter anticipated little trouble from Indians. He was practically a blood brother of the Delawares and Shawnees, and he noted with pleasure the precision of the guard mount of fur men under Stewart's sharp, military eyes. The Fur Company men, he saw, were of the same tough metal as those he had met in Missouri, Santa Fe and Taos. In one of them, the braggart Moses (Black) Harris, he saw a rival of the *great* mountain men— Jed Smith, Jim (Old Gabe) Bridger and Broken Hand, himself.

Stewart's chief hunter and close friend was a *métis,* or half-breed, named Antoine Clement. Half Cree and half French-Canadian, he was an even deadlier shot with the the fine Manton rifle which Stewart had imported from Europe for him than with his American Hawken.

Captain Andrew Drips was no stranger to Sutter. He was one of the most able partisans, or fur-brigade leaders, in the West, along with Lucien Fontenelle and William Henry Vanderburgh. While the flamboyance of the Jim Bridgers and Jim Beckwourths caught the public's attention, they would have to scramble to keep up with Drips. He had partnered with Fontenelle in a post at Bellevue, just a few miles downstream from the site of Omaha, where he married an Oto woman. (Four years after he marched with Sutter, Drips' ability was recognized by President Tyler, who appointed him Indian Agent for the tribes of the Upper Missouri.)

But the churchmen were as motley a bag of pilgrims as Sutter had ever seen. They had twenty-two horses and mules but only a single wagon, William Gray's. Each missionary was outfitted with a gun and a hunting knife, but Sutter learned that Cushing Eells refused to load his arm. However, he tolerated one of the others loading his piece for him when he drew his stint of guard duty. In his letters home Eells wrote, "It has been a trial to me to carry weapons of war." After only a few days of the incongruous crowding together of travelers on the immense plains, Sutter was all too familiar with the missionaries—and their quarrels. Sutter's careless Christianity must have been a trial to the group. But, if theirs was a state of grace, he was definitely not interested in it. Not only were they self-righteous but they were irritable with one another as well as with their involuntary traveling companions.

Elkanah Walker was a six-foot four-inch, stoop-shouldered man of thirty-three years. Shy and apparently afraid of offending everyone within sight and hearing, he seemed never to dare open his mouth except to grumble at his bride or to shift the omnipresent cud in his cheek in order to better fire tobacco juice at some unsuspecting clump of sage. Walker was studious, if less ostentatiously so than Gray. Otherwise, he was completely unlike that petty and "techy" churchman. His wife, Mary, along with Myra Eells, was the journal keeper of the religious party. To Elkanah's muttering annoyance she was always scratching in her diary. Cheerful and vigorous, Mary was tolerable company, Sutter found. She was a human being, something which could not be said for her companions. Sutter sometimes rode beside her to pass the time and to spare her the immediate company of the more annoying Bible bearers.

Sutter did not care for William Gray, the self-appointed leader of the missionary band and Marcus Whitman's secular agent of 1836. Gray had been sent east for reinforcements, and his recruits were forced to acknowledge his claims to leadership, however grudgingly. Gray had delusions of intellectual grandeur. He wanted to be called Doctor Gray, though he had no more earned his Hippocratic degree than First Under-lieutenant Sutter had really won his captaincy. Gray had survived sixteen weeks of medical school in Fairfield, New York. (Once in Oregon, Whitman quickly stripped him of the title.) On the trail, he made no bones about the fact that he considered Walker ill adapted for the Oregon missions. He quarreled with Asa Smith, too, a man, like himself, of strong feelings and prejudices who had little confidence in his comrades. Gray had some talent in Indian languages, which interested Sutter intensely, but his personality ruled out any kind of friendship or communication between them. To Sutter, he seemed embittered, perhaps because of the problem of his wife. She was practically an hysterical invalid, later named "Weeping Woman" by the Nez Perces.

Sutter found the Walkers and Eellses more attractive. Eells was thick-skinned enough for Gray's criticism to bounce off. His smugness irritated Gray, who claimed that Eells lacked every one of the qualities required for a successful Indian missionary.

For men of peace, the clerical party acted as if they were combatants in a state of temporary and fragile armed truce. Sometimes couples teamed up against couples, sometimes it was every man of God for himself. Sutter would have added an "Amen" to Mary Walker's diary entry for May 27, had she shown it to him —"We have a strange company of missionaries, scarcely one who is not intolerable on some account."

Sutter and the other gentlemen of Drips' party went out of their way to make the wearying journey easier for the women. Several times they paid social calls, always bearing some of the Scot's delicacies for the table. On at least one occasion, Mary Walker reciprocated by serving them biscuits and cheese. George Rogers Hancock Clark and the hard-drinking William Preston Clark, sons of the explorer companion of Meriwether Lewis, were traveling with Drips. They helped the missionary larder by presenting Myra Eells with a brace of ducks. But factionalism ruled the day, so that when the Walkers killed and butchered a wolf-bitten calf, the Eellses and Grays refused to eat any of the veal, saying that the animal should not have been killed. And when Stewart, Drips and Sutter gave the missionaries some corn and fresh pork, Smith so acted the glutton that Mary Walker described him as "hoggish."

There was little danger on the march, but there was a great deal of fatigue and hardship. Driving rains, accelerated by the ceaseless wind of the buffalo prairies, penetrated even the thickest cloaks. The storm of May 12 was so heavy and continuous that Sutter, like all the rest of the party, was soaked to the skin. For days, his clothes would not dry out, even when hung before roaring fires of river driftwood and buffalo chips in the evenings. Stewart alone loved the rain, perhaps because it reminded him of Scotland. Most distressed by the soaked clothing and bedding, of course, were the women. Once, when Mrs. Smith entered the flooded tent, she found Mrs. Walker in tears. "Why, Mrs. Walker, what *is* the matter?" she asked. "I am thinking how comfortable my father's hogs are," was the reply.

Only Gray, of the churchmen, had any experience in the endless chores of plains and mountains—loading and unloading animals, making and breaking camp. The other men were nearly helpless, possessing neither the skill nor the muscle for the work. Walker's strength gave out early. Sutter saw him one day flat on his back, quite unable to get up, complaining to Brother Eells, "You must have more help, or you won't have me." By good luck, the missionaries were able to hire two men, a packer and a hunter, and with their help the greenhorns were able to keep up with Drips, Stewart, Sutter and the Clarks.

Sutter was thriving. Compared to the missionaries, of course, he was already an old-timer on the plains. The West delighted him, whether it was the passage of a herd of buffalo or the excitement of a river crossing in a clumsy, coracle-like bullboat of buffalo hide stretched over willow poles. The craft never capsized and never seemed in danger of sinking as long as the men were careful to pay the seams with a calking compound of buffalo grass and ashes.

At night, wagons were turned into the customary circle to corral the picketed horses and mules. Tents were then pitched atop oilcloth or India rubber groundsheets, on which buffalo robes had been laid as combination blankets and carpets. Folded Mackinaw blankets took the place of chairs in the cozy canvas quarters. Everyone rolled up in his bedding early, for all had to arise at 3:30 to let the stock out, under guard, to graze until 6 A.M. Then after breakfast—and prayers in the case of the missionaries—the emigrants spent half to three quarters of an hour in saddling their mounts and harnessing or packing horses and mules for another day's progress.

Although the sixty-odd people once rode for nine hours straight, they usually put in only three to six hours in the saddle before stopping at noon for about two hours. The animals were turned loose while the men and women had their dinner and rested up. While some washed dishes, others caught and saddled the animals for the remainder of the day's march. Before nooning or camping for the night, the caravan might stretch out for a good half-mile in length. To Myra Eells, it resembled a great funeral procession rolling across the plains. But, thanks to the experienced Drips and the vigilance of his men, Sutter knew there would be no funerals for this caravan.

Sutter saw fewer buffalo than he had expected. So, like the other travelers, he ran through his bacon and flour sooner than planned. When Drips finally led them into a bison range, he enjoyed green (fresh) buffalo meat every day and practically all day long. He noticed that the missionaries were growing lean, and not from deliberate asceticism. They were lucky to have even a little flour to stir up into a gravy to go with their buffalo hump or ribs. Sutter fared well enough and could not complain of real hardships, although he found discomforts frequent enough.

The Swiss and his fellow travelers followed the usual route, soon to be pounded into a highway—the Oregon Trail. It ran from the Kaw or Kansas River to the Big and Little Blue rivers, and from there to the Platte. For 120 miles Sutter rode along the fabled coasts of the Nebraska (Platte) River until he reached the forks. Beyond that point, the green nap of the plains began to wear through in places. Trees thinned out until only a few cottonwoods huddled on the sandy islands spawned by the Platte. Sutter helped to rout boredom by telling stories of Switzerland, regaling his companions with tales of St. Bernard dogs digging lost travelers out of Alpine snowbanks.

May 21 provided the greatest variation in the routine of the party. They reached the forks where wild mustangs swept close to the wagons, nearly stampeding the animals; and their noon campfire spread into a grass fire. But these were only preliminaries to the main event of that long day—the shipwreck of Stewart's fine wagon on a rough stretch of terrain. The capsized wagon spewed forth sweetmeats, port and brandy bottles, silver flasks and fancy toilet articles like a misshapen cornucopia,

51

strewing the sea of grass with the most bizarre jetsam it would ever see. Sutter knew that the Scotsman did not mind roughing it, but his scattered cargo demonstrated that he relished the amenities of civilization, the things which made life worthwhile, like mint juleps and English biscuits—even when on the wild frontier.

Following the South Fork of the Platte for a while, the caravan avoided its treacherous quicksands and forded it at California Crossing, then struck for the North Fork via Ash Hollow. They followed its shallow, silty, course into an area of deepening ravines in weather that grew bitter for the season. After passing Courthouse Rock, the first major monument of the journey, Sutter saw famous Chimney Rock on May 26. The next great landmark was Scott's Bluffs where he began to anticipate "civilization," of a sort, only sixty miles ahead—Sublette's Fort William, better known as Fort Laramie. There, where the Laramie Fork joined the North Fork of the Platte, Myra Eells was as impressed by the fortress as Sutter. Hardly had she passed through its main gate and into the courtyard when she was casting about for a complimentary metaphor. At last, she had it, writing, "It compares very well with the walls of the Connecticut State Prison."

Lucien Fontenelle welcomed his old friend, Drips, to the trading post and was a kindly and considerate host to the entire caravan. From Fort Laramie, Drips sent Black Harris ahead as a courier to the old Susquadee, or Upper Green River, rendezvous site, to warn anyone there that the rendezvous had been changed to the Popo Agie. (When Harris reached the Green, between Horse Creek and New Fork, he not only spread the word verbally but left a laboriously written message on the old ruin of a log hut there—"Come on to the Popoasie. Plenty of whisky and white women.")

Drips rested his stock for several days at Fort Laramie, giving the missionary ladies a chance to wash, bake, and to pay social calls on the wives (squaws) of the post's staff. For Sutter, the week was invaluable. His close examination of the fortified post

52

gave him many ideas for the California trading fortress which was already taking shape in his imagination.

West of the fort, the Platte Valley grew drier and drier and the plains more desolate as the gradient increased alongside the Black Hills or Laramie Mountains. But buffalo were plentiful, and there were explosions of color in the scarlet and white flowering cactus, the fruit of the occasional wild plum tree, and the flash of black and white in the sky made by a magpie wheeling about in his formal-dress plumage. On June 12, the company caught sight of the Rocky Mountains and, two days later, Independence Rock soared into view. Sutter knew it as the northern equivalent of New Mexico's Pawnee Rock. The party made camp there, so cold that they all bundled up in their winter clothes. If Sutter took the time to scratch his name on the great monolith, as he had etched his name on the window back in Europe, no trace has survived the rain and wind erosion of a century and more. The huge, whale-shaped mass of rock marked the site of the grassy-banked Sweetwater River, the Eau Sucre of the French-Canadians. This was the end of fifty miles of arid, saleratus-whitened flats and alkaline water ranging in color from that of strong lye to that of weak coffee. It was an unpleasant stretch in many ways, for alkali was the father of dysentery, as well. But the weather warmed and the river water was as sweet as its name. Also, there were juicy—and puckery—wild plums for the Swiss to eat on the way to Devil's Gate, the gap the river carved in a rocky ridge.

On June 21, 22 and 23, the caravan straggled into the Popo Agie River fur rendezvous and disintegrated. Sutter, glad to be rid of the missionaries, however temporarily, turned his attention to the trappers and Indians who rushed out to meet the new-comers. In the van was Black Harris. Sutter camped with the caravan in a tree-fringed meadow between the converging waters of the Wind River and the Popo Agie. Although he was eager to be on his way to California he was saddle-weary and badly needed the rest. He did not attend Sunday services on the twenty-third, for he was busy eying the handsome Shoshone girls and meeting men who would later become legends—Joe Walker, Robert (Doc) Newell, and Joe Meek. He found them all in good spirits—steeped in spirits, in fact. They were as full of high jinks as they were of Taos lightning or metheglin, the mountain man's mead, compounded of whisky and honey.

The raw good humor of the lusty mountaineers amused Sutter but appalled his missionary companions. On Independence Day, they seemed determined to set new records for drunkenness, while Drips and Joe Walker had a quiet dinner with the churchmen and their ladies, the latter decked out in their Sunday best. That night, the mountain men threw a big carouse. They gathered outside the tent of the unpopular Gray, indicating they intended to "settle accounts" with him. (They blamed him for the deaths of some friendly Indians during his eastward trip.) While Eells attempted to calm them down, Gray loaded his gun, determined to sell his life dearly. However, the drunkards' attention span proved to be short, and they wandered off to their squaws without doing him harm. But they were back the next day. This time, Sutter saw Jim Bridger lead what Mrs. Eells called "an apology for a scalp dance," his men stumbling along behind him, firing their rifles and pounding drums to salute the clergy. Fifteen to twenty mountain men jogged about the tents, drumming and firing as they danced. One of them waved a Blackfoot scalp like a battle flag. Myra Eells was disgusted by the uncouth display, especially by the gruesome trophy. She learned that they carried it to salute the news of an outbreak of smallpox among the hated Blackfeet. That night she wrote in her diary, "If I might make a comparison, I should think they looked like the emissaries of the Devil, worshipping their own master." On July 6, the trappers were still at it. Sutter saw a dozen of them leave their drinking and wenching to entertain the missionary ladies with another war dance. All painted up, Indian style, and whooping like redskins, they caused Mrs. Eells to write in her diary, "No pen can describe the horrible scene they presented. I could not imagine that white men, brought up in a civilized land, can appear so much to imitate the Devil."

Sutter was unable to find much in the way of supplies for his trip to Fort Vancouver. Flour was $2 a pound at the Popo Agie; sugar, tea and coffee all sold for $1 a pint. Calico, worth $.25 back East, brought $5 in the lee of the Wind River Mountains, he found. A shirt would cost him $5, and the real essentials of life—tobacco and whisky—demanded $3 to $5 a pound and $30 a gallon. He wondered how, with Taos lightning so dear, half the camp managed their marathon binges. The only spending which Sutter felt free to do was to purchase an Indian boy for a guide. He planned to move on to the old Green River rendezvous site, and from there on to Fort Vancouver. Sutter bought the lad from a trapper who had acquired him from Kit Carson. His price was steep—$100 in beaver orders, worth $130 there at the rendezvous—but Sutter thought him worth it, for Drips was going no farther west and a guide was essential. Moreover, the boy spoke a smattering of English and Spanish as well as several Indian dialects.

Sutter had no trouble in recruiting men to his banner, even as a bankrupt. Two German trappers at the rendezvous, Niklaus Allgeier and Sebastian Keyser, threw in their lot with him, joining the Mexican muleteer, Pablo Gutiérrez, the Indian boy, two Americans who had accompanied Sutter westward from the Delaware nation, and a German or Belgian cabinetmaker, who may have been the Wetler or Koch with whom he left Westport. In fact, he had to discourage volunteers for California. Interest in the Mexican territory was high. As Sutter recalled, "I could find plenty [of men] to accompany me to California but I would not accept them. They wanted to go as a band of robbers and said if I would take them they would rob the mission churches for me, and also horses and cattle."

On Sunday, July 8, the problem of Sutter's route westward was solved. Jovial Francis Ermatinger, a Hudson's Bay *bourgeois,* arrived at the Popo Agie with a brigade of thirteen trappers. He told the delighted missionaries, who were on the point of turning back, that he was there to guide them to Fort Hall. He had gone to the Green River to find Gray, whom he had met the year before, and there had seen Black Harris' sign. Sutter introduced himself to Ermatinger, a veteran of some eighteen years in Hudson's Bay service, and got his permission to accompany him to Fort Hall. Sutter considered himself extremely fortunate again to fall under the tutelage of men of the caliber of Drips and Stewart. He learned that Ermatinger had guided Nathaniel Wyeth east from Fort Vancouver in 1833 and had been the factor at Flathead Post near Thompson's Falls east of the Spokane River.

Ermatinger's companions were an equally interesting lot. There was Jason Lee of the Oregon Methodist Mission, who was on his way back to the States with a gentleman named F. Y. Ewing, the first of a long line of people to go to the Pacific Coast for reasons of health. Having recovered his health, he was returning to civilization. Also with Ermatinger were three half-breed sons of Thomas McKay, the factor at Fort Hall, and two Chinook Indian boys bound for school in the East. While Sutter watched, the westbound and eastbound clergy mingled delightedly, engaging in animated conversation. So excited were his religious trail companions, in fact, that they quite forgot to hold Sunday services that day. Lee passed on the good news that Oregon missionaries Whitman and Spalding were sending horses and provisions to Fort Hall and Fort Boise to help the reinforcements on the last leg of their journey. The ladies brought out the unbroken remains of their fine china to show Ermatinger their appreciation of his offer to guide them. But the Hudson's Bay man insisted on using a tin cup and plate, saying, "Take away your little earthen cups. They gave me one of the little things once and I swallowed it right down with the contents."

Sutter was always intensely receptive to information, to new ideas. He soaked up suggestions—and retained them—like a Florida sponge. Reverend Lee may have been almost as welcome a visitor as Ermatinger. In him, Sutter met an outstanding frontier missionary, a man who had the skill to sow the seeds of civilization in the wilderness. Probably he passed on some of his ideas about transforming Oregon's migratory hunting society into a stable agricultural one. If so, just as he had influenced Marcus Whitman and Henry Spalding at Waiilatpu and Lapwai, so, too, he influenced Sutter in planning his Sacramento River settlement. He was ready to accept all of Lee's advice. The one thing he would not adopt, however, was his evangelism. Sutter had no interest in saving Indian souls in California.

After a last blow-out, the camps of the whites and Indians broke up on July 20, 1838. But Sutter, Ermatinger and the missionaries were already long gone. Timid and refined Myra Eells confided her fears of the trail ahead to her diary: "The gentlemen tell us we have not begun to see the danger and hardship of traveling." How right they were!

The first day out from the Popo Agie rendezvous, Ermatinger's party rode for seven hours. They forded three streams and covered twenty-two miles before camping. Captain Ermatinger had supper in the Eells' tent. On Friday, the unlucky thirteenth, they made sixteen miles but a mule tumbled down a ledge, broke the crupper on its packsaddle and threw the loosened pack up on its neck. Fortunately, it was not injured. Next, the missionaries' dog had to be abandoned because of his painful, blistered, feet. It was exhausting terrain; Mary Walker wrote, "I have not felt so weak since I left the States." Sutter rode past rugged bluffs of red sandstone and camped on the Sweetwater on the fourteenth, on the other side of the watershed from the Popo Agie. From Ermatinger he learned that he was now on the very backbone of America. That night, a herd of buffalo thundered by, so close to the camp that for hours there was no sleep for Sutter and the other pilgrims.

The next day, the women were so terrified by the high country they were entering that they often shut their eyes to forestall faintness as they skittered along dangerous slopes above deep ravines. Eells, Sutter noted, was growing fatigued and discouraged and Asa Smith looked even worse. But Ermatinger hurried everyone along, reminding them that they were in dangerous territory and tarrying could be permanent. Sutter kept no record of the time it took to cross the Rockies, but if Reverend Smith's figures were accurate, the party made the 327 miles between rendezvous and Fort Hall in just two weeks of the hardest kind of riding. The *bourgeois* gave them only two full days to rest and to dry meat during the passage. Sutter and his companions averaged better than twenty-three miles a day; twice, they covered thirty miles in a day. And once, they negotiated a bone-wearying forty-five miles before sundown.

On the fifteenth, Sutter had his view of South Pass and, like all travelers, was disappointed by its lack of grandeur. He could hardly believe that the gentle descent led to the Pacific drainage.

The following day was the longest Sutter ever put in in the saddle. The poor women were exhausted, for they insisted, of course, on the highly proper but excruciating sidesaddles. When, after ten and a half hours and forty-five miles of travel, Mary Walker got down stiffly from her horse, Sutter saw her collapse in a faint. Thirty-five miles of the march had been across waterless plain. Here, Sutter either saw or heard of the set-to between Joe Meek and Reverend Smith. (Brother Eells later denounced the story as "outrageously false.") Meek, chasing his runaway Nez Perce squaw and daughter, Helen Mar, came upon the Smiths just as their strength was ebbing away. Mrs. Smith was standing by their drooping horses, weeping over her husband, who lay on the ground. When she begged Meek for water, he replied that he had none but kindly offered her some whisky from the "kettle of alcohol" hanging from his saddle horn. She refused it. Smith, still lying on the ground, croaked that he was dying. Infuriated, Meek tongue-lashed him: "You're a damned pretty fellow to be lying on the ground there, lolling your tongue out of your mouth, and trying to die. Die, if you want to; you're of no account and will never be missed. Here's your wife, who you keep standing here in the hot sun. Why don't she die? She's got more pluck than a white-livered chap like you!" After lifting Mrs. Smith back into her saddle, Meek continued: "I'm not going to leave her waiting here for you to die. There's a band of Indians behind me on the trail and I've been riding like hell to keep out of their way. If you want to stay and be scalped, you can stay!" As they rode off, Meek made one last try to rouse Smith: "You can follow us if you choose or you can stay where you are. Mrs. Smith can find plenty of better men than you."

Whatever the truth of the tale, Sutter noted that all members of Ermatinger's party, the "dying" Smith included, staggered safely into camp on the Green River, horse-belly deep and crystal clear.

Fording the Green on the seventeenth, they camped on its banks to enjoy gooseberry pie and sauce. They were beyond the buffalo range now, so this dessert was a real treat after meals of jerked meat. On the next day, they left the Green River to pass over a terrifying mountain ridge to the Bear River drainage. There they camped in a beautiful basin. On the nineteenth, they dropped through fertile country of grass, springs, pines and streams full of fish. The water was the finest that Sutter and the Easterners had ever tasted. The air was cooled delightfully by the snow banks still hugging the flanks of the mountains. One of the men caught a delicious one-pound trout for dinner. Naturally, the pilgrims' spirits rose in this country. They felt better prepared to face the dangers of the steep country ahead. On Friday, they nooned at a saline spring where Sutter collected crusted salt to season his meat. From there, they continued along precipices to a creek which emptied into Bear River. During the day, Ermatinger's hunters killed a bear and even a buffalo which had wandered far beyond its normal range.

Sunday, July 22, 1838, brought to camp the filthiest, most brutish Indians that Sutter had ever seen, members of the Bannock tribe. They were peaceful enough, the braves not even waging war on their fleas and body lice. Only a few possessed buffalo robes. They crowded around the tents in their nakedness, eyeing the horrified white women. One squaw busied herself removing lice from the head of her child, only to pop them into her mouth to crunch like peanuts. Walker attempted the impossible. He did a little missionizing. Although they could understand hardly a single word of the sermon he preached to them, the soiled audience paid him the courtesy of rapt attention. When the Christians broke into a hymn, the Indians were delighted.

At last, on July 24, Sutter reached Soda Springs (alias Beer Springs) via the banks of Bear River. Everyone was sick of a steady diet of buffalo jerky, so the ladies used soda water from the springs to make bread which they baked in tin reflector ovens. Joe Meek was still tagging along and was tantalized by the aroma of freshly baked bread. The ladies were willing to give samples to the Indians, but Meek was beyond the pale. However, he bullied a Nez Perce into singing an encore after a hymn had been rewarded with a biscuit, then took the delicacy away from him and gobbled it down. From their biscuit camp the travelers moved due west across a lava-rock country to the Portneuf River, a tributary to the Snake, and from there to a camp on Ross Fork.

When Ermatinger broke his camp at 4:30 A.M. on July 27, he sent his guide, Baptiste Dorion (son of Meriwether Lewis's guide of 1805, Pierre Dorion) ahead to announce their coming to Fort Hall. Sutter gallantly accompanied Mary Walker, who was suffering from a painful toothache. It was steep country through which they wended their way to the Hudson's Bay post, built in 1834 by Nat Wyeth near Pocatello. One slope which they descended was pitched like the roof of a house. Prudently, Mary Walker put off her fainting spell until she and Sutter were safely at the bottom of the mountain. And still they reached the fort an hour before her husband. The jolting ride not only tore Elkanah's wedding coat but shook him up so much that it stopped his watch.

At the gate set in the white adobe walls, Sutter and the others were welcomed by Thomas McKay, stepson of the legendary chief factor of Fort Vancouver, Dr. John McLoughlin. With McKay was a group of Nez Perce Indians. The travelers set up their tents outside the fort but the kindly McKay offered them a room, into which the Grays moved. Fort Hall was hardly hospital-clean (Mary Walker likened McKay's laundry room to a pigsty), but the ladies pitched in to catch up on their washing. Mary Walker's tooth was extracted at the fort and, relieved of pain, she joined the others in enjoying the luxury of the cellar-cool laundry while the sun glared mercilessly outside. McKay treated everyone to a meal at a real table again, a table some 1,709 miles from Westport and spread with hard bread, salted tongue and ham from Fort Colville. On Sunday, the twenty-eighth, Eells preached to fifty or sixty people, including a half-dozen Nez Perces.

At the fort, the missionaries were persuaded to leave their cattle, to make their march easier. The promised supplies and horses from Whitman were there. But it was a dwindling party that continued westward with Sutter. Joe Meek stayed behind; he wanted to join up with Joe Walker. Ermatinger remained at the post. The hired hunter was sent back to the States to carry word to Jason Lee of the sad deaths, in childbirth, of his wife and infant. Sutter and the others rode out of Fort Hall on July 31 after the *bourgeois* warned the Swiss to pose as a "King George man," or Britisher, since the Indians did not like the "Boston men," or Americans. Like the others, Sutter expected the worst. The route was said to be rugged; there were Indians; they had no guides. Gray was in nominal command.

To the surprise of Sutter and all his trailmates, the weather was pleasant and cool. Instead of the lifeless desert which they had feared, they found the arid country below the Portneuf and Bannock rivers to be almost as full of ducks and rabbits as it was of crickets, crows and mosquitoes. On August 1, they camped at the falls of the Snake River—American Falls. Continuing down the south bank, they met a band of friendly Snakes camped on

61

the Raft River. Since Gray was in charge, there was no traveling on the Sabbath. Sutter rested with the others on August 5. But that day two Indian guides, dispatched by Ermatinger, caught up with them.

Riding through the perpendicular-walled canyon of the Snake, Sutter reached Salmon Falls on the ninth, where he found an encampment of Digger fishermen. Here, the impatient Gray left the party to push impulsively ahead with only his wife and hired man. Sutter and the others, moving at a slower pace, reached Fort Boise on the fifteenth. The post, which had been built by McKay to keep an eye on Fort Hall before it was absorbed by the Hudson's Bay Company, seemed to Sutter like paradise. He was welcomed by the genial, rotund and middle-aged factor, Francis Payette, who offered Sutter and his fellow travelers butter, pumpkins, milk, fresh turnips, green corn, turnip sauce, melons, salmon, sturgeon, boiled pudding and pumpkin pie. Sutter found in his host a sort of wilderness gourmet who delighted in setting a groaning board for half-starved travelers. Perhaps Sutter's later warm hospitality at New Helvetia was, in part, in emulation of this simple, generous factor.

On the seventeenth, Mary Walker celebrated their good fortune by inviting Captain Sutter and Captain Payette to tea. The Swiss never forgot those good times at Fort Boise. Thirty-eight years later he recalled, "How glad we were to come to a resting place where we could get something decent to eat!"

On Monday, August 20, Payette saw the party off for Rev. Marcus Whitman's mission at Waiilatpu, near Fort Walla Walla. The next day, Sutter saw signs of kindlier country ahead in the form of chokecherries, elderberries and sumac. On the twenty-third, he and the others were given a scare when Indians stole three of their horses. But there was no attack. Still they were vastly relieved when they found at Lone Tree a Cayuse Indian sent by Whitman to guide them in.

Sutter was treated to a demonstration of Indian resilience and stoicism on the twenty-fifth and twenty-sixth. The Nez Perce wife of one of their hired hunters, dropped out of the party to give birth to a daughter at sunset. She had traveled twenty-five miles that day. Her husband and the Smiths stayed with her near Powder River. The remainder of the party saw her come into camp about 10 A.M. Sunday, proudly bearing her new-born baby. Sutter marveled at her stamina. She had not slackened her pace, nor had her husband excused her from her nooning chores of collecting firewood and kindling fires. She had prepared dinner, too, just before giving birth to her child.

Cornelius Rogers, the only bachelor among the missionaries, was thrown from his horse on the twenty-seventh and injured. When he began to lag behind, Smith bled him, which naturally did him no good. The Smiths therefore volunteered to stay with him while Sutter and the others pushed on past the Cayuse village to reach Waiilatpu at two in the afternoon of August 29. Once again, he was amazed by the feast held to welcome them. This time, he sat down to melons, pumpkin pie and milk. The house was crowded with forty or fifty curious Indians, all of whom insisted upon shaking hands. Some of the Cayuse hands which Sutter shook that day would be reddened with the blood of the Whitmans in the massacre which took place in that very house nine years later.

On the thirtieth, the Smiths came in with poor Rogers. That day, Sutter took leave of kindly Whitman and his trail companions of so many months. As a gesture of friendship, he presented his treasured, leather-bound pocket French-English dictionary to Elkanah Walker. More likely, his gesture was meant for Mary. Although the inscription on the flyleaf read "Elkanah Walker, presented by Capt. Sutor," the legend was in Mary's hand, not her husband's. The would-be captain of California agriculture did not leave without first examining Whitman's adobe house, his melon and vegetable gardens, and his corn, wheat and potato fields.

Sutter next visited Fort Walla Walla, where he was received again with the traditional kindness of the Hudson's Bay Company by factor Pierre C. Pambrun. The Canadian told him that he had had a good education and had served in the British Army. So thoroughly had he become acclimatized to the frontier, however, that when Sutter prepared to leave the fort, Pambrun tried to tempt him to stay by saying, "I am sorry you are going now. I have just killed a fat mare." No lover of horsemeat, Sutter nevertheless recognized the gesture of a gentleman, if not a gourmet of Payette's caliber.

With the help of a guide provided him by Pambrun, Sutter reached The Dalles, a mission and trading post on the Columbia River. When he asked the missionaries for a guide to the Willamette River Valley, one of them, Daniel Lee, insisted upon being Sutter's pilot, himself, explaining that he had just purchased some horses from the Indians and was going to the Willamette to exchange them for cattle. Sutter set out with Lee, but hardly were they into the Cascade Range before Allgeier and Keyser came to the Swiss to complain about the course Lee was setting. "How he lies!," one of them exclaimed. "Lies?" countered Sutter, astounded at their dissatisfaction. "Why, he says nothing." But the Germans shook their heads and insisted, "See how he twists and turns about. He will bring us, at this rate, back to our starting point."

So impatient and rebellious were his two companions that Sutter decided to humor them. Besides, he was becoming impatient to reach California before the end of 1838. Polite as ever, he made his excuses to Lee and then struck directly across the Cascades with his men. It was the wildest country he had ever seen, Alps and Rockies included. At times, he and his men had to clamber up and down mountain slopes on all fours and to lower their horses down precipices on ropes. And, once, the current of a stream in flood carried away Sutter's horses and would have drowned them were it not for the quick responses of Gutiérrez.

The night that Sutter camped near the base of Mount Hood, he had nothing to offer his men but dried fish. Nor was there grass or water for the animals. Fortunately, soon after starting out again in the morning, the animals scented water and bolted for it. On September 9, just six days out of The Dalles (if Sutter reckoned correctly) they reached Jason Lee's Methodist mission. If so, it was a new world's record for the Cascades passage. No one at the Willamette believed him until he showed them a dated letter from one of the missionaries at The Dalles. With the blind luck of a greenhorn, Sutter had blundered through the mountains in express time. Daniel Lee, for all his trail experience, did not arrive at the Willamette mission for eight more days.

The missionaries were delighted with the charming Sutter. In their record book one of them wrote of the Swiss, "His visit among us has been of a truly pleasant character." Sutter rested his men for two or three weeks, but he turned a deaf ear to the missionaries' suggestions that he settle there. It was California or nothing. But he did promise one day to return to Switzerland via Oregon to collect his family and friends, and to drive cattle to the Willamette and visit his Methodist "neighbors" on the way.

Winter was not far off. It was time to move on if he was to make the beginnings of his New Switzerland in 1838. Sutter left his horses at the mission and continued his journey down the Willamette and Columbia by canoe. He arrived at Fort Vancouver in early October, just six months after bidding good-bye to his Missouri friends.

William Drummond Stewart had kindly provided Sutter with letters of introduction, which he presented to James Douglas, chief trader at Fort Vancouver, who was acting as chief factor during the absence of the legendary Dr. John McLoughlin. McLoughlin had sailed in the spring to England for a furlough. Douglas rivaled his superior not only in competence but in kindness, too, and he made Sutter feel very much at home. A West Indian Scot, he was strongly built, tolerably well educated and an excellent trader. He wrote well and Sir George Simpson, governor of the Hudson's Bay Company's Northern Department of Rupert's Land and the Columbia, thought him the equal of McLoughlin. Sutter found him very fair, firm of mind and sound in judgment.

Douglas delighted in showing off the fort to Sutter, who found it as self-sufficient as any castle or walled city of medieval Europe. It was a community, not just a trading post. Whether or not Sutter realized it consciously, Fort Vancouver influenced his plans for his own settlement on the Sacramento. He inspected the bakery, granary, storehouses, smithy, cooper's shop, flour mills, stockade, boat sheds and salmon house, salting away ideas like the very salmon he saw. Sutter was pleased with everything except for the crowded bachelors' hall of the fort, which was his headquarters during his stay. The company men turned the air inside blue with their "stiff pipes of tobacco." After months on the trail, he found it stifling and recalled, years later, "They smoked a great deal of tobacco and for this purpose they had a hall in which I could scarcely remain without suffocation."

Sutter intended to hurry overland to California from the Columbia. But Douglas soon changed his mind, pointing out the difficulty of a winter crossing of the Siskiyou Mountains even if the Indians should not give him any trouble. He urged him instead to winter at the fort, then to push on to California with a party of men who were going to the Mexican settlements for cattle in the spring. Sutter was too impatient to agree to this, but he did compromise to a certain extent. He abandoned his plan of marching over the Siskiyous to the Sacramento Valley, and instead asked Douglas for passage on the company's annual supply ship, *Columbia,* to Hawaii. Sutter decided to gamble on finding a California-bound trader in the harbor of Honolulu, to which he could transfer from the Britain-bound *Columbia.* Douglas agreed, asking only £15 for his cabin accommodation and £6 for quarters in the crew's forecastle for Sutter's eight followers.

The *Columbia* sailed on or about November 11, 1838, and after a comparatively peaceful voyage, the captain brought her past Diamond Head and safely into Honolulu harbor. On the ship, as it sailed for England, was a report by Douglas about Sutter, dated October 18. It was matter-of-fact and succinct: "The object of his visit is not exactly known. All that I can learn of his history is that he derives his title from a commission formerly held in the French Army and has no connection whatever with the U.S. Government. He left Europe with a respectable fortune, invested it in business and was unfortunate during the late commercial pressure in the United States. At present, he proposes to drive cattle from California to the Willamette."

CHAPTER IV

———————

THE SUPERCARGO

O N Sunday, December 9, 1838, the barque *Columbia* lay at anchor in Honolulu roads, twenty-eight days from the Columbia bar. Sutter disembarked and took an exploratory stroll around the tropical town. He saw native women going to services at Kawaiaho Church, the Westminster Abbey of Hawaii, dressed in beautiful silk dresses though barefoot. After his walk, Sutter returned to the barque in time to meet George Pelly, whom he took to be Her Majesty's consul but who was actually only the Honourable Company's representative in the Sandwich Islands. However, he often acted in lieu of the British consul, Richard Charlton, who may have been absent from Honolulu when the *Columbia* arrived. Shortly afterward, Sutter also made the acquaintance of the U.S. consul, John Coffin Jones. Most important, however, he was introduced to William French, Hawaii's leading Yankee merchant, who, Sutter soon learned, maintained all but a monopoly on island goods.

The *Sandwich Islands Gazette* took notice of Sutter's arrival (misspelling his name as "Shuiter"), although the paper was much more interested in the barque's cargo of 60,000 board feet of lumber and the superior-grade flour and Columbia River butter in her hold. From one of his new friends, Sutter learned, to his dismay, that he had just missed the sailing of the *Bolívar Libertador* for California. Worse, he found that there was no other sail in the harbor bound for California, nor any likelihood that there would be for months. One of his German companions found work as a cabinetmaker and was able to put aside a little money. This was more than Sutter could do, since he had to play the role of gentleman and entrepreneur. However, thanks to his genuine personal charm and to the letters of recommendation provided him by James Douglas of Fort Vancouver, he was warmly received by Honolulu's small business community. His stay in the islands would be pleasant enough, but it would stretch to four months—far longer than he had planned.

One of the first merchants encountered by Sutter was Faxon D. Atherton, who was amazed when Sutter related a rumor (which proved to be very incorrect) he had picked up in the States, to the effect that Congress had appropriated $50,000 in March 1838 to build an American fort on the Columbia River! However, on Wednesday, December 12, he passed on something more tangible to Atherton—his own plans for California. He told the American that he was going to take a look at the country in order to find a place suitable for locating a colony of settlers which he hoped to bring from Switzerland.

By the end of the year, Sutter was one of the commercial family, and he dined on Christmas Day at the hotel in the company of Atherton, British Consul Charlton, and U.S. Consul John Coffin Jones.

Sutter read a story in the *Hawaiian Spectator* by Hiram Bingham, the pioneer missionary to the Sandwich Islands, which greatly disturbed him. According to Bingham, Sutter's trail companion of the past summer, Rev. William Gray, had been attacked in 1837 by a party of Sioux, led by a Frenchman. Because of France's lusting for the Marquesas—and the Sandwich Islands, too—anti-French feeling was high in British and American circles. Sutter, the Francophile, could not resist a reply. He protested the story, politely—for he was aware of Bingham's immense prestige—but firmly in a letter, dated March 28, to the committee of editors which had taken over the *Sandwich Islands Gazette*. It appeared in the mourning-ruled issue of April 6. The paper was edged in black because of the sad and untimely death of Princess Kinau, King Kamehameha's half-sister, the governess of Oahu.

To make his statement more impressive, Sutter wrapped himself in the tricolor. "As I was formerly an officer of the Swiss Guard in the French service, I consider it my duty to defend the honour of the French nation. Hence, I am compelled to correct the accusation that a party of Sioux had been commanded by a Frenchman." He went on to explain the circumstances of Gray's trip east. The preacher had arrived at the fur rendezvous in the Green River Valley with five Flatheads, a Nez Perce, and a half-caste boy. Impatient as usual, he would not wait for the break-up of the rendezvous but had hurried on with his original party augmented by only three men, an American, a German and an Iroquois. This he did, said Sutter, despite the warnings of experienced men who told him that he was exposing his little party to great danger. Gray reached the Platte and, on the frontier of the Sioux and Pawnee country, was attacked, defeated and robbed by a Sioux war party. *But,* insisted Sutter, it was commanded by a half-breed, not a Frenchman. The war party's leader had been the son of a Sioux woman and DuChesne, trader John B. Sarpy's interpreter. "Consequently," he continued, "the Sioux party was not commanded by a Frenchman but by a three-fourth Indian."

Sutter reported that the four Flatheads, the Nez Perce (a chief's son), and the Iroquois were all killed. Gray was wounded in the head and the party's eighteen horses taken. Sutter did not give the details of the sensation the ambush caused among the Flatheads and Nez Perces until Pierre Pambrun was able to calm them down. Nor did he mention the hostility shown Gray at the

Popo Agie by the mountain men for what they believed to be his sacrificing of their Indian friends. But he did report the stinging taunt with which the half-breed warrior bade Gray farewell at the Platte, inviting the missionary to return again in 1839— with another herd of horses for him to steal.

Perhaps the letter, with its glowing reference to his imaginary French military career, enhanced Sutter's already winning combination of good manners and letters of recommendation. In any case, he soon had substantial credit. The ledger of French and Greenaway Company eventually devoted a page and a half to Sutter's account. While outfitting for his California adventure, he ran up a bill of $3,008.68. (Ten years later, French would present him with a bill for the sum and be paid by Sutter from the proceeds of sales of Sacramento lots.) It was, perhaps, the most important grubstake in the entire history of California.

The only vessel riding at anchor in the harbor was the eighty-eight-ton brig *Clementine*, built at Mahé in the Seychelles Islands. The vessel was for sale but there were no takers. Sutter stretched the truth once again in his memoirs, claiming that he bought the ship. Actually, he got William French to charter her for a trading voyage. The brig was freighted with a cargo of provisions and general merchandise for the Russian colony of New Archangel, Alaska, and French then signed Sutter on as unpaid supercargo.

The *Clementine*'s master, Capt. John Blinn, resumed command and, on April 20, 1839, hoisted anchor and pointed the vessel's prow toward Sitka. Sailing with Sutter were nine or ten Hawaiians, or Kanakas, two of them women; the others were all experienced seamen. With him also were the two Germans and his Hawaiian bulldog. On April 27, the *Sandwich Islands Gazette* bade Sutter *aloha*.

Sitka proved to be no barren outpost. Sutter enjoyed the social life of the Russian-American capital and stretched his stay there to a good month after the *Clementine*'s cargo was unloaded. He enjoyed conversations, in French, with the governor, Admiral Kauprianoff, and his wife, the former Princess Menchikoff. He spoke German to the storekeeper and practiced his faulty Spanish on the chief clerk. There were many feast days, sometimes three in a single week of the Julian calendar, and receptions, balls and banquets were given at the slightest excuse. Sutter had the privilege of dancing with the governor's lady, and he immensely enjoyed the pomp and splendor of the little court. The only thing which disturbed him was his clumsiness on the dance floor. He complained, "I was obliged to dance Russian dances which I had never seen before."

Perhaps it was Admiral Kauprianoff who decided Sutter upon the exact site of his settlement, for the two men discussed various expeditions to Alta California. During his stay at Fort Vancouver, Sutter had acquired a good idea of the course of the Sacramento River, and it may be that he had decided to locate on it even before he met Kauprianoff. But he pumped him for further information. Sutter knew that Michel Laframboise led Hudson's Bay trapping parties there every year and had done so since 1832. Doubtless, James Douglas had told him, too, of Jedediah Smith's exploration of the Buenaventura and Rapid Rivers, as he had named the Sacramento and American. And, somewhere, Sutter had picked up the story of another explorer's having gone upriver as far as the Sacramento's junction with the American.

The passage from Sitka to the Golden Gate proved to be a rough and hungry one. Lowering weather turned into gales which struck the *Clementine* savagely as she coasted the Oregon shore. The as-yet-unnamed Golden Gate was muffled behind fog banks but, thanks to a map, which Kauprianoff had given Sutter, Captain Blinn was able to find the great bight inside the Farallon Islands. He crept gingerly into the Golden Gate and the brig's anchor sank into the mud of Yerba Buena Cove on July 1, 1839. Sutter was in his new home.

California's growth in population and agriculture—there was no industry of any kind—was as slow and creaking in the 1830's as the rude *carretas* which traveled its Camino Real, the single road in the entire province. A setback to even this slow pace was the secularization of the missions in 1834. When they were placed under civilian control, they decayed like papayas in the sun. The civil administrators neglected the mission buildings, and once the roofs fell into disrepair, the adobe walls melted back into the ground from which they had sprung. Their herds of longhorned cattle ran wild. The tamed Indians reverted to barbarism and savagery, many of them becoming horse thieves for a living.

The California which Sutter saw for the first time in 1839 was already in decay, its sole (pastoral) economy running down, its government a virtual anarchy of endless *coups* and attempted *coups.* Yerba Buena, the "metropolis" of the north, would not claim a population of even 500 persons for another seven years.

The Swiss adventurer arrived in Yerba Buena Cove just three years after Richard Henry Dana, the gifted author of *Two Years Before the Mast,* who had described its desolation to the world:

> To the westward of the landing-place were dreary sand-hills, with little grass to be seen and few trees and, beyond them, higher hills, steep and barren, their sides gullied by the rains. Some five or six miles beyond the landing place, to the right, was a ruinous *presidio* and some three or four miles to the left was the Mission of Dolores, as ruinous as the *presidio,* almost deserted, with but few Indians attached to it, and but little property in cattle. Over a region far beyond our sight there were no other human habitations except that an enterprising Yankee [William A. Richardson, actually an Englishman], years in advance of his time, had put up, on the rising ground above the landing, a shanty of rough boards where he carried on a very small retail trade between the hide ships and the Indians. Vast banks of fog, invading us from the North Pacific, drove in through the entrance and covered the whole bay, and when they disappeared, we saw a few well-wooded islands, the sand-hills on the west, the grassy and wooded slopes on the east, and the vast stretch of the bay to the southward. . . . The few ranchos and missions were remote and widely separated. . . . The entire region of the great bay was a solitude. On the whole coast of California there was not a lighthouse, a beacon, or a buoy.

74

A small boat approached the brig from the shore. From it, a Mexican officer scrambled up the jacob's ladder and onto the deck. His welcome was anything but the warm *aloha* Sutter had received in Hawaii. He informed Sutter and Blinn that they could not land at Yerba Buena (later San Francisco) because Monterey, the capital, was the only port of entry. Sutter answered glibly, plausibly and politely. "I am aware of the fact but I was driven in by stress of weather, and I was out of provisions. I did not enter the port intentionally."

Sutter showed his letters from Fort Vancouver, Honolulu and Sitka first to the lieutenant, Don Juan Prado Mesa, then again when ships' captains Gorham Nye and John Wilson came aboard with merchant Nathan Spear. It was Sutter's good Swiss luck to have a fine letter of introduction from U.S. Consul John Coffin Jones of Honolulu to Mariano G. Vallejo, commanding general and military chief of Alta California. Vallejo was not only Prado Mesa's commanding officer, he was Captain Wilson's brother-in-law! Moreover, Spear, the leading merchant of Yerba Buena, took Sutter's part with the lieutenant and the *alcalde,* pointing out that Sutter had obviously arrived in distress. The overwhelmed Prado Mesa finally relented enough to allow Sutter and Blinn to stay forty-eight hours in order to make repairs and to refill the water casks. He could do no less for a man described by a U.S. consul to his commander as "a Swiss gentleman and a first-class man, honored for his talents and reputation."

Blinn quickly put carpenters and sailmakers to work, and by the Fourth of July he was ready to sail. The Americans of Yerba Buena tried to persuade Sutter to remain in order to join in the Independence Day celebration. But Prado Mesa would not extend the time limit and Sutter, on his very best conduct, made his apologies. Determined not to jeopardize his plans by even a single misstep at the outset, he gave the order to sail.

Next day, the *Clementine* anchored in the open harbor of Monterey. Going ashore, Sutter was met by David Spence, justice of the peace, who offered him lodging. He gratefully accepted the offer and remained in the house of the Scot who was, he found, one of the most influential foreigners living in the Mexican province. Sutter showed his letters to Spence, who then escorted him to an audience with the governor, Juan B. Alvarado. Spence remarked to Alvarado, in Sutter's behalf, "No one has, ever before, come with so many letters." Sutter explained his intention of becoming an *empresario* on the northern California frontier by settling colonists on the Sacramento.

Governor Alvarado was pleased with both Sutter's manner and his plan. As the Swiss recalled their discussion, "Alvarado was very glad that someone had come who wanted to settle in the wilderness of the Valley of California, where the Indians were very wild and very bad." But Alvarado was a little doubtful that his visitor could carry out his project. After all, the Swiss's resources were limited. Besides supplies, some trade goods, small arms and three cannon, he had only a handful of Kanakas, signed up for three years at ten dollars a month, with which to conquer a wilderness. Thus, when Sutter came to the point and asked the governor for a grant of land, Alvarado put him off. He advised him to select and improve a tract first, then to return to Monterey in a year. At that time Sutter would be eligible for Mexican citizenship and, he promised, he would then give him grants to the unoccupied land he had chosen.

Some of Alvarado's hesitation was due to the fact that Sutter was not the first to plan such a settlement. As early as 1811, the Sacramento River plain had been marked for colonization by Fathers Ramón Abella and Buenaventura Fortuni, who explored its lower reaches. But the Spanish Empire was in decline and nothing came of it. In 1829, Abel Stearns and George Ayres planned to settle the area, but Stearns' penchant for meddling in the politics of now-independent Mexico caused him to be expelled by Governor Victoria. Even Hall J. Kelly, Oregon's pioneer, toyed with the idea of exploring and settling the great river basin and, in the next few years, Irishmen, Prussians and American Mormons would design ambitious settlements which never materialized. Alvarado could not be blamed; he did not yet know Sutter's mettle.

The governor did see that Sutter's plan, if successful, would prove a godsend in buttressing the frontier which he was trying to maintain against Indians, Russians, Americans and British. Sutter seemed to have no fear of the hostile rustlers who, Alvarado warned him, would not welcome him to the no-man's-land from which they launched their raids on the horses and cattle of San José and other settlements. And, before terminating the interview, the governor advised Sutter against settling in the territory commanded by his jealous uncle, Mariano G. Vallejo. Despite their kinship, General Vallejo was the governor's major rival. Alvarado put it clearly to Sutter; his uncle kept his area under military ordinances which, he was sure, Sutter would find incompatible with his plans for living independently on the frontier.

On July 3, Spence wrote a letter of recommendation which Sutter hoped would grease his way into the general's good graces. It was a model of the genre, introducing him as "an excellent person, of good character and [one who] desires to be a neighbor of yours. For this purpose, he is going to look for a ranch. He is bringing with him some useful men—artisans." Spence knew how swiftly Mexican-Californians dropped their hostility when foreigners turned out to be carpenters or boatwrights. Sutter's cabinetmakers might prove to be aces up his sleeve. Spence's letter, of course, was backed by the one written for Sutter by U.S. Consul Jones to Vallejo. It read in part: "Captain Sutter is going to California with the intention of remaining there if he finds the country comes up to his hopes, and you will do me a great favor if you will assist him in every way that may be in your power."

With two such letters in his pocket, Sutter felt equipped to beard the redoubtable Vallejo in his Sonoma "castle." He had Captain Blinn sail for San Francisco Bay, where the *Clementine* dropped her hook again on July 7, at about the point where Montgomery and Clay streets would one day meet. From the deck, Sutter gazed at the shore, picking out the *casa grande* of

Capt. William Richardson, at once the pilot, harbormaster and captain of the port. Next, his eyes sought and found Jacob Leese's frame building (which would, later, house the Hudson's Bay Company store) and a scattering of other wooden and adobe structures. He could identify only a few of them—John Fuller's home and the wine cellar and *cantina* of Victor Prudón, who, Sutter knew, was an important man often called upon to draw up official papers because of his excellent command of Castilian. Sutter's eyes roamed the shore but found nothing resembling a wharf in the entire harbor. All goods had to be lightered to the beach in small boats. Nor were the harbor defenses impressive. The *presidio* of San Francisco boasted a small garrison to serve the old battery, but Sutter saw that it was only a token force, for show.

Supercargo Sutter had no freight for Yerba Buena, so it was only a matter of unloading his equipment and men from the *Clementine*. He did not think he could take such a deep-draft vessel up the Sacramento, so he released the brig to Captain Blinn, who loaded her with barrels of beef and beans and set sail on August 10 for Honolulu.

Meanwhile, Sutter was rowed across the bay with Captains Richardson and John Wilson. They proceeded up the twisting slough of Sonoma Creek to the Sonoma *embarcadero* where they left Wilson's boat crew and joined Vallejo's *vaqueros,* who awaited them with saddle horses. With the cowboys as guides, they rode to Vallejo's headquarters, adjacent to Mission San Francisco de Solano.

Vallejo welcomed the men but was a little stiff with Sutter, just as he had expected him to be. He tried to persuade the Swiss to settle near Sonoma rather than far off in the great central valley, praising the great tracts of unoccupied land around Suisun Bay, Mount Diablo and the Napa Valley and insisting that there was absolutely no need to go to the far wilderness of the upper Sacramento. Sutter understood that the general wanted to keep an eye on him. Captain Wilson tried to be helpful at this juncture, offering Sutter his own Sonoma cattle ranch, stock included, at a very low price. When Sutter declined, without any hesitation, Vallejo's brother-in-law exclaimed in exasperation, "Well, my God! I'd like to know what you really want!" Sutter pacified Wilson as best he could, for he could not confess that he wanted to put as much distance as possible between himself and the general. Instead, he explained, "I prefer to be on a navigable river." This satisfied Wilson and Vallejo enough for them to drop the argument. "In reality," Sutter confessed later, "I had information that my neighbors of that [Sonoma] valley had a way of marking other people's calves that I did not like. I noticed, also, that the hat must come off before the military guard, the flagstaff, and the Church. And I preferred a country where I could keep mine on. In other words, where I should be absolute master."

Leaving the sea captains with Vallejo, Sutter went to pay a courtesy call on Fort Ross. He carried greetings to the commandant from Admiral Kauprianoff in Sitka. At the Edward Manuel MacIntosh ranch, near Bodega, he secured fresh horses and continued on over the steep Coast Range to the first outpost of the Russian colony, about halfway between Bodega and Fort Ross. This way station was a farm with two wooden houses, in one of which he found a room set aside for travelers. There he joined a guide sent down from Fort Ross and continued on to the seaside bastion.

Governor and Baron Alexander G. Rotcheff received him most warmly and introduced him to his wife, the lovely Princess Helena de Gagarin. (He had eloped with her years before, when the Tsar's court would not hear of her marrying beneath her station.) Sutter presented his letters to the baron and, while his host glanced at them, Sutter sized up the fort, finding it a compound surrounded by a palisaded wall of split redwood timbers, which looked to him to be about twenty feet high. There were about fifty buildings and sheds, all of heavy redwood timber. Sutter thought the post compared favorably with both Forts Laramie and Vancouver.

When Rotcheff finished his reading, he took Sutter on an impressive tour of his industrious settlement. Mechanics and laborers of various kinds were at work, for Rotcheff allowed a modest trade to be carried on with the Mexicans. While showing his guest the fields of grain and the truck gardens, the baron explained that they were becoming more important every year as a food source for Alaska. He mentioned, too, that seal and sea-otter hunting, the original impetus for the settlement, were declining. But Sitka's wheat, barley and vegetables came from the foggy little outpost on the coastal shelf north of the Slavianka (now the Russian) River. Even the hay for Kauprianoff's two cows was imported from California's redwood coast.

The most impressive building was the Greek Orthodox church, with its cupola topped with a distinctive slant-armed Russian cross. But more interesting to the future colonizer was Fort Ross' great threshing floor of redwood timbers. And he responded to the pride and enthusiasm with which the Princess showed off her twenty-foot greenhouse in a beautiful garden lying behind the fort. While dining with the governor and his lady in the manager's house, Sutter learned that Rotcheff was a writer and translator of plays for the Russian stage. Before bidding his new friend good-bye, Sutter told him that he intended to settle on the upper Sacramento River plain. Rotcheff responded, "If I can be of any service to you, command me."

Returning to the MacIntosh place, Sutter spent the night there. Next day, he and the *vaquero* returned via Sonoma to Yerba Buena. Once back in the sleepy port, he made his way to Nathan Spear's store and home, Kent Hall (named for the superstructure of the old *Kent,* out of which Spear built it). Sutter chartered the twenty-ton schooner *Isabel* from Spear and William S. Hinckley as well as Hinckley's yacht, the *Nicholas,* supposedly once the pleasure craft of the king of Hawaii. Sutter rounded out his flotilla by buying Wilson's four-oared pinnace. He chose William Heath (Kanaka Bill) Davis to command his little fleet, with a Dublin-born Irishman, Jack Rainsford, as master of the *Isabel.*

Sutter's credit, supported by his letters of reference, remained good, and he had no trouble lading his craft with provisions, seeds, agricultural tools, muskets, rifles, powder and lead. Nor was there any problem in crewing his vessels. Sailors who had jumped ship and were rotting on the beach at Yerba Buena were eager for a change of scenery. He signed on four or five of them to reinforce his party of about thirteen.

On August 8, 1839, Capt. George Vincent played host to a farewell party for Sutter aboard his Boston ship *Monsoon*. Recalling it later, Sutter wrote theatrically, "All were here to bid me goodbye, as to one whom they never expected to see again."

CHAPTER V

THE EXPLORER

EARLY on the morning of August 9, 1839, Sutter dropped down the jacob's ladder of the *Monsoon* and into his pinnace. He moved his little squadron away from the ship's side and out onto the broad surface of the bay. The course which he had his pilot, Davis, set was due north first, then northeast to bring the craft past Mare Island and through Carquinez Strait, a narrow passage hemmed in by hills which were grassy but bare of trees except for a few evergreen oaks crouching in marshy meadows. When he passed tiny Seal Island and reached Vallejo Bay, Sutter had his Kanaka oarsmen pull him to shore. The schooners followed his lead to a landing on the south shore, where he docked to pay a courtesy call similar to his visit to Vallejo. This time his host was Don Ygnacio Martínez, owner of Rancho Pinole. Martínez was destined to become Sutter's nearest neighbor, only sixty miles away.

Sutter was calling not only to observe the amenities but also to try to purchase cattle and horses for his settlement. Martínez agreed to deliver the animals to him once he was settled on the Sacramento. Next morning, Sutter led his small fleet out again

on an easterly and northeasterly course in Suisun Bay toward a
bewildering maze of low-lying, overflowed islands and peninsulas.
He was entering the great delta shared by the Sacramento and San
Joaquin rivers. (Two years after his maiden voyage in these waters, Lt. Comdr. Cadwalader Ringgold, U.S.N., would suggest
that Suisun Bay might more aptly be named Bay of Islands.)

The boats proceeded deeper and deeper into the tule marshes
of the delta where, eleven years earlier, Jedediah Smith had set
twenty-eight traps and immediately caught twenty beavers. The
rounded Montezuma Hills on the north shore, covered with ripe,
straw-colored wild oats, receded from view. Taking his bearings
from Mount Diablo, rising gloomily over the marshes, Davis
guessed badly at Tongue Shoal. Just beyond that shallow reach
the true entrance of the Sacramento River lurked, but it was
masked by Point Sherman, wooded Burnett Island, and the Chain
Islets. Mistakenly keeping the huge bulk of Sherman Island,
which separated the mouths of the two rivers, on his port beam,
Davis led the vessels past Hammond and Weber islands and the
mouth of the slough destined to be called False River. He avoided
that trap only to fall into a much greater one. Unwillingly, he led
Sutter up the San Joaquin River.

Sutter was in no position to correct Davis. He knew far less
of the lay of the land and the drainage of the central valley than
Spear's seventeen-year-old nephew. Kanaka Bill, so-named because he was half Hawaiian, had taken the *Isabel* into many of
the bays, sloughs and streams opening out of San Francisco Bay
while collecting grain, cattle, hides and tallow from ranches for
his uncle or returning wheat flour to them. But he was thoroughly
lost now. He had to depend on the British explorer Edward
Belcher's rude map and inaccurate account: "Two considerable
rivers fall into the Bay of San Francisco, of the which that in the
north is the largest and is called by the Spaniards the Río Grande.
This river, the missionaries say, is the finest in the world and is
navigable by the largest vessels; at the same time, its banks are
fruitful, the climate is mild, and the population numerous. The

missionaries frequently make excursions upon it in large, well-armed, boats in order to get recruits for their faith in which, however, they seldom succeed, the inhabitants being brave and well-armed." Actually, the Sacramento River was virtually *terra incognita,* not only to the *padres* but to such men as Vallejo, Alvarado and Martínez as well. It was, in fact, a no-man's-land, claimed by Mexico but held by Indians of various tribes, united only in their hostility to the civilized.

The voyage was a taxing one, though Davis quickly realized his mistake and wasted only two days in ascending the wrong river, perhaps as far as present-day Stockton. But to Sutter it seemed to take a week. Writing in the 1870's, he recalled, incorrectly, "I was eight days in finding the entrance to the Sacramento after I reached Suisun Bay." Each night, he grouped the boats at the shore before going inland to reconnoiter and select a campsite. No matter how fine a site he chose, rest was almost impossible for his men because of the astonishingly thick clouds of mosquitoes that descended upon them. Returning to Suisun Bay, Sutter and his men coasted its northeast shore again, poking in and out of bays and sloughs in an exasperating search for the elusive Buenaventura-Sacramento. Then, as Sutter remembered, "One night, after sundown, after having searched again all day in vain, I said, disgruntled, to my people, 'Now, let us go in here and camp for the night.' And then, when I was in, I saw a great opening and said, 'This is the River Sacramento.'" It was probably the deep East Fork or, possibly, the Middle Fork. Sutter would have been suspicious of the shallow westernmost channel.

The Swiss left notes in prominent places to guide the two larger vessels, as his pinnace explored the delta lands. When they caught up with him on the open river, he shifted his command from the pinnace to his flagship, joining Kanaka Bill and Rainsford on the *Isabel.* The little fleet continued its way slowly up the twisting, multi-channeled river, winding away from humpbacked Mount Diablo at last. Sutter was pleased with the Sacramento—once he found it. The three channels merged into one deep bed at Baker's

Reach, and he noted that its banks grew higher and higher as he progressed. The flat fields beyond the riverside fringe of sycamores, cottonwoods and elms appeared well suited for agriculture. The river bed, he found, was composed of mud, clay and sand, with virtually no rocks to threaten a vessel. Even running aground proved to be only a minor mishap, since neither the grounding nor the easy refloating seemed to injure a hull. The only snags or sawyers that he saw were close to the river banks, never obstructing the main channel. Sutter guessed that they might be perilous in the spring and winter floods but not in summer, when they could easily be seen in the lower water and avoided. There was no need for Davis to heave a lead line, with the shallow draft of Sutter's vessels. The lowest channel was a full ten feet deep, as compared with the San Joaquin's one fathom.

While he observed the scenery, Sutter carried on spirited conversations in his heavily accented English. He quickly convinced young Davis that he was an accomplished and educated gentleman and revealed to the impressed youngster his grand design. He would build not just a settlement on the Sacramento but a real fort which would serve him as a defense against the Mexican government, if need be, as well as against Indians, "in case any hostility should be manifested in that quarter." Certain that Vallejo would attempt to meddle in his affairs, to keep him in his place, he was determined to be prepared for him. Sutter told his shipmates that he intended to form a large colony of Swiss on the river. His hard-working countrymen would then spread out to develop and civilize the entire Sacramento Valley.

Once out of the reed marshes, the passage was a relatively easy one. The prevailing northwest winds were no trouble. Barring the mosquitoes, it was practically a pleasure cruise. There were no Indians to be seen but no lack of Indian sign along the river. Sutter had spent enough time among the redmen to know something of their ways. He recognized bunches of white feathers tied

86

to tree branches overhanging the shore as religious offerings. He understood that many Indian eyes watched his passage, from hiding. The Indians bided their time until Sutter was only ten or twelve miles below the mouth of the American River. Then, suddenly, 200 armed warriors appeared in a clearing. Their bodies were painted yellow, black and red, and they made threatening gestures at the pinnace. His men wanted to open fire on the savages, but Sutter ordered them to keep quiet and not to shoot unless he expressly directed them to do so. Alone and unarmed, he made for shore. Banking, rashly, on the surety that there were runaway San Jose Mission Indians among the throng, he called out in garbled Spanish, *"Adiós, amigos! Adiós, amigos!"* However upside-down the greeting, it served to demonstrate his peaceable intentions. Two of the Indians came forward to talk to Sutter in pidgin Spanish which was almost as bad as his own.

By telling them that there were no Spaniards in his party and by assuring them that he had not come to make war or to carry off captives as slaves, Sutter pacified the natives. He said that he only came to live among them as a friend. He then produced his agricultural tools and trade goods and proposed a treaty. One of the two Spanish-speaking ex-mission Indians he sent off in a canoe with a letter to Davis and Rainsford, for the schooners were lagging behind him. The other man he took into the pinnace as pilot and interpreter. He had the two men parley first, however, with their fellow tribesmen to tell them all to come and visit his camp, promising them presents should they do so. The warriors, who were of Chief Anashe's Walagumne tribe, appeared satisfied with the pow-wow and melted into the underbrush.

The accounts of Sutter and Davis differ somewhat as to exactly what happened next. Davis stated that the boats anchored off the site of Sacramento that afternoon and were soon surrounded by 700 to 800 Indians in tule canoes. Again, the whites and Polynesians prepared for an attack. But none came. The boats then entered the American River and the men landed and pitched their tents while Sutter saw to the mounting of his brass cannon, just in case the Indians should choose combat. Sutter's own memory had it that he took the boats past the mouth of the American, frightening off hundreds of Indians from a nearby *ranchería,* then sailed on up the Sacramento to enter the Feather, rather than the American, River. Since the Feather was wider at its mouth than the Sacramento, he entered the former in the pinnace. Ten or fifteen miles of progress convinced him that he had the wrong river, and he dropped back to the mouth to find his schooners at anchor.

Captain Sutter now faced an incipient mutiny. His men were tired and fearful of the unknown. He, too, was nearly exhausted but was eager to penetrate deeper into the wonderland of water and plain. That night, when he went to the little cabin of the schooner to sleep, his men demanded to know just how long he intended to lead them around in the wilderness. He refused to give them a straight answer then but promised them one in the morning. During the night, he mulled the matter over. He wanted to explore farther upstream, but he knew that he could not continue in the face of a mutinous crew. He surrendered, telling the men that he had decided to return to the American River. They floated down the Sacramento, entered that tributary and made their way up it as far as it was navigable for their keels. Then he gave orders for all his goods to be landed while he attended to the cannon.

Once his property was safely ashore, Sutter decided to put an end to dissatisfaction. He assembled all hands and told them that he was dispatching the schooners to Yerba Buena in the morning for more provisions. All those who wished to sail were free to do so. Announcing that their pay was ready, he told his audience that he wanted none but contented men with him, even if it meant being alone in the wilderness with his loyal Kanakas. Six of them decided to return with Davis and Rainsford, leaving Sutter with three whites, his Hawaiians, and one Indian. During the night he drew orders on Nathan Spear for the men's pay, in goods. He had little cash. Indeed, there was hardly any in all California. Hides—"California banknotes"—were the customary currency. They were worth $1 in cash or $2 in trade at Yerba Buena. Prices of trade goods were so inflated on the Boston sailing ships which called at San Francisco Bay that Sutter observed, "He who went on board with $100 in money or hides could carry away his purchases in a pocket handkerchief."

But Sutter had no time to worry about his erstwhile employees and their buying power. He had to make peace with the Indians, who now came in to see him. He gave them beads, blankets and shirts. They brought him in exchange some sore-backed horses which he was certain they had stolen from California *rancheros.* (He bought them at a very low price in order to please their Indian "owners," then, in an inspired piece of public relations, pastured them till their sores healed and turned them back to their real—and grateful—owners.) He then treated the Indians to a show of his military power by saluting the departure of the *Isabel* and the *Nicholas* with a cannonade, firing a nine-round salute, "to show the Indians the effect of powder and shell. I planted my guns and fired at a target. They didn't care to have them tried on them." William Heath Davis described the historic salute and the reaction to it:

As the heavy report of the guns and the echoes died away, the camp of the little party was surrounded by hundreds of Indians, who were excited and astonished at the unusual sound. A large number of deer, elk and other animals on the plains were startled, running to and fro, stopping to listen, their heads raised, full of curiosity and wonder, seemingly attracted and fascinated to the spot while from the interior of the adjacent wood the howl of wolves and coyotes filled the air, and immense flocks of water fowl flew wildly about, over the camp. Standing on the deck of the *Isabel,* I witnessed this remarkable sight, which filled me with astonishment and admiration, and made an indelible impression on my mind. This salute was the first echo of civilization in the primitive wilderness so soon to become populated and developed

89

into a great agricultural and commercial center. We returned the salute with nine cheers from the schooners, the vessels flying the American colors. The cheers were heartily responded to by the little garrison and thus we parted company.

Now Sutter could get down to the business of empire-building. It was August 13, 1839. The first order of business was food, so he sent one of his white employees, along with an Indian guide, for game. They were soon back with an elk. Next, he led his men inland a quarter of a mile to a gentle rise. There he attended to the problem of shelter. He had them erect the tents, then set his Kanakas to work building two Hawaiian-style grass houses, or *hale pili*. His white workers helped by building the frames, but the skilled islanders attended to the crucial thatching.

While his Hawaiian grass shacks were taking shape, Sutter wrote the first of what would become a veritable barrage of letters. Few understood better the power of the pen than Capt. John A. Sutter. Letters of introduction had given him his start in California. A continuous correspondence might secure his position, if permanent ties could be made with the Mexican-Californian residents who were his neighbors. In lame and halting Spanish, he wrote first to Don Ygnacio Martínez to ask for the promised horses and cattle. He particularly needed draft oxen to transport everything from the riverbank to the knoll. He wrote, "The mosquitoes eat us nearly up here, and without the oxen we cannot do anything." He also wanted more milk cows and beef steers for meat than he had originally requested. He offered Martínez goods in exchange for animals. For the first time of a thousand, he assured Martínez that he would be pleased with his bargain. He also asked for beans, wheat, dried meat, Indian corn (for seed), and lard. Most of all he needed saddles, no matter how old and battered. Already he was demonstrating his peculiar sway over simple people, like the Hawaiians and California's so-called Digger Indians. Not only were a number of Indians in his employ before he had even raised a permanent structure, but he had already turned two Indians, Clemente and Julián, into *vaqueros*. And no self-respecting cowboy would ride bareback.

With only tents and two Hawaiian shacks in his settlement, Sutter at once demonstrated the hospitality which would become legendary. He invited Don Ygnacio's son and his friend, Octavio Custot, to come up with the stock and visit him.

Once the grass huts were completed, Sutter set his laborers to building a one-story adobe. About forty-five feet long, it contained a blacksmith shop, a kitchen and his own sleeping quarters. The roof was of tules, thatched by his islanders. They finished the job in the nick of time, thwarting the late autumnal rain. During the first weeks of residence there, Sutter did not stir far from this adobe headquarters. But he was not by any means at leisure. He was hunting, making the settlement secure, and wooing the friendship of Anashe and other chiefs, liberally passing out brightly colored bandannas and handkerchiefs, glass trade beads and small bags of his precious Hawaiian sugar. Anashe, particularly, became a friend and ally.

Sutter won the alliance of local tribes but never their complete confidence. Thus, though he tried to learn all about the history of his tribe from Chief Anashe, Sutter got little out of him other than that his people had once been powerful but had been greatly reduced by disease, probably smallpox. "They dislike to impart much of such valuable information to white men," said Sutter. Anashe's reticence was apparently due to a superstition that bad luck followed the divulgence of tribal lore.

At the end of September, Martínez had still not delivered the animals; far worse, he had taken Sutter's two cowboys into his own employ. Sutter managed to hold his temper—he was in a poor position, after all, to scold Don Ygnacio. Instead, he asked the *ranchero* to pay him the seven *pesos* each that Clemente and Julián owed him. Still, he tried to be obliging, reaffirming the invitation to his son: "If Don [Vicente] José Martínez wishes to come here when the cattle come, he can, easily, on the launch, and also choose from my goods what he likes best. In case he does not come, I will go to your house in a short time."

Sutter's letters secured the dried meat, butter, beans, rope, candles and ox yokes he needed, but Martínez was excruciatingly slow about sending the animals themselves. Moreover, Sutter was having Indian trouble for the first time, and caused directly by Martínez. His kidnapping of Sutter's two Indian *vaqueros* had caused the flight of many of his Indian workers from Sutter's little settlement. They feared the Mexicans and told Sutter they were sure that Clemente and Julián were prisoners. Sutter wrote urgently to Don Ygnacio, asking him to "send these two Indians in my boat. . . . Then I will be able to serve you with all the Indians that you may need."

Sutter's patience eroded away and was replaced by a festering anger which erupted on October 22, 1839, when the stock arrived. He found the herd short one cow and two heifers, so he deducted from his bill eight *pesos* for the missing cow and eight more for the two missing heifers. Since his two Indians were still virtually Martínez' captives, he also deducted their pay for one and a half month's work. Because he had advanced young Vicente Martínez eight *pesos* in silver, he deducted them, too, from what he owed Don Ygnacio. Warming to his task, he wrote the *ranchero,* "I must tell you also, with a good deal of sorrow, that I am not satisfied with the manner in which you have treated me in the matter of the oxen, mares and tame horses. The mares arrived all unbroken, a thing which annoys me very much, with the greater reason that I had put all my confidence in you, thinking that you would serve me with all exactness, as I expected of a gentleman." Heedless of his very precarious foothold on the shore of the American River, Sutter proceeded to infuriate his creditor further by adding, "The wheat which you sent me is so full of maggots that it has infested my whole house and spoiled nearly all of my flour. I would not have believed that you would have been capable of selling me such wheat!"

After furiously insulting him, Sutter nevertheless had the gall to ask Martínez to pick up some butter and seed for him at Don Antonio Suñol's ranch! He assured his correspondent that he would pay, and dangled as part payment a quantity of calico and a Scotch cape. For the rest, the supremely confident, and not a little arrogant, pioneer wrote, "We will settle on my next trip."

When next Sutter wrote Martínez, it was to accuse his son of stealing the missing cow! As if deliberately provoking the man upon whom he depended for survival, Sutter then dismissed Don Ygnacio's complaints about his overvaluation of the Scotch cape by saying, "I did not come to this country to open a shop. Besides, you can buy cheaper in the house of Señor Nathan Spear, who is my agent." At least, Sutter was honest enough to give him a note for what he owed him, 361 *pesos* and 6 *reales*.

By now, Martínez was furious with Sutter. He demanded full payment but got nothing for his pains but another insulting letter: "I truly believe that you ought not to complain for, since you failed in the quality of the animals which you sent, there is no reason why you should wish to exact the fulfilment of a contract in which you were the first to fail. . . ." With the maddening inconsistency which would mark him during his entire California career, Sutter then tried to mollify Martínez: "This slight misunderstanding in our business ought not, nevertheless, to cool our friendship. For you know well that the latter is one thing and [business] interest is another."

Although Sutter was Mexicanized enough to close his letters with such flowery phrases as "your affectionate servant who kisses your hands . . . accept assurance of my high and distinguished considerations . . . I pray God to preserve your life and those of your family for many years," he was anything but polite in the body of his letters. He made an enemy of Vallejo not only by welshing on debts but by his arrogance. When Vallejo wrote, asking him if Spear would pay him, on Sutter's behalf, in silver, Sutter snapped in reply, "Shall he pay a part of it in silver, or not? For me, it is all the same. Nevertheless, I might have acted differently if you had not failed in good faith and loyalty in sending me the articles about which we have already spoken a good deal. In consequence of this, I do not believe myself under obligations of fulfilling a debt to my entire satisfaction which, in fact, I had the intent of fulfilling. But your conduct was the cause of mine."

Sutter was on a collison course with his *Californio* neighbors but was faring considerably better in his relations with the Indians and his Kanakas. Experienced boatmen, the Hawaiians were good builders and laborers, as well. He was genuinely fond of them, and they would prove to be his most loyal associates in California. "I had undertaken to pay them ten dollars a month," he recalled, "and to send them back to the islands after three years, at my own expense, if they wished to leave me. These men were very glad to go with me and at the expiration of their time they would not leave me. Two of them were married and brought their wives with them. These women made themselves very useful by teaching the Indian girls to wash and sew. . . . I could not have settled the country without the aid of these Kanakas. They were always faithful and true to me."

Taking nothing away from the several white men who stuck by him, the success of the infant colony of New Switzerland was due largely to the loyalty of Sutter's islanders. Kanaka Harry eventually became his major-domo at the Hock Farm, a satellite of Sutter's Fort. Maintop succeeded to the command of Sutter's launch, the *Sacramento,* which kept the colony in touch with civilization. (It was Maintop who gave the Sacramento River seasonal names. In the winter it was *Muliwai Konaloli,* or Turbulent River; in the summer, *Muliwai Ulianianikiki,* Dark, Smooth and Swift-flowing River.) Harry's brother, his name unknown to us, served Sutter well, until his drowning in Suisun Bay in 1847. Harry's brother-in-law, confusingly, was known by the same name as his sister, Manuiki. Sam Kapu and his wife, Elena, as well as Ioanne Keaala o Kaaina (called John Kelly by the Americans) who married a Maidu girl, were also among Sutter's first and most devoted colonists.

Dearest to Sutter of all the islanders was the girl, Manuiki.

Some of his associates, notably Heinrich Lienhard, insisted that she was Sutter's common-law wife and bore him several children, none of whom survived infancy. According to Lienhard, Sutter— a regular wilderness Don Juan—tired of Manuiki and gave her back to Harry as a wife, devoting his *droit du seigneur* to young Indian girls living in the fort. Like Laufkotter, Lienhard had a Teutonic ear for scandal and was always quick to deprecate the man who offered him protection, friendship and hospitality.

Whether or not Sutter was a California Don Juan, there is little doubt that Manuiki was his mistress. On February 22, 1840, he wrote William Heath Davis, "If you have any gold earrings left, I wish you would send me three or four, if they are not too high priced." It is most unlikely he meant to lavish gold earrings on Indians delighted by glass beads.

Life was good, if still not yet easy, as 1839 dwindled away to nothing at the settlement Sutter was already calling New Helvetia—New Switzerland. Buildings of adobe were going up, ground was broken for wheat, and he had cut a road to an *embarcadero* on the deep-water Sacramento, as well as to the American River's shore. Sutter had planted his colony well; he knew that it was going to prosper. Although its growth was almost imperceptible that first rainy winter, the roots of New Helvetia were worming deep into the sandy soil, steadily gaining strength. Paradoxically, Sutter was also cultivating a bumper crop of enemies in men who might have been his friends—Vallejo, Suñol, Martínez. Vallejo, particularly, was more than irritated by the arrogant Swiss, more than jealous of his success. Long before anyone else, Vallejo recognized New Helvetia as a threat to the entire Mexican province of Alta California. The day after Christmas, 1839, he wrote to his brother, José de Jesús, to warn him not to lose sight of the colony of foreigners which, though founded with the permission of the departmental government, was in conflict with its existing laws. Don Mariano's own estimate of the potential of Sutter's New Switzerland was ominous—"This establishment, with its treacherously venomous exudations, is extremely dangerous."

CHAPTER VI

THE FOUNDER

THE year 1840 opened quietly for Sutter and, fortunately, stayed that way, allowing him to consolidate his position on the American River. This in spite of the fact that California was rocked violently by what came to be called the Graham Affair. A teapot tempest, it nevertheless was heard of in Washington and Whitehall, and rendered all foreigners in California highly suspect. One of the backwoodsmen who had migrated to California before 1836 was a Kentuckian named Isaac Graham, who drifted into the territory from the Rockies or New Mexico, where he had been trapping. Graham set up a distillery at Natividad, turning out a California version of Taos lightning, made from wheat. He was soon the terror of Natividad, the Pájaro Valley and Branciforte (Santa Cruz), since his red-eye and his talent for personal leadership attracted to him a band of lawless roughnecks, largely Americans with a sprinkling of British subjects, either fur trappers like himself or beached sailors.

In 1837, Juan B. Alvarado had made the mistake of asking Graham for aid in his conspiracy against Governor Gutiérrez. Alvarado won but found himself saddled with an unruly company

97

of American riflemen whom he wished to heaven he had never recruited. When they were drunk, their conduct was particularly bad, and, since they were almost constantly saturated with whisky, they were forever in trouble with the local authorities. In 1838, Graham himself was ordered to serve eight months on the chain gang for killing cattle on the Gómez rancho. He and his men were insolent to the local *alcalde* with impunity, because of their deadly rifles, but they went too far when they wandered into Monterey and began to badger the governor himself. He was not about to let them turn Monterey into another Taos. Complained Alvarado, "I was insulted at every turn by the drunken followers of Graham. When walking in the garden, they would come to its wall and call upon me in terms of the greatest familiarity, 'Ho! Bautista; come here. I want to speak to you.' Bautista, here; Bautista, there; Bautista, everywhere!"

Alvarado's offended dignity led him to believe a rumor that the *gringos* intended to overthrow the government of Alta California. (When its editor learned of the affair, the *Sandwich Islands Mirror* snorted, "What! Seventy foreigners, scattered along the coast more than 500 miles, to take the country!" Yet the idea was not far-fetched; the Bear Flag Party of 1846 was no more formidable.) Whatever schemes, if any, lurked in Graham's booze-soaked brain, Alvarado moved quickly to prevent a revolt. He ordered Prefect José Castro to apprehend all the foreigners involved in the suspected plot. Castro surprised the *rifleros americanos* and arrested sixty of them. None was killed and only one was seriously wounded in resisting arrest. Some of the others, including Graham, were roughly handled, of course, and later, inspired by a lust for damages, told tales of brutal treatment. Castro marched forty-five of the foreigners aboard the *Jóven Guipuzcoana* and escorted them to San Blas, Mexico. Here, in a comedy of errors, *he* was arrested and court-martialed but was eventually released. Meantime, the prisoners rotted in cells in nearby Tepic.

In June 1840, Captain J. B. Forrest stormed into Monterey Bay with the U.S.S. *St. Louis* to denounce the arrests and demand the release of the men. Alvarado tried to calm him, but when the British government made representations via its Tepic consular agent, the Mexican government backed down. All the exiles, except the four actually charged with conspiracy, were released and at least eighteen of them returned to California. The four, including Graham, were kept in Mexico until the summer of 1842. They were then fitted out in fine clothes and given free passage to Monterey. When they arrived in July, neatly dressed and armed with rifles (and even swords!) by an embarrassed and frightened government, they looked better, more sober and as arrogant as ever in their lives.

Sutter, wisely, kept entirely clear of the Graham affair and may have been the inspiration for Alvarado's protest against Lieutenant Forrest's near-ultimatum. The governor reminded the naval officer that Graham and his men were lawless fellows and that he had no wish to disturb the many Americans and other foreigners in California (such as at New Helvetia) who "pursued honest industry." Sutter contented himself with commenting on the crisis to a neighbor, Dr. John Marsh at his Pulpunes rancho near Mount Diablo.

Marsh had no trouble, either, although he was a fugitive from the law in the United States. He had led a Prairie du Chien unit in the Black Hawk War, until it was discovered that he was selling arms to the Indians on the side. Fleeing first to Santa Fe, he had then made his way to California. Sutter was never able to get along with Marsh, although he corresponded with him and, naturally, managed to get himself indebted to him. But then, Marsh had few friends. Still, the Swiss loaned him copies of the *Hawaiian Spectator,* although declining to part, even temporarily, with his medical book, which the quack doctor coveted. Lied Sutter, "Someone must have taken it and forgotten even to return the same." By June, Sutter was sounding Marsh out on the purchase of cattle for New Helvetia, promising to pay two-thirds in goods and one-third in beaver skins or cash. He said he expected funds, shortly, from Honolulu.

There was, of course, no mail service in Mexican California in 1840. But Sutter sent a flurry of messages to his far-flung neighbors by runners. He continued to wrangle with Martínez, growing more insolent as he felt increasingly secure at New Helvetia: "I am very much surprised that you are still annoying me in regard to a matter which I thought was concluded long ago, and all accounts with you settled. . . . If you have forgotten the laws of trade, I can still teach them to you. And do not think to frighten me with your threats!" But he was turning increasingly to Don Antonio Suñol, a rancher of the *contra costa,* to supply him with corn, wheat, peas, beans, flour and fowl (for which he paid in beaver), since he had alienated Martínez.

Sutter was two people altogether. Guilty of a reckless arrogance, he would write to Martínez' son, to whom he owed money, and who asked for it: "It surprised me very much that a person who prided himself on being a gentleman should act in such a way. . . . I beg, in future, you will not repeat such contemptible acts." Yet, paradoxically, at the same time, his kindness and hospitality was making New Helvetia a magnet for all the rootless men in northern California. Rocky Mountain trappers drifted into his service, as well as sailor-deserters from Yerba Buena. Don Octavio Custot, whom he had earlier dismissed as "a trifling fellow," not only attached himself to Sutter but became his chief clerk after Vallejo threw him out for stealing sugar. ("Anything to spite Vallejo," may have been Sutter's motto of the moment.)

Sutter had little trouble with the Indians in 1840. He allowed scores of them to crowd into his establishment. His only precaution was a brace of pistols displayed conspicuously on his table. But one night his overconfidence nearly betrayed him. He was chatting with Custot when he was startled about midnight by a scream of pain and a cry, *"O, Señor!"* They rushed outside to see what the trouble was. There Sutter found an Indian held prisoner in the jaws of his Honolulu bulldog. No sooner had Custot dragged him inside the adobe than he and Sutter heard another shriek. They found a second Indian trapped in the bulldog's jaws.

Sutter questioned the two sternly and they confessed that they were part of a band who planned to murder Sutter and his men and seize the settlement.

Instead of making an example of them, Sutter sewed up their wounds with silk thread and let them off with nothing more than a sharp dressing-down. (Sutter was not unwilling to kill Indians, but he was most reluctant to eradicate his work force.) He warned them that if he ever found them plotting again, he would punish them swiftly and terribly. Yet shortly he found other Indians concealing weapons under the very blankets he had given them. "When I asked them why they wanted to kill me, who had treated them well, they answered that they simply wanted to plunder." Sutter gradually forced honesty upon his Indians by assuring them that thefts or other depredations would be punished by death. By skillfully tempering severity with kindness, Sutter, with very little force at his command, managed to pacify the Sacramento frontier by 1840. Robbery was virtually unheard of at the settlement. A visitor of that year said of him, "He was probably the best Indian tamer and civilizer that I know of or ever heard of."

When the Chucumnes withdrew from around New Helvetia and showed fight, Sutter knew what to do. He mustered a tiny force—six white men—and marched them some twenty miles to the Cosumnes River. There he made a surprise attack on the Indian camp by night. With no casualties on their side, he and his squad killed six of the warriors. The leaders of the tribe begged for mercy—and received it. "If you will come back to your village and attend to your work as before," Sutter told them, "all will be forgotten." He had no more trouble from the Chucumnes. In fact, they became not only good servants and workers, but also soldiers in the praetorian guard which he was forming. At first, he paid them for their work in merchandise, largely shirts and mission blankets. Later, he had his blacksmith "mint" coins of a sort—a currency composed of tin pieces, stamped with a star, with holes punched in them to indicate the number of days an individual had worked. The Indians traded their tin discs at

Sutter's store for whatever goods they needed. Naturally, the unscrupulous white hangers-on at the settlement did not hesitate to bully or cheat the Indians out of their pay, but Sutter protected them by refusing to accept the tin pieces except from Indian hands.

The secret of Sutter's success in pacifying the Indians was the same as the "how" of his arrogance toward Martínez and the Mexican-Californians. (The "why" of his deliberate rudeness is another, and unanswered, question.) He was able to maintain an air of complete independence—an independence that thoroughly impressed would-be Indian raiders—because he was busily transforming New Helvetia into Sutter's Fort. During 1840, he had his Indian laborers begin to build an eighteen-foot-high wall of baked adobe bricks. Two and a half feet thick, it was virtually cannon-proof. The compound which it enclosed was 320 feet long on the north and south, 160 on the west, and 140 on the east. It was far larger than Bent's Fort (180 by 135 feet) and Fort Laramie (150 by 150 feet), although only half the size of Fort Vancouver. Sutter's bastions, from which peered the muzzles of his cannon, were of double strength, with walls five feet thick. Underneath each tower was a dungeon.

At times, Sutter had as many as 1,000 Indian workers to feed, and he solved the problem efficiently, though his technique offended some of his visitors. He filled long wooden V-shaped troughs with *atole,* boiled corn, or some other kind of mush, and they ate like domesticated animals. Sutter was also criticized for "turning his Indians out to graze" by travelers who did not realize that the natives considered sweet clover as much of a treat as acorn meal or grasshoppers.

Inside the compound, Sutter had his men build *Casa Grande,* a large three-roomed structure, as his headquarters, to replace his original adobe (destroyed by fire during the winter), as well as a barracks for his Indian troops, a bakery, a mill, a blanket factory and various workshops. Because of the stink of the hides, he located his tannery on the American River, well beyond whiffing distance of the fort. Beyond his walls, he had his laborers throw up houses for his *vaqueros* and for visitors. Building a castle, however rude, was a difficult task, he discovered. As he told John Marsh on June 18, 1840: "It is a great trouble to make a new establishment in this country. If I had not already commenced, I would not begin again. But now I do all I possibly can to make it, at once, as large and extensive as possible. But it wants a great deal of patience and preseverance."

Sutter was pleased, and amazed, that his launch never capsized or swamped in the turbulent Sacramento River or on the often stormy bay. It once took him seventeen days to get upriver from Yerba Buena, but a normally fast trip was only a matter of seven days, and, in her way, the pinnace came to be as dependable as a Black Ball packet. He had to crew her with inexperienced Indians; only the Kanaka helmsman was a real sailor. But the boat kept his vital lifeline open.

In August, the pioneer welcomed reinforcements after the *Lausanne* landed five recruits from the Columbia River at Bodega. The Spanish officer in charge there forbade the landing, giving as his reason the exposure of the Graham plot. But Governor Rotcheff, Sutter's friend, arrived from Fort Ross in time to take the Americans' part. According to witnesses, he told the lieutenant and his handful of Mexican soldiers to leave, if they did not wish to be killed or taken prisoners. The plucky officer insisted that he would not yield. But on July 16, he led his force away, feeling that he had at least saved face, and the Americans came ashore. Sutter was delighted to welcome his old comrades Gutiérrez, Allgeier and Keyser as well as two strangers, Peter Lassen and William Wiggins. Others who joined his banner at about this time included Robert Ridley, who had been with his 1839 "fleet," whom Sutter named master of his pinnace. Perry McCoon became his major-domo, to oversee his herds, and John Chamberlain, an Irishman like McCoon, was named blacksmith. An ex-sailor, Bill Daylor, was signed on as cook but Sutter soon found him to be a troublemaker. John Sinclair, a Scotsman, somewhat fond of the bottle, had also joined him by this time.

These reinforcements were doubly welcome to Sutter, because in October he had his first real Indian crisis. A band of San José Mission Indians under Chief Acacio showed up at the fort with passports signed by José de Jesús Vallejo, administrator of the secularized mission. Ostensibly, the converted Indians were on a trip to see relatives and friends. They begged Sutter's permission to trade for some feathers and baskets at a nearby Indian *ranchería,* and some hoped to secure women by barter. Sutter had no objection. However, the Indians were warned that the women must go with them of their own free will. He approved the request of his Indian second *alcalde,* Julián (the cowboy finally restored by Martínez), who wished to go along. Sutter told him to supervise the bartering and to warn the Christian Indians that they must not fight with his *gentiles,* or wild Indians.

Sutter went about his business but was interrupted by an old Indian who had run all the way from the Yalecumne *ranchería.* To his dismay, Sutter learned that the visitors had raided the village. Very likely, they had done so because Julián knew that almost all of the men were away, working for Sutter, leaving the women of the village unprotected. Sutter listened carefully as the old man told how they had attacked his village, killed the five able-bodied men left there, and kidnapped the women and children for squaws and slaves. Years later, Sutter would recall, "It was a common practice in those days to seize women and children in order to sell them. This was done by the Californians as well as by the Indians." (He did not add that it was so customary that he himself indulged in it from time to time.) When the angry chief of the Yalecumnes left his men working in Sutter's fields, and stormed into the fort to accuse him of having ordered the attack, the Swiss held his temper, saying simply, "Wait for tomorrow morning and I will get you your wives and children back."

On the morning of October 15, 1840, Sutter led a punitive expedition out of the fort. It was no six-man squad this time. He had the twenty best white men from the fort, plus a host of Indians. Moving his force quickly over the flood plain, he overtook the raiders about thirty miles from the fort, where a *laguna* drained into the Sacramento River. Exactly what happened then, other than his complete victory over the war party, is not clear. He wrote a report to José de Jesús Vallejo, and in English because he was afraid he would make too many mistakes in Spanish, but it was a thoroughly confusing account of the action and its outcome. He reported that he had the prisoners locked up in his bastion jail. But later, in the memoirs which he provided the historian Bancroft, he admitted to having fourteen of them executed by a firing squad for shooting the five Yalecumnes and dashing out the brains of the old women at the captured *ranchería*. He also told Bancroft that the Mexican government had, at the time, thanked him for his stringent measures. To Vallejo, in his broken English, he wrote that he wanted "to show others an example; more, to see what bad actions get for recompense."

Sutter wanted no more so-called civilized Indians around his fort. He wrote José Vallejo, "I am very sorry to tell you that ... when a party of Indians of the mission comes here, they make, all times, a disturbance in my people. They don't like to work anymore and a great many stories was told to them. It would be better to give them no more permission to come here, and let us all in peace."

Sutter was beginning to feel his strength. To him, 1840 seemed a vintage year. Everything had gone right. He had stayed out of the Graham trouble; he had quelled all Indian uprisings; he had become almost solvent in December by paying off Martínez; and his fortress was well under way. In August, he had gone to Monterey to take his oath and on the twenty-ninth was naturalized as a Mexican citizen. In September, Secretary of State Manuel Jimeno Casarín had signed the document making him judge (justice of the peace) and official government representative for the Sacramento District of Upper California.

Sutter expended enormous energies that year, even entering the fur trade, though he was aware that he could not yet confront the Hudson's Bay Company's formidable California brigades, mainly because he knew that he could not count on the jealous Mariano Vallejo to back him up with an armed force. Alexander Simpson, of the company, was led to write to Dr. John McLoughlin on October 1, 1840, from aboard the *Columbia:* "I saw Capt'n Sutter and ascertained that he has actually obtained from the Civil Government a right to exclude all trapping parties and is named for that purpose the *Alcalde* (Magistrate) of the Frontier. But his appointment is not acknowledged by the Military Commandant and he [General Vallejo] avowed to me that he had neither the will nor the power to interfere with our trapping party."

CHAPTER VII

THE SETTLER

SUTTER consolidated his control over the Indians in 1841 and advanced his farming and trapping frontier. He had secured a trusting creditor in Barcelona-born Don Antonio Suñol. Since Suñol had served in the French Navy before jumping ship in California in 1818, the two corresponded volubly in French. Sutter was much more polite with him than with Martínez because of their mutual love of France. Sutter was no less eager for supplies, however, and no less reluctant to pay for them promptly. From Suñol he got seed wheat and peas to sow, plus corn, beans and white Columbia wheat with which to feed his men. He also ordered from him raw sugar, dried meat, cocoa, cheese and onion seeds. Sutter was confident that he could pay off Suñol from his agricultural returns or his newest venture—fur trapping. Sutter had advanced large amounts for traps and provisions to his chief trapper, Joseph Gendreau, and his men, and had no return as yet. He confessed to Suñol that three months of trapping had paid little or nothing, and admitted to Marsh, "I don't know how and when I can get my pay from Joseph Gendreau." But he was full of plans and had several smiths at work making traps enough to outfit four canoes. He asked Suñol to lend him an oxcart to pick up tools at Natividad in order to speed up the trap-making. Optimistic as ever, he promised to pay for everything in beaver pelts —*"A la fin de la chasse à castor, je serai capable de vous payer tout."*

After ordering 6,000 feet of redwood lumber from Suñol and 2,000 from another source with which to complete his fortress, Sutter asked his Spanish friend for the loan of some horses for an important mission. The tributaries to the Sacramento were too high to ford, so he went downriver as far as Suñol's ranch on his launch. From there Sutter, two *vaqueros* and two armed companions, rode via the Livermore Pass to Mission San José. After changing mounts, he continued on to the capital where, on May 15, 1841, he presented his petition to the governor. He asked for the vacant lands of New Helvetia in order to colonize and foster civilization on the frontier. He represented twelve families of settlers besides himself, he said, and he made a good case for his colony: "This settlement, from its position, proves to be a strong barrier against the incursions of the savage tribes into the villages and as a school of civilization either to the wild natives or to those [once] under the care of the missions."

Governor Alvarado was greatly pleased with Sutter's progress. In the patent that he issued him, the governor expressed his satisfaction with the Swiss entrepreneur: "He has sufficiently proved his assiduity, good behaviour and all other qualities . . . , his truly patriotic zeal in favor of our institutions having reduced to submission a number of savage Indians born on those frontiers." This compliment delighted Sutter, who accurately considered himself gifted at handling the Indians. In later years, he liked to recall, "I subjugated all the Indians in the Sacramento Valley. I had frequent fights with the Indians, and had frequently to punish them for stealing cattle. . . . At this time, I had power of life and death over both Indians and white people. The Spaniards were very much surprised when they saw my Indian soldiers, especially because one of them could read and write, which many of them could not do."

Alvarado gave Sutter eleven square leagues of the rich Sacramento Valley, not counting overflowed lands within the general bounds of the grant. The New Helvetia patent was bordered on the north by three eroded remnants of volcanic cones, the Tres Picos or Prairie Buttes (today called Sutter Buttes, or Marysville Buttes). The Sacramento River bounded the grant on the west, the Feather on the east, and the line of 38° 49′ 12″ on the south. Alvarado attached certain conditions to the grant, but none of them distressed Sutter. He was allowed to fence his land but not to injure any river crossing or road and, above all, was not to interfere with the free trade and navigation of the rivers. Since Alvarado had inherited the Spanish government's paternalistic policy toward the Indians, he was obliged to caution Sutter to maintain the native Indians in the free enjoyment of their possessions, without troubling them, and to reduce them to civilization only through prudent measures and friendly intercourse. He warned the Swiss against making hostilities against them without previous authority from the government.

Sutter left Monterey in high spirits. Not only had he won his land grant, he was also followed by a half dozen new recruits. His exuberance was a bit dampened, however, when he discovered what hard drinkers they were. Just before he left the capital, he mustered his men, including a cooper, the first Negro to settle in the Sacramento region. Several ships' captains also gathered in front of David Spence's house and, surveying the motley group, one of them exclaimed to Sutter, "My God! How can you manage such vagabonds?" Sutter explained that he had made it clear there would be no liquor at New Helvetia. And when he somehow got the men to the fort, he flatly refused them spirits despite their pleading. At Christmas and on the Fourth of July 1842 he gave in to their demands for a barrel of whisky. But they behaved so badly that he refused them on the next holiday. The result was a mutiny. A sailor whose opinion Sutter respected suggested that he give them a barrel, then go off on a long hunt. He did just that, returning to find the liquor exhausted, the men dried out from their binge, and everyone back at work. Sutter never again tried a temperance policy at the fort. As early as October 1840, he had been making brandy for his own use from wild grapes brought him by the Indians, and in September 1841, he secured machinery from Suñol for an improved still.

Sutter's modest recruiting campaign caused him further annoyance when a complaint was filed against him for hiring a deserter from the United States Exploring Expedition, which was then on the coast. He made excuses, then returned to the press of business, sending John Sinclair to purchase supplies from Hawaii and putting off creditors with promises of thick, rich beaver pelts to come.

Sutter was plunged into depression late in July when he learned that the Russians, eager to sell the no longer profitable Fort Ross, had turned down his offer. He had bid only for the cattle, and his friend Rotcheff had to write him that they had decided to accept an offer for the entire establishment, real estate and stock. No names were mentioned, but Sutter guessed that his rival was no other than Vallejo. He confined his disgust with the Russians, who would sell their property to a man who had insulted their flag, to a ranting letter to Suñol. This revealed their true character, he grumbled, after they had told him they would rather burn the buildings to the ground than sell them to any Mexican-American official. *"Seulement les Russes peuvent agir comme cela,"* he said sourly. "In order to make some 1,000 piastres or more, they are not ashamed to make such a transaction. . . . I would have preferred not to have had any dealings with them."

An unexpected visit roused Sutter from his blues. William D. Phelps, the old ship's captain who called himself Webfoot, decided to pay a call on his new friend, who had regaled him with glowing accounts of the beauty of the Sacramento country. On July 27, 1841, Phelps set out upriver from San Francisco Bay in a ship's cutter with six oarsmen. The other captains and supercargoes who had been eager to accompany him at first all backed out before he cast off, making such flimsy excuses as "It's a bad season of the year ... the river is low, ... the weather is hot, ... the mosquitoes are ravenous, bears numerous and the Indians are cannibals." The country around Sutter's Fort still had the reputation of being a savage wilderness, at least at the San Francisco Bay *embarcadero* in the summer of 1841. Phelps sent a note from his Sacramento River landing, and Sutter rushed saddle horses back with his major-domo. As his friend approached the main gate, Sutter fractured the heat of the day with a cannon salute. He treated his visitor to a display of flags and a feast of venison, cooked in several different ways. Sutter took him on an elk hunt and after otherwise entertaining him for a week, gave Phelps a collection of Indian artifacts including finely woven baskets, bows and arrows, and feather blankets.

Shortly afterward, Sutter's routine was again broken. Lt. Comdr. Cadwalader Ringgold of the Wilkes expedition led six boats from the U.S.S. *Vincennes,* anchored at Sausalito, up the Sacramento to the fort. With him were some fifty men and an Indian pilot. The fleet of small boats camped on Sutter's Sacramento River *embarcadero* on August 23, 1841. Sutter was expecting them, having been alerted by his Indian allies. As he explained, "Whenever strangers came into the valley, my Indians gave me notice of their approach, telling me whether they were white men, as they called Americans, or Californians, and always giving me a good description of their appearance." He had dispatched a white clerk to determine exactly who his visitors were, then sent horses to the riverbank for the convenience of the naval officers. When they rode up to the fort, he saluted them with his cannon and greeted them warmly. Sutter's reception was not pure sociability; their visit strengthened his position greatly in Indian eyes, as he was quick to admit—"It made a very good impression upon the Indians to see so many white men visiting me."

Ringgold told Sutter of his duties, exploring and measuring the Sacramento and its major tributaries, while Sutter, of course, filled his ears with fables of his French military service. He was honest in extolling the richness of his land grant, however, except that it grew in the telling from eleven square leagues to thirty. The admiration of the Americans for his energy and good management in settling in the very midst of hostile tribes flattered him immensely. Sutter was proud of the good will which he had won from the redmen but admitted having had to shoot nine Indian raiders. This led Commodore Charles Wilkes to comment later, "Indeed, he does not seem to stand upon much ceremony with those who oppose him in any way." (Wilkes' officers, in reporting on his supreme authority in the region, directly contradicted Sutter's own statement to the historian, Bancroft. They claimed that he not only judged and punished the Indians but also married and buried them, whereas Sutter told Bancroft, "I had no clergy, no church. At burials and marriages I officiated myself . . . [but] the Indians I did not marry or bury. I was everything—patriarch, priest, father and judge.")

In any case, the American officers reported that Sutter treated his Indians well and paid them, in goods, for their work. At that time Sutter's new adobe was almost finished, as well as his extensive corrals, and fort workmen were busy making additional adobe bricks for the walls. The Americans observed that his farmland was already extensive but, like everyone else's, had been largely ruined by the drought of 1841. After showing them his distillery, Sutter treated the officers to his potent wild-grape pisco.

Sutter enjoyed a long chat with Ringgold. He told him of increasing his fur trapping, of his plans to bring his family over from Switzerland, and of his concern over General Vallejo's jealousy. Sutter seemed convinced that the general meant to try to dislodge him by force, and was preparing a stiff welcome, which explained his hurry to complete the outer walls of the fortress. Ringgold not only felt that it was too late for Vallejo to oust Sutter but doubted the intensity of their antagonism: "The reality of the hostility said to exist between the two rival administrators seems doubtful, at least to the extent reported by the residents."

Sutter passed on to Ringgold considerable information (and some misinformation) about the nine tribes which he identified with the New Helvetia area, telling him, for instance, that they spoke only two dialects, one east of the Sacramento and one west of it. One evening he had some of his Indian boys put on the White Mask Dance. To the naval contingent, it resembled descriptions of Pawnee dancing but the music was more harmonious, "almost Polynesian." Perhaps Sutter's Kanakas exerted some musical influence over the local natives.

Sutter loaned Ringgold a guide to take the boats up the Sacramento. At one bend, Ringgold saw the remains of an Indian village destroyed by Sutter in retaliation for its warriors' having stolen his cattle. He was said to have killed only a single brave but to have taken twenty-seven captives in the battle and to have forced the others into exile beyond the limits of his territory.

Game larger than quail and curlews grew scarce as the boats ascended the river, possibly because of overhunting by the Hudson's Bay trappers who came yearly to the valley. From a point near Sutter Buttes, Ringgold turned back, reaching New Helvetia again on September 4. To his surprise, he found the Russian schooner *Constantine* at the *embarcadero*. Rotcheff was with Sutter, offering him the whole colony of Fort Ross!

The next day was payday and the Americans joined the Russians in watching Sutter giving his workers calico, vests, shirts and trousers through the head men, who spoke a little Spanish. Only men and boys were working for him, but he explained that he hoped to have light work for the squaws in a year or so. On the sixth, Ringgold said good-bye to his genial host. The visit was marred only by the disappearance of four deserters. Recalled Sutter, "Ringgold sent me word, asking me if I could have them arrested. I hunted for them and attempted their arrest—nearly at the cost of my life—but I did not find them." It is very doubtful that the Swiss made any such attempt. He badly needed workmen, and hardly were the boats out of sight before he had put one of the seamen to work in his tannery.

113

Ringgold passed on a fine impression of the Swiss pioneer, which led Commodore Wilkes to write of him, "In his manners, Captain Sutter is frank and prepossessing. He has much intelligence and is, withall, not a little enthusiastic. He generally wears a kind of undress uniform, with his sidearms buckled around him."

Sutter now turned his attention to other important visitors. Besides Rotcheff, he played host to the French explorer, Count Eugène Duflot de Mofras. Supposedly studying the commercial possibilities in California, Duflot was actually a French spy whose mission was to determine whether California could become part of the French sphere of influence and possibly the last of a chain of French colonies stretching from the Marquesas, Society and Sandwich islands to the mainland. Duflot got along very well with the Russians and, indeed, claimed that it was he who got them to reconsider Sutter as a buyer for Fort Ross. But Governor Alvarado was thoroughly unimpressed by the nobleman: "He believes that the inhabitants of this country are brutal Indians whose duty it is to prostrate themselves before him and that he, the count, should hesitate to allow them to be honored with his presence." The Francophile in Sutter rose to the surface, of course, and he made Duflot most welcome at New Helvetia. He was disproportionately flattered by the count's attentions and, in his customary boasting about service under Charles X of France, found himself stretching his enlistment to twelve years.

The Frenchman made detailed notes on Sutter's Fort, even to counting the number of cannon. He noted that Sutter had taken advantage of a slough to protect his fort's north side with a natural moat. Nor did he miss the gallery topping each wall to form a parapet for Sutter's sharpshooters. However, by now Sutter was exchanging his long-held dream of military glory for a different goal. He would, he resolved, be a gentleman-farmer—an emperor of agriculture. He showed off his grain fields and talked of putting in cotton, rice and indigo to transform New Helvetia into a true plantation. He predicted that he would soon be exporting large quantities of butter and cheese. Although they had been blasted by the drought, he showed the Frenchman his vegetable gardens and got him to agree that grapevines and olives would prosper on his higher ground. Sutter's fisheries interested the count, too, and his host explained that the enormous salmon were not always taken on hooks but often netted, speared or even stoned when trapped in fish weirs. The master of New Helvetia expected large profits from his salmon fishery as well as from his grain and furs. He told Duflot that he intended to bring his family, soon, to the fort, along with a group of Swiss colonists.

Duflot de Mofras was much impressed with Sutter and his fort. Aware of the impending transfer of Fort Ross, he predicted that Sutter's Fort would become a great settlement thanks to its access to the sea, both directly and via the Sacramento River and San Francisco Bay. He was properly awed by Sutter's capacity for hard work—"No branch of business is overlooked by this pioneer, who must pay off within a short time the amount he owes the Russians for the purchase of their livestock and farms."

Duflot made too much of Sutter's affection for France, however. It was easily understandable, for Sutter told him how much he wanted French and French-Canadian settlers at New Helvetia. (He neglected to mention that he wanted settlers of every other nationality, too.) Perhaps Duflot made too much of the Dubosc case, too. A *Bordelais* named Pierre Dubosc was killed by an Indian on the Edward MacIntosh ranch near Fort Ross. Vallejo all but ignored the murder, letting the culprit escape. Sutter, however, sent posses to scour the countryside. Although he had to abandon the hunt after releasing one suspect, he proved his desire to revenge the murder of the Frenchman. Sutter's zeal may have been as much the result of his sense of duty or his ego— he was proud of his office of justice of the peace—as of his love for France. Nevertheless, such proof as the Dubosc case and his willingness to welcome French missionaries at his fort convinced Duflot that Sutter considered himself a Frenchman. Rotcheff passed on to William Heath Davis the praise which the count showered on Sutter: "He spoke of Sutter in the highest terms and thought his establishment and operations in the Sacramento Valley would people and develop that immense country sooner than it could otherwise have been done, as he believed Sutter would induce a large immigration to that point by the numerous letters he had written home to his own country and to the United States."

Aware that Vallejo expected Fort Ross to fall into his hands like a ripe plum, Rotcheff collected Sutter at New Helvetia and took him to San Rafael, where they transferred to horses for the ride to Bodega. There, aboard the *Helena,* an agent of the Russian company made the formal offer. For $30,000 and a down payment of only $2,000 in cash, the fort, lock, stock and cannon-barrel, was Sutter's. The Russian asked for the first three installments in produce, chiefly wheat, and only the last one in cash. Sutter agreed to pay $5,000 in wheat for the first two years and $10,000 in wheat the third, and to guarantee payment by mortgaging his New Helvetia property.

After a champagne dinner aboard the *Helena,* with many toasts saluting the new owner of Russian California, the parties to the contract embarked in a small boat for Yerba Buena to have the document witnessed and registered by the *alcalde.* Four brawny men crewed the boat in a difficult passage against the tide. A high sea was running, and Sutter always believed that he narrowly missed drowning on the trip. He remembered saying to Rotcheff, "Your tyranny over your men is so complete that they will carry you to destruction if you tell them to." So impressed was Sutter with the Russian sailors that he asked if some could remain in his employ. The officer, convinced that Sutter would not be severe enough with them, told him that he would be unable to handle them. But, according to one source, a few Russians did stay on at Fort Ross to work for Sutter in dismantling the stronghold.

Just why Sutter was so eager to possess Fort Ross still puzzles California historians. It was no bargain, since he understood that

116

he was buying only the stock, buildings and equipment, not the land. The contract specified that the land was *not* being transferred to him—because, in Mexican eyes, the Tsarists had never owned it. Of course, he secured the Russian schooner *Constantine,* which he wanted to add to the Yerba Buena–New Helvetia run. And he was scoring a *coup* over Vallejo; that was worth a good deal. But perhaps the answer to his rash bid was his hope to break the legal point stipulating that he had not purchased the land on which the Russian buildings stood. He secured a duplicate deed, not registered, which stated that Fort Ross and Bodega were "delivered to his indisputable possession with all the lands." Somehow, legally or otherwise, Sutter hoped to switch deeds. He was probably gambling on his friendship with Alvarado and the prevalence of the bribe in Mexican politico-legal matters. He made no secret of his 1841 plans in his 1876 memoir: "After I had bought Fort Ross, I informed the Mexican government of my purchase and asked for a title. I was informed, however, that the Russians had no title to the land and hence no right to sell it to me. If I had had a few thousand dollars of ready cash, I could easily have secured the legal title. Money made the Mexican authorities see anything."

There is little doubt that Sutter made a colossal blunder in buying Fort Ross, under the terms of the purchase. He was plunged into a morass of debt from which he would never really be able to extricate himself. What, exactly, did he get in return? About 1,700 cows, calves and oxen, 1,000 horses and mules, and 2,000 sheep were added to his herds. He also received many tools to make his great granary dream a reality, as well as plows, carts, corrals, a tannery, a dairy, a boathouse and two hide kayaks, a fishing boat and a canoe. Two windmills and a millstone capable of grinding twenty *fanegas* of wheat a day came to him, also a horse-powered mill and stone and two machines, one for beating tan bark and one for grinding it. The fine threshing floors which he had admired in 1839 were now his. In addition to cannon captured in Napoleon's retreat from Moscow, there were houses, storehouses, barracks—in short, all the lumber he needed to complete Fort Sutter. Besides Fort Ross itself, Sutter owned all of the portable property at Bodega and at three nearby Russian ranches.

Although the final signing of the contract before Yerba Buena *Alcalde* Francisco Guerrero did not take place until December 19, 1841, Sutter sent his chief assistant, Robert Ridley, as early as September 28 with men to begin driving the Russian cattle and horses to New Helvetia. He had the bad luck to lose about 2,000 head in crossing the Sacramento, but the carcasses were fished out of the river and flayed, and Sutter made something on the hides. He sent the *Sacramento* to ferry lumber from the buildings at Fort Ross, as soon as they could be dismantled, for construction at New Helvetia.

Meanwhile, other visitors arrived overland at the fort. On October 19, Lt. George Emmons led thirty-nine men into the settlement. He was one of Wilkes' lieutenants from the Willamette. With him, besides naval personnel and civilians who attached themselves to his party for protection, were a number of travelers, including Titian R. Peale of the famous Philadelphia family of scientists and artists.

Sutter welcomed the naval contingent with the same old story of devoted service in Charles X's Swiss Guards. One of the midshipmen was deeply appreciative of Sutter's hospitality: "We were most hospitably and kindly received by him. There was no ostentatious display, no pomp or ceremony, but an easy and polite demeanor on the part of our host that made us feel perfectly at home." He noted that Sutter treated his Indians well but was disgusted by "the filthiness of their looks; their natural inclination and habits [which] are such as to prevent their advancement in civilized life." Peale, on the other hand, commented, "We saw about forty Indians at work, who appeared smiling and contented." Looking over the establishment, the same observant midshipman estimated that Sutter had 2,000 horses and mules, 3,000 cattle, and 1,000 sheep. (Ringgold's figures had been 1,000 horses, 2,500 cattle and 1,000 sheep; Duflot's, 1,500, 4,000 and 2,000. Sutter did not really know how much stock he possessed; he never found the time and men to inventory his herds properly.)

On October 21, Emmons split his party. Sutter loaned him his launch to take the sick and some others downriver, while a land party started across country, guided by a Californian. With winter coming, Sutter knew that the days of visitors were over. He begged Suñol for shingle nails to complete the roofing of his house before the rains, and hurried the transfer of lumber from Fort Ross. Vallejo did not interfere with his movements from Fort Ross, for which he was grateful. (As early as September 19 he had written Vallejo, "Do me the favor to permit them [his men] to pass the frontier to Ross and to put no obstacle in their way.")

Sutter was being kept busy as a magistrate. He was holding Henry Bee prisoner for the murder of John (Black Jack) Wilson. Since Wilson had been an unsavory character and Bee's friends had posted $1,000 as security for him, Sutter took the irons off but kept Bee in custody until instructions should arrive from Governor Alvarado.

As the winter of 1841 approached, Sutter was uneasy, fearful of attack by a Mexican force. Yerba Buena merchant Nathan Spear claimed that Sutter was saying publicly, "I will not be the aggressor but woe to those that shall do me harm!" Doubtless referring to the rumors of impending attack, Sutter wrote General Vallejo that "some very curious reports come to me which made me, first, a little afraid. But, after two hours, I got over the fit." In a letter to merchant Jacob P. Leese, however, Sutter exposed his real anxiety: "Very curious reports come to me from below. But the poor wretches don't know what they do. I told Mr. Spence to explain to those ignorant people what would be the first consequence of their doing injury to me. The first French frigate to come here will do me justice!" Once again, Sutter was hiding behind the tricolor. "These people don't know me yet. But soon they will find out what I am able to do. It is too late now to drive me

119

out of the country. One first step, if they do anything against me, is that I will make a declaration of independence and proclaim California a *république* independent of Mexico. I am strong now. One of my best friends, a German, comes from the Columbia River with plenty of people. Another party is close by, from the Missouri. One of the party has arrived here. Some of my friends and acquaintances are among them. They are about 40 or 50 men of respectability and property. They come in the intention of settling here."

Although he reported to Leese that "the whole day and night we are under arms," he asked him to tell Vallejo that he wished to remain his friend. Sutter was beginning to realize that his principal enemy in California was not Don Mariano but the militant, suspicious, xenophobic General José Castro. He told Vallejo, via Leese, that he appreciated his past kindnesses. In fact, he said, "If he would join us in a *république,* in such a case I would like it very much." The mercurial Sutter, alarmed by Castro, meant these gestures as overtures to Vallejo. The time was not yet ripe, but a *rapprochement* would eventually come.

In late 1841 Commodore Charles Wilkes accurately assessed the situation in California: "The state of society here is exceedingly loose; envy, hatred and malice predominate in almost every breast and the people are wretched under their present rulers." But Sutter told Leese, certain to pass the word on to the governor, that there would be no problems coming out of New Helvetia—as long as Don José Castro left him alone. All that he wanted from the government was security. Never a pussyfoot, he laid down a bold warning aimed at Alvarado, Vallejo and especially at Castro: "I am strong enough to hold me till the couriers go to the Willamette to raise about 60 or 70 men. Another party I would dispatch to the mountains and call on hunters and Shawnees and Delawares, with whom I am well acquainted. The same party then to go to the Missouri and raise 200 or 300 men more. That is my intention, sir, if they let me not alone. If they will give me satisfaction and pay the expenses which I have had to make for my security here, I will be a faithful Mexican. But when this rascal, Castro, comes here, a very warm and hearty welcome is prepared for him. Ten guns are well mounted to protect the fortress, and two field pieces. I have also about 50 faithful Indians who shoot their muskets very quickly."

CHAPTER VIII

THE DEBTOR

B Y 1842, Sutter had exhausted the entire reservoir of good will he had found upon his arrival in California. Thanks to his boasting and insolence, he was on bad terms with the entire corps of Mexican officialdom. Almost his only "friend" was the cantankerous, miserly quack, John Marsh. Although Sutter could never feel close to Marsh, the doctor loaned him a Spanish novel and a book on practical agriculture. Sutter appreciated the latter especially, but still he did not reciprocate with the medical book Marsh coveted. Since he had to treat all the sick at the fort with absolutely no medical training or experience, Sutter didn't dare let it out of his hands.

He was grateful, too, for Marsh's diverting the first overland immigrants, who arrived at his Mount Diablo ranch, to Sutter's Fort. The fort was always short of manpower; on any given day Sutter could use sixty or seventy more white men than he had. But Marsh's chief value was as Sutter's informant. When the doctor warned that there was talk of punitive action against New Helvetia, Sutter told him, "I am in a state of war here," and added, "I will be very thankful to you for sending me a courier if you

123

hear of any movement, and happy to pay any expense." Then he tried to entice Marsh into his hazily conceived Republic of California. Evanescent as it was, this plan should be considered to be the child of Alvarado's 1836 Free and Sovereign State of Alta California and father to the Bear Flag Republic of 1846. "I wish very much to see you, that we could have an interesting talk over many circumstances and, particularly, of the situation of the foreigners here in California. In a case of hostility, I am able to do a great deal."

With his inexplicable, maddening arrogance, Sutter managed to alienate General Vallejo once and for all. Vallejo was almost as angry with him as was José Castro. Drawing upon data given him by the Indian chief, Francisco Solano, and others, Vallejo dictated a letter to the Mexican government damning Sutter's actions and motives. So emotional and angry was he that his secretary, Victor Prudón, had to cover the paper with erasures and interlinings as the general searched for precisely the words to make the case against Sutter as strong as possible. He warned Mexico City that the insufferable Swiss was calling himself Governor of the Fortress of New Helvetia, was issuing arbitrary commands and was making frequent, despotic campaigns against the Indians. Since slavery had long been abolished in Mexico, Vallejo made a point of informing the government that Sutter was compelling adult prisoners to work in his fields, while he sold off children orphaned by his campaigns. Sutter, charged Vallejo, had also shot Indians without consultation or law and, worse, had dared to make threats of sedition.

The future did not look bright for New Helvetia. Sutter was more heavily in debt than ever before, thanks to his acquisition of the white elephant, Fort Ross. Still unpaid were French & Co., Suñol, the Hudson's Bay Company and many others. His farm at New Helvetia was as yet no agricultural empire but a shoestring operation—and one badly frayed and knotted by the drought of 1841. The winter of 1840–41 was the worst in memory. Almost no rain fell in northern California between February 1840 and

October 1841. Sutter saw the familiar specter of poverty grinning at him once again. But sublime optimist that he was, the Swiss threw himself into a new venture that might be his salvation. If wheat farming would not make him rich, perhaps trapping would do the trick.

Sutter was no greenhorn. He knew that the only form of legal tender in cashless California, aside from cowhide "banknotes," was beaver. And the prime pelts of his area were so heavy that a man could carry only ten or twelve skins at a time. He also was aware that each prime skin was worth one pound sterling per pound of its weight in New York or London. Each year saw 3,000 skins, which could have been his, taken from the region of the Sacramento and the San Joaquin to be sold for an average of three *piastres* a pelt. He had picked up considerable knowledge of the fur trade during his Santa Fe and Popo Agie days, and he relished a meal of beaver tail as keenly as the next mountain man. But he studied the animals and trapping anew. Every year, he found, Jean McKay, Francis Ermatinger or Michel Laframboise led a Hudson's Bay brigade into the environs of New Helvetia to trap. From the start Sutter had been able to buy moccasins, shirts and leggings of fine deerskin from the trappers' squaws, but the men refused point blank to sell him any of their beaver. They explained that to do so would be a high crime in the eyes of the company. Sutter must have licked his lips when he heard that in the single season of 1830 McKay had taken 4,000 beaver in just six months of trapping the sloughs and marshes of Suisun Bay.

Shouldering the Hudson's Bay Company aside would not be easy, but as early as the summer of 1840 Sutter had taken the first tentative steps in that direction. As official representative of Mexico on the Sacramento, and following Alvarado's orders, he had issued an edict to the company, forbidding its trappers to take beaver and land otter any longer in the Sacramento-San Joaquin area. The governor had indeed told him to put a stop to hunting in the region by Columbia River men. But he had neglected to tell Sutter that Hudson's Bay trappers were the sole exception to the rule. The company had signed an agreement with the governor in 1837 which, to formalize a *fait accompli,* legally allowed the brigades to continue trapping.

Between 1840 and 1842, Alvarado blew hot and cold on the expulsion of the company. Actually powerless to force them out, he let his patriotism and pride suffer, as did Vallejo. When James Douglas had come down from Fort Vancouver in 1841 to soften up both men, he discovered, to his surprise, that Vallejo—"the redoubtable Blue Beard"—was by no means a bad fellow. By guaranteeing him a royalty of half a dollar on every beaver killed in California, Douglas won Vallejo's permission to continue to hunt furs on the frontier northeast of Sonoma. Douglas had not found Alvarado as easy to tame, but he was finally able to report to his Hudson's Bay Company superior, Sir George Simpson, on March 25 that he had succeeded in his mission. "My communications were coldly received by the governor, who was displeased at our having pertinaciously maintained a hunting party on the frontiers in defiance of his repeated orders to the contrary. I coaxed him into better humour. . . . We are now free to do business generally in the country, both as merchants and hunters."

Thus, while Sutter was busily recruiting trappers, securing horses and canoes, and urging his smiths to make more beaver traps, the company was consolidating its position in California. Douglas had got permission from the governor for the company to establish a store and Hudson's Bay Company headquarters in Yerba Buena. No time was lost; on August 27, 1841, William Glen Rae had arrived and by September 9 had purchased Jacob Leese's establishment for $4,600. Soon, despite Alvarado's backing Sutter up to the point of asking Douglas to withdraw company brigades from any settled area (and Sutter's Fort had advanced the Mexican frontier by more than 100 miles to the northeast), rumors were flying of new company footholds throughout the province. One of U.S. Consul Thomas O. Larkin's informants passed on word that the company was dickering with Alvarado for a thirty-two-mile-square grant in *"los Tulares,"* the San Joaquin Valley. Chief Trapper McKay, already in command of 120 hunters in California and 40 to 50 more en route on the *Columbia,* would become the Sutter of this domain. It was said that McKay would stock the grant with 100,000 cattle and 6,500 sheep. One Californian wrote Larkin, "The Hon. Hudson's Bay Company are playing the Devil with the California cattle, if not with California, itself. It is very easy for the government of California to admit these privileges within its limits, but will it be easy for the government to drive them out, should they, hereafter, desire their expulsion? *Pienso que no!* [I think not!]"

Although Sutter had won no victory over the company, except a limited one—and that one on paper only—neither had the company been able to eliminate him as a rival in the two years following Douglas' visit to Alvarado. As 1842 lengthened, Sir George Simpson began to view this "territorial potentate" as a major obstacle to company expansion in California. This meant, too, that the stubborn colonizer was a block to British hegemony on the coast,—now an arena of fierce competition with France and the United States. Sir George damned Sutter's wisdom in choosing the superb location of Sutter's Fort. On the direct route to both Missouri and Oregon, it was admirably situated for fostering and maturing America's ambitious designs on California, designs toward which, Sir George realized, Sutter was now leaning despite his previous loyalty to France. At the same time, it blocked settlement by the Mexicans of the best parts of their own country, the rich Sacramento and San Joaquin valleys. Simpson predicted, with great accuracy, that if he had the talent and courage to make the most of his position, Sutter could turn California into another Texas with his "bullying the government and letting out Indians on hire."

In 1841 and 1842, California was virtually crowded with Hudson's Bay men. Besides all the fur trappers, Sir George Simpson and Dr. John McLoughlin arrived from London. And while

Douglas was there on a formal visit, Francis Ermatinger was traveling about the country, in disguise, as a spy! But theirs was a losing battle against Sutter and his trump card—American immigration. Ironically, from the establishment of the company's store in Yerba Buena, Hudson's Bay influence in California began to decline. This was in spite of its attraction to company men, many of whom talked of retiring there. Douglas had even written Sir George Simpson, "California is decidedly one of the finest countries in the world, surpassing all that poets dream of beauty and fertility. . . . The government is arbitrary and feebly administered, otherwise I would make it my home in preference to any other country I know." When Francis Ermatinger dropped his disguise, he, too, became a California enthusiast. He took up a position at Fort Hall as unpaid propagandist, urging Oregon-bound immigrants to strike for California rather than the Willamette. If Ermatinger was really trying to save Oregon for Britain rather than to win California for the United States, as has been claimed, there was no doubt about the attraction of Sutter's new California for his colleague, Michel Laframboise. The French-Canadian left the Hudson's Bay Company to go to work for Sutter.

Although Sutter boasted of shortly reaching his goal of having 8,000 traps, the hunt did not go well in the early months of 1842. He was able to send his agent forty-one pounds of beaver skins in January, but just two months later he was forced to send Dr. Marsh the rifle of one of his luckless trappers to pay off a debt. In April, he dispatched ninety-seven pelts, at $2.50 a pound, to Suñol, and forty-two skins, weighing seventy-seven and a half pounds, in May. But he confessed, "Beaver hunting will be very poor this year as I have only recruits for hunters and [Henry] McVicker, who commanded them, stole a good part of the hunt and sold the skins to Dr. Marsh and others." He told Suñol that McVicker (one of the "plotters" arrested with Isaac Graham in 1840) was at the camp of the Canadians, ready to go to the Columbia with them. "Some of these Columbia hunters had dealings in beaver and other skins with my men— and stole

128

Capitain A. Sutter

Gründer des Fort Neu Helvetia am Sacramento & der Harmoni am Federfluß, so wie auch Eigenthümer vom Fort Ross am Hafen von Bodega in Ober Californien

The stereotype of Capt. John A. Sutter is that of a portly burgher, founding American California in middle age. Actually, Sutter was a lean and dynamic adventurer when he came to California, who looked remarkably like the South American liberator Simon Bolivar.

Late in 1834, John Sutter arrived in St. Louis, Missouri, and settled into the German and Swiss community there. But he found Missouri far too tame a frontier for his adventuresome spirit and, after two seasons in the Santa Fe trade, decided to gamble his future on a colony in northern California which he would call New Helvetia—New Switzerland.

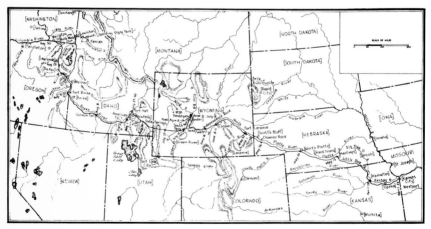

Reprinted by permission of the publishers, The Arthur H. Clark Company, from First White Women over the Rockies, *Vol. III, by Clifford M. Drury.*

Captain Sutter's route to California was a long and roundabout one. From the right bank of the Missouri, he marched with fur traders and Oregon missionaries across the High Plains via the Platte and over the Rockies via South Pass, to the Willamette. From there, he continued by canoe to Fort Vancouver, near the mouth of the Columbia, then by ship to Hawaii, back to Sitka, Alaska, and finally to San Francisco.

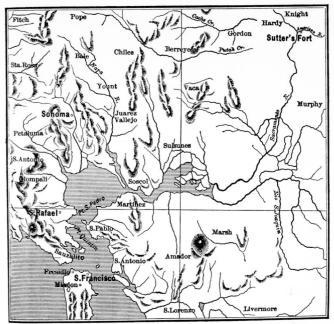

California Historical Society

John Sutter's choice of a site for New Helvetia, of Sutter's Fort, was superb. It was beyond meddling distance from Mexican San Francisco and Sonoma, dominated the route to Oregon, controlled virtually all inland navigation, and was the bottleneck through which all trans-Sierra American immigration had to pass.

Idaho Historical Society

Sutter's Fort was not a copy of any particular fort the Swiss pioneer had seen but rather the end product of study of a number of posts, such as Fort Hall (above) and Fort Vancouver, through which Sutter passed on his route to California.

Within only a few years of his arrival, Capt. John A. Sutter was not only the wheat king of California but also its cattle king, with 4,500 head in the care of his Indian *vaqueros* and Mexican *mayordomos*.

Not only was John Sutter the major pioneer in California agriculture and mining, but he also began the state's fishing industry by establishing a salmon fishery on the Sacramento and Feather rivers and barreling salmon for export.

From 1841 until 1849, the High Plains west of the Missouri River were crossed by hundreds of wagon trains whose members knew but one destination—Sutter's Fort. Within only a few months of the arrival of the first company, in 1841, Sutter's generosity became proverbial, and despite the reversals he suffered, he never failed to provide for the worn and hungry travelers who arrived at New Helvetia. The warm welcome at Sutter's Fort, which they knew would be forthcoming, served to keep up the morale of immigrants on the long march westward.

Typical of the rough-hewn adventurers who flocked to Sutter's banner at New Helvetia in the early 1840's was Peter Lassen. Like so many other friends and associates of Captain Sutter, the Dane had a falling-out with the pioneer and decided to set up his own establishment. Lassen's rancho, far up the Sacramento Valley from New Helvetia, came to be a small-scale New Helvetia on the trail to Oregon. Mount Lassen and Lassen National Park are named for Sutter's one-time friend and hired hand.

G. M. Waseurtz af Sandels, the traveler and writer who called himself the "King's Orphan," sketched Capt. John Sutter's newest property, Fort Ross, in 1843.

California Beaches & Parks

Captain Sutter blundered in buying Fort Ross, the Russian bastion on California's Redwood Coast. He placed himself so deeply in debt that it took the Gold Rush to get him out—and then it was too late; Sutter was finished as a major figure in California society.

Ansel Adams Photograph, Redwood Empire Association

AYUDANTE GENERAL MICHELTORENA.

Cuartel maestre en la Angostura.

Gen. Manuel Micheltorena, governor of Mexican California, was a handsome and dignified gentleman who won John Sutter's allegiance completely. When the governor was threatened by civil war in 1844–45, Sutter marched to his rescue with a crack foreign legion. But, unfortunately for Sutter, Micheltorena was a sham. After allowing himself to be "defeated" in a virtually bloodless battle—arranged so that he might save face—he abandoned California to the rebels and, in so doing, abandoned Sutter to a downward spiral of fortune.

John Sutter made many rivals and enemies after his founding of New Helvetia. One of them was Dr. John Marsh, who practiced medicine without a license and who practiced deception with great skill in Sutter's grand army of 1845. A conscript soldier in Sutter's foreign legion, which marched in aid of Governor Micheltorena, Marsh spread desertion and mutiny through the ranks, bringing about the army's collapse.

California Beaches & Parks

Manuel Micheltorena's carriage was a great improvement over California's crude *carretas,* but it slowed the ailing governor—and his right-hand man, John Sutter—enough in their pursuit of rebels in 1845 that their army became open to dissension, mutiny and final defeat after a long and rugged march down the Coast Range to Los Angeles.

Sutro Library

some. As long as the company comes to this country, beaver hunting will be a failure." Although McVicker did not desert Sutter for Fort Vancouver, but drifted back to the Santa Cruz area where he had lived when a crony of Isaac Graham, Sutter felt compelled to write to Suñol: "I wish very much that you would teach that foreigner a good lesson. I am beginning to discharge many of the foreigners because I do not want so many in my employ; because so few among them are trustworthy." Shortly afterward Sutter had to discharge one of his own men for selling a horse to the Canadians. Next, he had trouble with some of the French-Canadians who had attached themselves to him. He wrote Suñol, "We have three Frenchmen who intend to leave here. One among them, Big Nicholas, wanted to kill me one day and caused me a lot of trouble."

Trapping was no panacea; even Sutter could see that. He returned to his letter-writing campaign, staving off creditors with the customary flood of promises to pay. He cast about for new enterprises to satisfy new markets, sending Suñol a quantity of deer tallow which, he assured him, was carefully prepared for overseas shipment and lamely explaining that his fur trappers had taken deer on their last hunt, rather than beaver, because "it pleased them more." And he was not above involving himself in the dirty business of slaving Indians, promising Suñol, in a June letter, some "little Indians."

But still the creditors closed in inexorably. The worst threat came from Suñol's brothers-in-law, the Bernal boys, who were threatening to come to New Helvetia to seize his cattle in order to settle a debt. "This would be futile," lied Sutter to Suñol. "That would be nothing but making war uselessly, and dispute without end." Most of his cattle were gone, he claimed—not without reason. He was increasingly moving his stock from New Helvetia to his Hock Farm on the Feather River. This maneuver not only got his herds a little farther beyond the reach of the Bernal brothers but released more prime land around the fort for wheat. Another angry creditor was Rae, of the Hudson's Bay Company store, who wrote Larkin that Sutter owed him $3,400 but that he doubted he would see a farthing of it during 1842.

Not all the news in 1842 was bad for Sutter. Busy harvesting his wheat, he exclaimed, "Thank God! It looks like a good crop." He was able to deliver 1,200 *fanegas* of the 1,500 promised the Russians. Wild grapes were so abundant that he toyed with the idea of turning his pisco brandy into a kind of cash crop. And to Suñol he spoke of another California industry in which he planned to pioneer, lumbering. "I have a splendid place near here for a saw and flour mill which is to be constructed in a short time. The builder of the mill assures me that he has never seen as good a site in all California." Unknown to him, the "short time" would stretch to almost six years, and the site of his still-born lumbering industry would, by a curious twist of fate, hold the golden seeds of his ultimate ruin.

While Sutter was fighting off creditors, Sir George Simpson was warning the governor and committee of the Hudson's Bay Company in London:

> This person [Sutter] . . . has recently settled on the Sacramento, falling into the Bay of San Francisco and, I understand, was formerly a soldier in the French Army, afterwards a grog-shop keeper in St. Louis, U.S., whence he decamped in debt, accompanying a band of American trappers to the Snake country, whence he found his way to Fort Vancouver, thence to the Sandwich Islands and thence to California, where he has contrived to obtain credit to the amount of nearly $100,000. I am sorry to add the Honourable Company are among his creditors to the amount of $3,000 to $4,000. Now that he has, I may say, defrauded almost every one with whom he has come into contact, he has seated himself down in a stronghold on the Sacramento, surrounded and protected by a body of runaway sailors, vagabond trappers from the United States, and other desperadoes, bidding defiance not only to creditors but even to the public authorities and laws of the country. I am this particular in noticing this man's proceedings because he has lately sent threatening messages to our trapping party under the command

of Mr. Ermatinger, now hunting on the Sacramento, with a view
to drive us from that part of the country. Our operations there
are carried on under the sanctions of a license granted to us by
the authorities of California so that if Sutter should attempt to
follow up his threats of expulsion by an overt act of violence
(which is very improbable), it is feared the banks of the Sacramento may become the scene of violence and strife.

August 1842 was a dark month. One of Sutter's creditors attached the schooner *Sacramento,* and threatened to cut the fort's
lifeline. September was even blacker. Sutter learned that Suñol
planned to come to the fort with the Bernal brothers in order to
seize cattle to settle Sutter's debts to them. He hurriedly wrote
Suñol to express his shock, admitting that he had been expecting
him to come up to discuss business matters but begging him not
to bring along a lot of men. With a few companions only, he
would, of course, be welcome. However, Sutter, alarmed, rushed
his chief clerk, Charles W. Flügge, to Suñol to stall him. He told
Suñol that Flügge had full power to act for him and complained,
"The rumors circulated here are very disadvantageous to me. . . .
I beg you, again, not to give credence to all the stories that my
enemies tell you. They have injured me greatly."

When Suñol refused Sutter's arrangements and demanded immediate payment in cattle, Sutter sent him still another stalling
letter. Gambling for time, he promised to round up 200 to 300
cattle for him, *if* he would lend him a few cowboys. He dangled
some beaver pelts before his correspondent's nose, too, reminding
him that summer was ending and the beaver season beginning
again. Sutter's instinct was right; his gamble paid off. He soon
was able to send Suñol not only deer tallow but sixty-nine beaver
skins and a furious letter: "The stranger who told you I write you
letters only to pass the time, and that I will pay you when it
pleases me, I declare an infamous liar, whoever he may be!"

Good news for Sutter was the increasing number of immigrants
reaching California, many of whom found themselves drawn to
New Helvetia. Three families came south with Lieutenant Em-

131

mons and his expedition. A trickle of men, like Theodore Cordua, founder of New Mecklenburg, a copy of New Helvetia, came from Hawaii. But the real harbinger of things to come was a young man named Jacob (Jimmy) Johns, who wandered, lost, into Sutter's Fort while the rest of his companions, of the Bidwell-Bartleson party, camped at Dr. Marsh's place. The party was the van of the vast wave of immigration which was soon to sweep aside not only Vallejo and Castro and the grandiose plans of men like Duflot de Mofras, but even Sutter himself.

Sutter issued passports to the new arrivals over the protests of Vallejo, who considered himself the only person in the north qualified to issue such documents. In performing this service for the newcomers, John Sutter became guarantor of their good conduct. But this did not at all disturb him. He readily assured the government that such men as Charles M. Weber (eventual founder of Stockton) would not subvert public order and tranquillity. Although far from contrite for his previous bad manners, Sutter also tried at this time to patch up his differences with Vallejo, writing him, "I am very much obliged to you for the assistance and for the good advice which you had the kindness to give to my people when they went to Sonoma with the animals [from Fort Ross]. If I can serve you in any way, dispose of me freely."

More and more, Sutter found himself sympathizing with the Americans rather than the Mexicans in California. His Francophilia was cooling. Writing U.S. Consul Larkin to recommend two of his old Missouri comrades, he cemented a friendship which became an instrument of empire. "I am all the time happy to do everything for an American citizen when it lies in my power and so I think you will do the same." Whether or not Sutter was aware of it, Larkin was already trusting him as an informant and practically as an ex officio U.S. Vice Consul for New Helvetia, although Sutter still wore the uniform of the Mexican government in his role of magistrate and militia officer. Sutter's relationship with Consul Larkin was second in importance, for his career, only to his friendship for John Bidwell.

Bidwell was a talented, utterly dependable young man who would one day be a gubernatorial and Presidential candidate. Hailed in his old age as California's "Prince of Pioneers," Bidwell was a mere twenty-two years old when he arrived at Sutter's Fort in November 1841. He found Sutter the very antithesis of Dr. Marsh, whom he described as "one of the most selfish of mortals." Wrote Bidwell, "Sutter received us with open arms and in a princely fashion, for he was a man of the most polite address and the most courteous manner, a man who could shine in any society. . . . Everybody was welcome—one man or a hundred, it was all the same. He employed men not because he always needed and could profitably employ them, but because in the kindness of his heart it simply became a habit to employ everybody who wanted employment. As long as he had anything, he trusted anyone with everything he wanted, responsible or otherwise, acquaintances and strangers alike."

Sutter liked Bidwell's looks and hired him on the spot. He spent five weeks teaching him Spanish at the fort, forbidding him to go farther than fifteen miles up the river. In that short time, an enduring friendship was born. Bidwell became Sutter's strong right arm. Sutter found in him the absolutely loyal and trustworthy man he had so long needed to aid his efforts.

Sutter first put Bidwell in charge of Fort Ross, replacing Bob Ridley. There he moved everything portable within fourteen months and was so thorough that he even made cider and dried apples from the fruit trees. Next, Sutter made him manager of Hock Farm on the Feather River. There, in charge of Indian adobe brickmakers and two French-Canadian sawyers, Bidwell began putting up buildings for Sutter and generally expanding farm operations.

What Sutter needed was fifty men like Bidwell. Dark clouds were lowering over New Helvetia. The inclement political weather was due, at once, to Sutter's arrogance toward the Mexican government and to the steady arrival of American immigrants. Alvarado, Castro and Vallejo were all alarmed, and Vallejo sent his aide, Prudón, to Mexico City to witness, personally, to Sutter's behavior. It was meanwhile reported to Larkin that President Santa Anna was taking action himself. Not only was he raising an army to invade Texas but was sending 500 soldiers to Alta California under a new governor, his crony, Manuel Micheltorena, with orders "to put Sutter in order or root him out."

Santa Anna did not yet march on Texas. Nor did the United States declare war on Mexico, yet. (To his embarrassment, one Thomas ap Catesby Jones, U.S.N., waged war, single-handedly, and captured Monterey after putting too much faith in an October 1842 war rumor. Sheepishly, he gave the town back and apologized for his rash actions.) But Micheltorena *did* sail with his 500-man expeditionary corps. By the time he reached Monterey in the fall, sickness and death had reduced his force to 300 men, most of them released jailbirds. Both Sutter and Vallejo, simultaneously, began to woo him. While Sutter was sending Flügge to intercept the new governor in Los Angeles, Vallejo was warning Micheltorena that the wild tribes of the Sacramento were rising and a band of foreigners, "of bad tendencies," was assembling at Sutter's Fort. Small wonder that Micheltorena was puzzled, for while Sutter thundered that he had the support of the Hudson's Bay Company trappers, Vallejo claimed the company had offered to help *him* drive the Swiss from the Sacramento Valley. Almost as ambivalent for the moment as Sutter himself, Vallejo then hurriedly explained that he did not intend to accept the Canadians' help—because he did not want Sutter and his friends to lose the money invested in New Helvetia. Only a paragraph after describing Sutter as "badly compromised" and a man with a "marked tendency to conspire," he was advising, "I consider it rather to the advantage of the government that his nascent colony should flourish there." The result was that Micheltorena adopted a wait-and-see attitude toward Sutter, despite the fact that Vallejo swiftly reverted to his old fear tactics, warning

134

the governor that his force at Sonoma was inadequate to repel an attack by Sutter, his Indians and his Missouri hunters.

To his surprise, Sutter found himself liking Micheltorena. He was, in fact, an affable and well-disposed man, but he was not firm enough with his *cholos,* as the Californians termed his chicken-thief soldiers. Word of the conduct of Micheltorena's ragamuffin force spread all over California. John Coffin Jones, former U.S. Consul in Honolulu and now a resident of Santa Barbara, wrote Larkin: "I hope to God they will be swallowed up by a flood or an earthquake. . . . With a few exceptions, wretched and miserable as are the soldiers, their officers—if there can be any beings more loathsome and despicable—they are so. What a prospect for California after the introduction of such a body of felons! It is intended, no doubt, to be made the Botany Bay of Mexico."

Sutter presented an appearance of power which impressed Micheltorena. But Bidwell knew the truth; behind the façade, he saw Sutter's empire in danger of crumbling into bankruptcy. And he understood the fatal cycle that plagued his employer: "His necessities compelled him to take all he could buy and he paid all he could pay, but he failed to keep up his payments. And, so, soon he found himself immensely, almost hopelessly, involved in debt." Fighting desperately for his existence, Sutter used every trick in his bag—honest and dishonest alike—to forestall defeat. He worked long and hard hours; there was no loafing at the fort. He procrastinated on payment of debts, overpriced his goods, gave false weights. He attempted to evade payment of fees on the Russian ships which called for his wheat. For the endless delays in delivery of beaver skins to Suñol he had a whole catalogue of excuses: the hunting parties were late; he had loaned his schooner to the Hudson's Bay Company; his launch had broken down. When he finally did deliver sixty-seven skins, he told the Spaniard that they weighed eighty pounds. Suñol was not surprised to discover that they weighed only seventy-five. In June of 1843 he delivered another twenty-five skins, but it was the last shipment of the season. When Suñol also asked him for spirits, Sutter had one of his inconsistent bursts of honesty, advising him not to buy any of the corn whisky which he was making because he did not age it and it "always has a bad taste."

From time to time, backed to the wall by bankruptcy, Sutter felt sorry for himself. When he was forced to pay one of his creditors in cattle, he mourned the thirty-one animals lost in crossing the Sacramento: "The crossing of the cattle has caused me a great deal of trouble and, doubtless, a far greater number would have been lost if boats, canoes, horses and men of mine had not been sent to the assistance of your men." Summer drought and winter floods alike worked against him. In June of 1843 he was optimistically informing his creditors, "Thank God, I shall have a fairly good crop again." In October, he was grimly swallowing these words, writing, "Had the harvest not failed this year, I could have paid off the entire debt."

Sutter tried feverishly to increase his beaver harvest. He was more optimistic than ever in the fall of 1843. He wrote Suñol that all his hunters were out and that soon he would send him a bale of furs. "I have a very good chance of being alone in the bay," he told him, "because Laframboise is not coming this year with his company, so destructive to the country. I have also added to my hunters, up to 40 men and, in a short time, I shall be able to equip another dozen. I shall not fail to send you beaver skins this year." When Suñol pressed him for payment, he reiterated, "I shall do everything in my power to satisfy you. Now, until next May, I cannot do any more than send you, from time to time, as much beaver as possible." The fact was, though neither Sutter nor the company realized it, northern California was just about "hunted out" of beaver. Hudson's Bay Company agent William Rae had reported from Yerba Buena in November 1842 that he had received only 254 beaver and 445 land otter skins. On August 27, 1843, he was writing to London, "The company trapping party under the charge of Mr. Laframboise left the Sacra-

mento a few days ago. They have made out miserably. I do not
think the whole hunt exceeded 650 otter and beaver skins."

Rae was getting worried about collecting from Sutter, too. He
received a letter from John McLoughlin which read, "As to Captain Sutter, he has acted so as to make it unnecessary for me to
comment on his conduct. We must get him to pay, the best way
we can." But Sutter was as slippery a debt-dodger as ever. He
not only put off the Hudson's Bay Company successfully, but got
Suñol to call off the Bernal brothers, who had threatened to complain directly to the government. After chiding them, in a letter
to Suñol, for even thinking of such a thing—"That would have
been a very disagreeable thing to me, as I am upon a very amiable
footing with His Excellency, the governor"—Sutter promised to
pay off all his debts by October 1844.

Sutter was not just boasting when he assured Suñol of the good
terms existing between the governor and himself. Micheltorena
had been much impressed by the master of New Helvetia. When
Vallejo wrote the governor in 1843 demanding to know exactly
what authority Sutter possessed, he was told the harsh facts of
life. The governor's Secretary of State replied: "Since he has
formed an establishment in that place, of considerable importance, the government held it to be proper to clothe the afore-
said Señor Sutter, on the 1st of September 1840, with political
authority making him justice of his establishment of New Helvetia
and its vicinity, so that he might prosecute and reduce Indian
thieves and pernicious people, observing in all cases the good order and tranquillity of the Indians who have established or may
establish themselves in that place."

Sutter ignored Vallejo's periodic tantrums and continued to
punish Indians, issue passports and write bonds for prisoners. But
most of his time was devoted to wheat, not documents. When he
replaced his crude California plows—crooked tree limbs with
their points shod with scraps of iron—with Russian plows, he
found them nearly as unsatisfactory. So he put his smiths to work

making improved iron plows, but his major weapon against blazing sun and unyielding earth was manpower. Day after day, he called from 300 to 400 Indian workers to a hearty breakfast of beef, bread and wheat or cornmeal gruel by ringing his Russian bell and rolling a beat on his Mexican militia drum. He killed four or five beeves a day to keep his laborers in good shape. Every day but Sunday, a day of rest although Sutter required no religious observations, he sent his army of workers into the fields to harvest the precious wheat. They were armed with a strange array of clumsy tools. Sickles and scythes were almost nonexistent. To some he gave kitchen or skinning knives; others carried sharpened lengths of barrel hoops. Too many had to pull up the crop by hand, until the rough stalks cut and bloodied their hands so badly that they begged him for willow branches, split to produce some semblance of a cutting edge, for the reaping.

The Swiss had tried to raft one of the great Russian threshing floors all the way from Fort Ross to New Helvetia, when he found that the parquet floor of redwood was so snugly locked with nails that dismantling was virtually impossible. The *Sacramento* lost her tow, however, and the sixty-foot wooden arena broke up on the rocks, a total loss. Sutter was forced to fall back on an earthen-floored thresher, little more than a circular, adobe-walled corral. He had his whooping *vaqueros* drive 300 to 400 half-wild horses onto the floor, atop a week's—or even a month's—harvest. The dashing horses churned and beat down the wheat. At his command, the cowboys would reverse the direction of the circling horses, the braking and skidding of their hooves efficiently turning the mass of grain and broken straw. An hour of this and Sutter would have 2,000 bushels of wheat threshed. But separating the grain from the chaff—and the horse manure—was a more difficult operation. The winnowing might take a month. Luckily, although rain failed in California, the trade winds rolled off the Pacific with clocklike regularity. Sutter's Indians pitched countless shovelfuls of grain and straw into the air, letting the light trash blow aside as the clean flow of heavy grain cascaded to the ground. His only fanning mill was the valley of the Sacramento, up which swept the wind from the Golden Gate.

All day long, four mules, changed every four hours, plodded in a circle, drawing a banshee-screaming flour mill. Yet it was barely able to keep up with the appetite of Sutter's small army for coarse, but sweet and nutritious, bread. At times, he had to keep the mule-powered mill and the bake oven going night and day to feed his wards and workers. By dint of such round-the-clock activity, Sutter was able to hold his own during 1843. So determined was he to rescue his enterprise from ruin that he neglected the socializing which he enjoyed. When the scholarly Swedish traveler, Dr. G. M. Waseurtz af Sandels, visited him, Sutter was so distracted by his wheat harvest that he could spare him little time. Yet the Swede wrote, "Although he was very busily employed in distributing orders for the day, he most hospitably received me and made me at home under his roof." Sandels did not get to know him well, although he called Sutter "my interesting friend," because of his frenetic activity. Years later, Sutter more or less apologized, saying, "I do recollect the scientific Swedish gentleman. But I was much too occupied at the time with other concerns to devote any time or attention to his statements. My crops were ripe and it was imperative that they should be gathered as quickly as possible."

Sutter did not forget his good manners, however, and he invited his guest to join him at breakfast. Used to having tough chunks of beef roasted on ramrods over an open fire, Sandels could not help contrasting the fine meal he enjoyed with Sutter— tender steaks, bread and butter, tea, eggs and *frijoles*—with the porridge the Indians were gulping down outside: "They fed more like beasts than human beings." Sutter put on a good face for his visitor, but Sandels noticed tell-tale signs of trouble in the American River "citadel." He saw how small was the vegetable garden and how meager the harvest—"the wheat was next door to failure." Riding about the fort, he noted the cracked soil and the tinder-dry grass, sparse on the baked plain. There were no flowers and the smoke of grass fires under the relentless sun explained why his host was so wrapped up in his harvest. At the fort itself, for all its cannon and uniformed Indians, bread was in short supply. Sandels did not fail to observe that Sutter was grinding part of his precious supply of seed wheat. And the latter's cheerful insistence—"We find peas a good substitute for coffee, and acorns still better; indeed, it is difficult always to tell acorn coffee from good coffee"—did not fool him. Sutter was as hospitable as ever, but he was finding it difficult, toward the end of 1843, to live up to the reputation he had earned from such accounts as that of Lieutenant Emmons: "Everything that the heart could wish was supplied from the bountiful storehouse of this large-hearted, generous, man . . . and for all this the noble man declined any compensation."

Sutter's open-handed hospitality to travelers was part of his character, intimately bound up in his concept of personal honor. No matter how hard-pressed he might be by his foes, drought and debt, he could never refuse a request for help. Meanness and miserliness simply were not in him. His charity was tangled in his pride and in his enjoyment of his role of *patrón*. As sensitive as a feudal lord, he would rather starve than lose face. But it was more than face-saving. One of his aides stated that it gave Sutter great pleasure to administer to the needs of exhausted pilgrims—and pleasure was important to the sensualist in Sutter. But more, the passing years revealed his major weakness, a tender heart. Such compassion could easily be exploited on the frontier. When just this happened, during the Gold Rush, Sutter was ruined. But in the balance sheet of his paradoxical character, generosity—indeed, magnanimity—stood out large. Even his most jealous enemies were forced to abandon as hopeless the task of running it down.

Sutter's preoccupation with crops, furs and debts did not absorb his entire attention. He still had time to thwart Vallejo's attempts to turn the new governor against him. As far as Micheltorena was concerned, there were no grounds for complaints

against Sutter or his dependents, and a firm friendship developed
between them, though Sutter was unable to leave his demanding agricultural chores to pay His Excellency a visit until October 1844. Meantime, he kept his good will, jettisoned his own
hare-brained scheme for an independent *république* and ignored
American immigrant Lansford Hastings's far-fetched plan for a
California Republic. Sutter put all his political chips on Governor Micheltorena, abandoned his recent militancy, and returned
to the fence-mending that had kept him out of the Graham affair
in 1840.

He was well repaid. Micheltorena followed up his friendship
with complete jurisdiction over northern California east of the
Sacramento, whereas Vallejo had to share authority to the west
of the river with Jacob Leese, charged with civil matters. With
this reassurance from the governor, Sutter expanded his program
of settling newcomers all over the Sacramento Valley. At the
same time he renewed his peace offensive against Vallejo, stating
that their sacred bonds of friendship had been cut by treacherous
flatterers. "I repeat, I am entirely disposed to obey superior orders," he assured the general. Soon Sutter was acting as if their
friendship had never been ruptured, and Vallejo was selling him
—on credit, of course—a loom and 150 bushels of wheat.

Sutter worked harder than ever. He recalled, in the 1870's,
"My head was full of business, night and day. Bidwell was about
the only man I ever had who could assist me much." In a letter
of 1843 to Marsh, he commented, "I have no clerk at present. . . .
Now, everything lies on my back." At times, he allowed himself
only two hours of sleep at night. When he was away from the
fort, he had to leave very detailed instructions with his chief
clerk, Pierson B. Reading. Thus, on April 24, 1844, he not only
had to remind Reading to get the smiths to make screws for the
Fort Ross windmills, and to keep an eye on the Indian night
guards, and to keep the men from dipping into the whisky, but
to be certain that Manuiki was safe from the Don Juan of the

smithy. He ordered Reading "to have a sharp eye on Chamberlain entering in the apartments of the girls."

Unfortunately, work proved no fetish against trouble as Sutter moved into 1844. The wheat crop was sickly and he confessed to Suñol, *"Encore, une malheureuse année* [Again, a bad year]." Next, William Rae filed suit to recover the money Sutter owed the Hudson's Bay Company. Rae's legal maneuver stimulated others to nip at Sutter's heels. Then, one of Larkin's associates had to be stalled. Sutter wove a tissue of white lies, in order to gain time: "I was fully under the impression that you had received payment, having made arrangements to that effect," and "I will, by the earliest opportunity, forward you the amount, in cash, or place it to your account with Mr. Rae." On the heels of Rae's suit, William Wiggins filed a complaint against Sutter with the governor for refusing to punish Peter Lassen for stealing a horse belonging to Wiggins. Claimed Wiggins, "When I asked him to punish the thief, he sneered at me and gave no answer. I hope you will ask the general, in particular, if there is any penalty for horse stealing and if Captain Sutter is to be allowed to treat men with impunity that apply to him for justice." Sutter's justice was a personal kind of reward and punishment, colored throughout by friendships and loyalties.

Bad news came not in threes during 1844 for Sutter, but in sixes and sevens. His schooner, *Sacramento,* was swept onto the rocks near Fort Ross. The captain and his men managed to save the vessel, but it was out of action all the summer and early fall. Next, he suffered a severe blow—the defeat of his hope that he would ultimately receive title to the land at Fort Ross and Bodega. To his distress, he learned that his friend, Micheltorena, had given grants there to settlers who were locating sawmills on the redwood coast. A bitterly disappointed Sutter briefly made a fool of himself, swearing emptily that if Bodega were not "returned" to him, he would call one of the Tsar's men-of-war to his assistance. Everyone ignored him. Sutter was still living partly in the past. No Russian—or French—gunboat was going to come to his rescue now, as the tide of American hegemony began to flow in California.

Sutter was still renting or selling Indians, usually orphaned children, to his neighbors. When he sent a group to Suñol to work off part of his debt, he swallowed his pride and apologized for the fact that some did not even have shirts to wear. "I have no an ell of *manta* left, to have some made." When the Indians passed Marsh's ranch, en route to Suñol's, the miser grumblingly killed two calves to feed them after billing Suñol for $6. Then he sneered at Sutter's men, who, he said, were "as usual, dying of hunger." This was an unnecessary dig at the man who had offered him a piece of land at New Helvetia and who promised him protection from stock thieves. Sutter's kindness was altogether wasted on the surly Marsh. There were only two men in all existence whom Sutter, no matter what he did, was never able to please. One was Marsh and the other, met in the spring of 1844, was John C. Frémont, the man who, more than any other, might be considered Sutter's nemesis.

CHAPTER IX

THE PARTISAN

A turning point—downward—for Sutter occurred on March 6, 1844. While strolling outside the walls of the fort, he was surprised to encounter a haughty stranger on horseback. The visitor proved to be the ambitious, conceited Lt. John C. Frémont. With Frémont rode his guide, Christopher (Kit) Carson. The two men explained to Sutter that they had pushed ahead of their main force of twenty-four men, which was dropping down the American River under the command of mountain man Tom Fitzpatrick. When Frémont reported that hunger and fatigue had forced him and his men to detour from his determined course, Oregon to the Arkansas River, Sutter immediately sent a *vaquero* and pack horse, loaded with foodstuffs, to refresh Broken Hand's party.

Sutter recalled, in 1878, the welcome which he had extended Frémont: "I received him politely and his company likewise, as if an old acquaintance." Kit Carson verified Sutter's recollection by saying, "We were well received by Mr. Sutter and furnished in a princely manner. . . . When we arrived at the fort, we were as naked and in as poor a condition as men possibly could be." Carson did not exaggerate. Frémont's thirty-three surviving horses, of an original herd of sixty-three, were pitiful, stumbling racks of bones. And the riders were as gaunt as their mounts.

By 1844, Sutter's loyalties were exactly divided. He dutifully reported Frémont's arrival to the Mexican authorities, as befitted an *alcalde,* but he also hurried word to United States Consul Larkin. Larkin had already heard garbled rumors of Frémont's coming and had asked Sutter what he knew of a U.S. boundary commission said to be wandering around the West. Sutter, in his naïveté, did not share the suspicion which most *Californios* instinctively felt toward the so-called Pathfinder. Reported Sutter: "The visit of this exploring expedition I attribute entirely to accident. For a month previous to their arrival, the company has subsisted on mule and horse flesh. The starvation and fatigue they had endured rendered them truly deplorable objects. With these facts and the assurance of Lt. Frémont, I can be of no other than the above opinion."

Micheltorena was not so sure that Frémont's visit was pure accident. He sent a military commission to Sutter's Fort, to treat with the American officer and to ask him just what he was doing in the department of Alta California. As Sutter recalled the sequence of events, "I had expected the soldiers and had hurried Frémont off before they came." When they arrived, Sutter treated them formally, even stiffly. Much later, he explained his restraint: "In my intercourse with American settlers, mountaineers, and trappers, I was frank and unconventional. I greeted them with a hearty handshake, although I always expected to be treated with respect. But with Californians and Mexicans I was more particular. I required them to pay the same deference to me as they were accustomed to pay to their own officers. Whenever they came within the walls of the fort, they were obliged to take off their hats, soldiers as well as officers. When the Mexicans came to look for Frémont, they found sentries at the gate of the fort and a guard at my door. Their officers, whom I quartered within the walls, asked me politely and humbly to permit their servants

146

to enter the fort." Sutter's answer was "Yes, but no soldiers." When the officers asked him one evening if the fort was built solely as a protection against Indians, Sutter answered bluntly, "No, it is against you Californians." He then reminded his guests that Vallejo and others were jealous of his settlement and resented his issuing passports to immigrant Americans.

Larkin wrote, asking Sutter to give Frémont every assistance. It was quite unnecessary. Sutter needed no urging; he was compulsively generous. He gave the men bread and their horses feed. He brought out new bridles and pack saddles from his storeroom. During Frémont's entire stay, until March 24, Sutter's forge was hardly ever cold, as his smiths hammered out shoes to refit the Americans' horses. The generous Swiss turned over to the Americans sixty mules and twenty-five fresh horses, all shod, plus thirty head of cattle, for beef. He loaned Frémont one of his young Indian *vaqueros* to be his cattle drover, then presented his supercilious visitor with his own fine, iron-gray saddle horse, named Sacramento. As Sutter said, "Captain Frémont found in my establishment everything that he needed."

Sutter showed Frémont the heart of his 49,000-acre spread, his vast fields of waving green wheat. He boasted that he had sowed 600 bushels of seed and that his irrigated fields would yield twenty-five bushels to the acre. He gladly answered all his guest's questions about California, whether concerning its geography or politics. He was hospitality personified. Yet, try as he might, the puzzled Sutter could not penetrate Frémont's cold reserve.

Frémont's coolness soon changed into hostility. The Pathfinder accused three of his men of the theft of some sugar. As Mexican magistrate, Sutter assumed jurisdiction in the case, which displeased Frémont. Then, Sutter tried the men and found them not guilty, infuriating Frémont, who had arbitrarily predetermined their guilt. Finally, Sutter compounded his error by hiring the men when Frémont discharged them! Before the Pathfinder left for the United States by way of southern California, Sutter had signed on five of his men. One of the sugar-theft suspects became

147

his best blacksmith. But Sutter's daring to "cross" him finished him with Frémont, although he managed to bottle up most of his resentment temporarily.

Frémont's brusqueness and inconsideration could not discourage Sutter. He delighted in feasting the Americans, who had been making do with horse meat, stewed dog and piñon nuts for too long. He gave them fresh-caught trout and salmon, venison, beef, ham, bear meat, smoked tongue, peas fresh from the garden, salads, fruits and even Rhine wine. The white wine would have soured in Sutter's mouth if he could have dreamed, that spring of 1844, that the next time Frémont would visit him it would be to depose him as lord of the Sacramento and to hold him a virtual prisoner in his own fortress.

Once Frémont was gone, Sutter returned his attention to California politics. The year 1844 was one of grants and settlement, Micheltorena approving thirty-three petitions for 600,000 acres in the Sacramento Valley alone. But it was also a time of war, or at least rumors of war. The rumors which had led Com. Thomas ap Catesby Jones to seize Monterey in 1842 continued unabated. In May of 1844 the Mexican minister of war predicted that the expected treaty annexing Texas to the United States would mean war. In July, Governor Micheltorena, following the minister's orders, moved his cannon and military headquarters from Monterey to inland San Juan Bautista, to be well out of range of Yankee sloops-of-war. He ordered all citizens between fifteen and sixty years of age, including naturalized foreigners, to enroll in nine companies of militia. Micheltorena named Sutter, of course, to the command of the Sacramento company. But Consul Larkin shrewdly guessed that Micheltorena could really count only on his 250 Mexican troops in any showdown and perhaps on some 150 California soldiers. He was convinced that the 1,000 militiamen had no zest for fighting in behalf of a government in which they took little interest and no pride.

When word came in September that Texas was not yet to be annexed, California briefly returned to normalcy. The customary rivalry between southern and northern Californians led to the former's loudly urging Micheltorena to move the capital from Monterey to Los Angeles. He paid them no more heed than had Alvarado. But separatism was, more and more, involved in the plotting and counterplotting of political partisans.

Fear of war with the United States did not keep the personal ambition of Castro and Alvarado from festering, either. Micheltorena's army of ex-jailbirds became an intolerable insult to the proud native Californians. With the distraction of a possible Yankee intervention removed for the moment, Micheltorena's rivals renewed their Machiavellian scheming. Already, the affable and indolent Micheltorena had lasted longer than many Californians had predicted. John Coffin Jones described him as the very last man the Mexicans should have sent to govern the department. Of course, Jones felt that *any* man's continuing long in the executive chair was a virtual impossibility. The French secret agent, Duflot de Mofras, flatly predicted that Micheltorena would suffer the same fate as deposed Governors Victoria, Chico, Gutiérrez and Carrillo. On the other hand, some men almost gave up hope that the governor and his rascally *cholos* would ever be overthrown. Even Jones was led to despair, "If there was a speck of courage or of moral honesty in the Californians, they would rise *en masse,* and drive those wretches from their shores. But no, these pusillanimous souls quail at the very thought."

Jones was wrong. Alvarado and Castro were about to strike. In an ill-concerted movement, they confronted Micheltorena. As early as January 1844, the governor had felt it necessary to arrest Alvarado for plotting. But he was persuaded to release his prisoner. One of Micheltorena's officers so succumbed to the incessant rumors of revolt that in March he staged an abortive counterrevolution. An embarrassed governor had to suppress it by putting his own partisans under arrest. Resentment grew on all sides with each passing day.

Many Californians could not believe that Castro would join Alvarado against the governor. After all, Micheltorena had been

Castro's counsel in his court-martial in Mexico for escorting Isaac Graham and his friends into exile. He had seen to it that Castro was exonerated, winning his friendship and gratitude, and later obtaining for him a commission of lieutenant colonel of cavalry. According to Don Augustín Janssens, a prominent rancher of the Santa Barbara area, "With his own hands, he had pinned the insignias of rank on him." Yet, he and Alvarado were old friends and *compadres.*

If Castro's true feelings were in doubt, there was no discounting Sutter's loyalty to the governor. The Swiss made two grave errors in 1844; he made an enemy of Frémont and he gambled all his stakes on Micheltorena. In July, Sutter organized a twenty-eight-man company when the governor sent out his war alert. He reported to Micheltorena that his artillerymen lacked only practice and that he had some Indians who could shoot as well as anyone. If Micheltorena would send him muskets, Sutter offered to form forty of them into a company of grenadiers. As a newly commissioned captain in the Mexican militia, Sutter was overjoyed at last to be able to play the soldier in earnest. He made his first appointments, choosing John Sinclair as his first lieutenant and Ernest Rufus as his second lieutenant. He reported to the governor that he had many men who were eager to serve, beyond those whom he had actually enrolled on the roster. This was not surprising; Sutter apparently spread the rumor that anyone refusing militia duty would be subject to ten years' service in the Mexican regular army. Rufus turned out to be a good soldier, but Sutter's judgment in Sinclair's case was bad. In remembering his 1844–45 campaign, he stated, "Only Sinclair, whom I had made my aide-de-camp, and Cordua, who served in the ranks, acted cowardly and backed out soon after we had started."

Deciding that it was time to pay his long-delayed visit to the governor, Sutter rode to San José with Bidwell and an armed escort. There, on October 19, 1844, British Vice Consul James A. Forbes informed him of a ripening plot against Micheltorena. Forbes urged a Vallejo-like policy of neutrality upon Sutter because, whatever the outcome of the impending civil war, he expected California to fall under British sway. He boasted to Sutter that there were British men-of-war lying off the coast at that very moment. Sutter's loyalty was personally to Governor Micheltorena and "nationally" to the United States, which he by now expected to take California in due time. Ambivalent as Sutter was, he had no ties at all with Britain. So he reacted immediately by writing to Reading, his chief clerk, whom he had left in command of New Helvetia. He told him to ignore all commands but those coming directly from him, and he ordered all of his stock sent to Peter Lassen's ranch or beyond, should a retreat become necessary. Sutter was not the bravest of men and, while bloody warfare seemed remote at the time, he worried over being made a prisoner. He directed Reading, "In case they should keep me, raise all the foreigners you can and a strong body of Indians and make a movement towards here. All the foreigners are very willing to assist me because all look on New Helvetia for their protection. Alvarado is in Sonoma now. Castro is, with 60 men, on the San Joaquin. In all cases, it requires your attention on every movement of this gentleman. Be on your guard! I will try my best to join you without delay." In a postscript, he hastily added, "The cannon; please to get mounted by Mr. Dutton."

As soon as he arrived in the capital, Sutter warned Micheltorena of the danger. It was apparently the first indication which the governor had of the gravity of the situation. He complained to Sutter that the native Californians treated him badly, although he had only the best of intentions. But he convoked a council of war, to which he invited Sutter. Before the session was over, the governor's new favorite had a guarantee of a second tract of land, the Sobrante Grant, in exchange for his promise of military aid. Micheltorena also gave Sutter extraordinary power to grant land himself, as a proxy for the governor by means of a general title. The papers confirming Sutter in all these rights could not be completed because of the absence of the Secretary of State, but Micheltorena gave Sutter his solemn word on the matters.

151

Sutter wanted an additional grant in order to tie together the two main blocks of his original New Helvetia settlement, which were separated by marginal or overflowed lands. He also considered the second grant partial compensation for his Bodega and Fort Ross losses. Mainly, he wished to reserve some new land for his family, which he still intended to bring to California. With perhaps a spark of prescience about troublesome days ahead, he even tried to transfer title to his lower grant, as distinct from his upper or *hoch* farm, to his son, John Sutter, Jr. But Secretary of State Jimeno Casarín had turned him down because John, Jr., was not a naturalized citizen or even a resident of California at the time.

Despite the consideration Micheltorena had shown him, Sutter growled his disappointment to Casarín's brother-in-law, William S. Hartnell: "I think since I am a citizen, my son, too, is a citizen. But it seems that Mr. Jimeno is against everything that comes from me." He intended to ask Hartnell to intercede in his behalf. Unfortunately, Sutter lapsed into the bullying tone which had once worked for him but which was now pathetically out of date. "It would be better for him to act somewhat more according to right and not according to favor. Otherwise, he might be very sorry for his procedure, for a time will come—and it is quite near—when Mr. Jimeno will be glad that I protect him. It is said that one good turn merits another." Sutter offered to pay Hartnell for his help and further assured him that, if he chose to take up land near New Helvetia, "I shall prove to you that it is a good thing to have a good neighbor. I shall assist you in every way possible." He assured Hartnell that Micheltorena was most favorably disposed toward him and that the only obstacle he faced was Jimeno Casarín's lack of cooperation. Sutter then proceeded, uncharacteristically, to feel sorry for himself: "Of course, very few people bother about how many benefits I have brought to the country and how many enormous sacrifices of all kinds I had to make to bring such good order and such a police system to this District. The thanks I get is that Mr. Jimeno still has, through

152

the influence of Mr. Leese, a part of the district which I con-
quered with much trouble and sacrifice of lives and in which I
civilized the people. Now it is being taken, without consideration
of all this, and is being torn away without knowledge of the
situation through pure hatred and prejudice." Then he added
darkly that settlers in the Sacramento Valley were displeased by
Casarín's refusal to give them land titles. "You may assure Mr.
Jimeno that this causes bad blood and that the people are all
quite wrought up against him and that they will not stand it much
longer. I have much trouble keeping them pacified."

But Sutter did not choose Micheltorena's side in the upcoming
struggle merely out of land lust. He was genuinely fond of the
governor. Moreover, he feared what his jealous rivals, Alvarado
and Castro, might do if returned to power by force. "I am well
aware of what we can expect if the Californians are to succeed
in their scheme. They will drive us foreigners out of the country
as they attempted once before, in the winter of 1840." Sutter's
neighbor, Theodore Cordua, accused Sutter of allying himself
with the governor for just one reason—to be forgiven for his past
offenses against the government. But, if true at all, this was only
part of his reasoning. There was also a lingering remnant of loyalty to the Mexican government, mixed up with pride and vanity
as well as patriotism. Finally, Sutter saw an opportunity to satisfy
his life-long craving for military glory.

Micheltorena received him with full civil and military honors.
He had Sutter to coffee several times and made him his guest of
honor at a Sunday supper attended by six officers and served by
the governor's drummer. Micheltorena flattered the Swiss outrageously. He mustered the troops for his review; he paid social
calls at David Spence's house, where Sutter was lodging; he entertained him at a balloon ascension. When the officers of Commodore Armstrong's U.S.S. *Savannah* paid a formal visit to the
governor, they were particularly impressed by the lone foreigner
of his suite. With his marked military bearing, courteous manners and great precision, Sutter carried off the role of dashing

captain to perfection. But, inside, he was gnawed, most unmilitarily, with doubts and worries to which he confessed only in his letters to Reading, back at the fort. "I have again noticed that something is brewing in this country. If they will only keep away until I am at home again."

Micheltorena warned his friend against going home by land and to be especially on the alert in Yerba Buena. Both men knew that their friendly intercourse had not gone unnoticed by the rebels. Sutter admitted, "I was with him at review and everywhere and it was regarded as extraordinary that a foreigner should be so intimate with him." He accepted safe quarters aboard the *Savannah* for his last nights at Monterey.

When he sailed for Yerba Buena on the *Don Quixote* with one of his Kanakas and a newly hired German smith and mechanic, he sent his escort and some newly recruited employees home by land. John Bidwell remained in Monterey, on Sutter's orders, not only to wind up his business affairs but to keep an eye on the political situation brewing there.

At Yerba Buena, Sutter had the misfortune to run into the Bernal brothers and dashed off another stalling letter to their brother-in-law, Suñol. "I can see that the business transaction between us is becoming more and more disagreeable to you. I am very sorry, but what can I do?" After promising skins and cattle, in due time, Sutter exclaimed, "This is all I can do and even the government cannot make me do anything else!" Perhaps he can be forgiven this outburst. At the very outset of his long-awaited military career he had had an attack of nerves, convincing himself that he had barely eluded men sent by José Castro to capture him when he boarded his schooner and sailed for New Helvetia.

Safely back in his fortress, Sutter unloaded the fifty muskets and bayonets which Micheltorena had given him, as well as twenty-five carbines and ammunition, and fifteen muskets and a keg of powder which he had bought from Larkin. Once Bidwell was home, he sent messengers to Sonoma, San Rafael and elsewhere, to recruit men to his growing army. Probably aware that

Vallejo would fence-straddle, at least until a victor should begin to emerge, Sutter nevertheless briefed the general on his actions. He said he was acting "to inform the foreigners and citizens who are in favor of the legitimate government to present themselves at this point to march, under your orders, to Monterey to protect General Micheltorena so that he may not again be obliged to capitulate to the rebels who are still under arms against him." The capitulation to which he referred was the Treaty of Santa Teresa, which had followed Manuel Castro's inciting the revolution by driving off the government herds. When Micheltorena had led a punitive force in pursuit, at Laguna Seca he had meekly surrendered to the rebels, reinforced by a legion of Americans led by Sutter's onetime employee, Charles M. Weber.

Sutter was confident that the Treaty of Santa Teresa was only a temporary armistice. He did not issue an ultimatum and insisted later that "all of the settlers in the Valley were enthusiastic for the cause and joined me heartily." Theodore Cordua was probably more nearly correct when he reported that Sutter had to recruit his troopers through a variety of "intrigues." His next move was to send one of his men to round up horses from the government drove in order to mount his volunteer cavalry. He then asked Vallejo for permission to carry out this *fait accompli,* to allow him to save face and possibly to keep an enemy from his back as he marched south to join up with Micheltorena. His explanation was, "We have not horses enough and you can do us a great favor by sending us at least 100 from the many you have." Next, he alternately cajoled and threatened the general: "It may be that, some day, you will have need of my arms and my people and then we will be your servants."

Some of Sutter's agents who recruited or impressed men and supplies were loud-mouthed bullies of Isaac Graham's stamp. They boasted that they would capture Alvarado and Castro, dead or alive. By the time these words reached these rebel leaders, rumor had attributed them to Sutter. When the story had made the complete round of the province, Sutter was supposedly boasting that he would bring the heads of Castro and Alvarado to Micheltorena on a platter. José Castro actually protested to his friend, the governor, whom he would shortly attack, insinuating that Sutter had armed not to defend Micheltorena but to take over California. Castro swore that he would resist Sutter to the death. He refused to believe, he insisted, that Micheltorena had authorized Sutter's warlike preparations.

Canny General Vallejo detected a secret understanding between the supposedly deadly enemies—Castro and Micheltorena. He was determined not to be made a fool of by a carefully staged military charade. While Sutter rashly mobilized for a forced march, Vallejo—to avoid taking sides—disbanded his military company at Sonoma on November 28, 1844. The best excuse he could think of on the spur of the moment was that he could no longer afford to maintain the force out of his own pocket. Still jealous of Sutter, however, Vallejo attempted to block his movement southward. He called his attention to the Treaty of Santa Teresa which, he said, had ended all opposition to the governor —although he forgot to mention that it was Micheltorena who had capitulated. Unwilling to tell Sutter of his suspicion of conspiracy between Castro and Micheltorena, he instead tried to halt him by pulling rank:

> Don Juan Vaca showed me a letter of yours in which you incite true patriots to join with you to march against the rebels and to aid the government. All the government being in full peace, I am obliged to suppose that the rebels only exist in your fevered imagination. If there were a rebellion, I, who occupy the first post on the frontier, and who hold myself to be a patriot, could never permit my subalterns to take the initiative in a matter which it is my place to direct. And you know very well, Señor Sutter, that if anyone, no matter how powerful he might be, should attempt to attack the government in the territory under my command, the authors of such an attempt would not be long in receiving at my hands condign punishment for such unheard-of daring.

This was pure bluff. His subaltern was not put in his place. Sutter was well aware that Vallejo had disbanded his military company; some of the men had even joined his cavalry. But what must have puzzled him was Vallejo's subtle interpretation of neutrality, which allowed him to be on all sides at once. He was astounded by one paragraph of Vallejo's letter:

> The movement which took place at Monterey was done at my direction. It was not good for the people of California that there should remain in their midst more than 300 criminals who were brought in the disguise of soldiers by the general to this land to maintain order and improve the morale of the inhabitants. Do you believe, Señor Sutter, that the wolf and the tiger would be suitable guardians to take care of sheep and lambs? Certainly not. I have also believed and still believe that the criminals and assassins who, unfortunately, form the Praetorian Guard of the general, are not the most suitable people to educate, inform and protect the inhabitants of California who, being endowed with simple habits, would succumb with extreme ease to the astuteness of such intractable guests. At Monterey, it was exacted of the general that his Praetorians should return to Mexico. He agreed to this. . . . I hasten to inform you of what happened because [Chief] Solano informed me that you were fomenting a military movement founded on an erroneous conception, and twelve days after the matter which caused your alarm was at an end.

If Sutter believed Vallejo's bizarre claim that Castro and Alvarado were his tools, he dismissed it. When he replied on December 17, 1844, it was to say:

> I would be much pleased if I could avoid an expedition which is not indispensable. . . . I know very well that Señor Castro and Señor Alvarado made an agreement to send away the troops and some of the general's officers. But I am also convinced that they do not wish the general to remain in the country. Of this, I have certain information by good authority. Now, if the affair is completely at an end, why is Señor Castro collecting men at San José? It is clear that he is going to break the agreement. I am

157

satisfied that you are for the legitimate government, as we are, and that, perhaps, you are ignorant of the plan which Castro and Alvarado have formed. But I, being well informed, can do no less than march to protect order for the general. I am very sure of your good friendship and, for that reason whenever you may consider my forces useful, I will aid you.

Before marching, Sutter dashed off one last note to Vallejo. In it, he chided him for his strong words against foreigners. Sutter predicted (incorrectly, as it turned out) that "when we march through the settlements, surely the greater part of the native sons will join us." As for his New Helvetia foreigners, he reminded Vallejo that three-fourths of them were naturalized Mexican citizens. And he added, pointedly, "I believe that we have the same rights as natives of the country."

Vallejo's intervention was futile. The governor's call to arms enkindled Sutter: "I have seen a true plan against the government, against every Mexican and foreigner. . . . To a brave man like you, orders are not given. To act is to conquer. . . . If you have not started, for any reason, without need of new orders, on learning that I move from Monterey to San José, you will march immediately."

Castro was as puzzled by the actions of Sutter and Micheltorena as was Vallejo. After the intermission of the Santa Teresa truce, the last act of the bogus revolt was not going as originally written. Perhaps Micheltorena had second thoughts about leaving California, or even shipping off his *cholos*. He was a master of indecision. When Manuel Castro had pronounced against his government, Micheltorena had written an ambiguous letter to Don José Castro: "My godson, a revolt has broken out at the Cañada de San Miguel among some hot-headed young men. This suits me but I do not wish for any personal persecution or vengeance. Put yourself at the head of this movement and we shall come to an understanding." Now he was calling upon Sutter for help. He had also violated the treaty by rebuilding his military strength and making use of the horses returned by the rebels to convert his infantrymen into cavalry. Perhaps Micheltorena was inspired by Sutter's patriotism or humiliated that some observers had attributed his collapse at Santa Teresa to cowardice. In any case, he dumbfounded José Castro by ignoring their "understanding." When Castro protested Sutter's militancy, the governor snapped, "If he marches, it is in consequence of your revolution. Just as you instigate some citizens to revolt against the legitimate authority, so others have moved in its defense."

Proof of continuing collusion between the supposed enemies, Castro and Micheltorena, is lacking. But many Californians besides Vallejo were convinced that the entire war was a farce. They were baffled, however, as to why Micheltorena did not turn over the government to Castro. Instead, he apparently doublecrossed Castro and called upon Sutter for help. Perhaps Micheltorena felt that the stage had not yet been adequately set by his explanation of the surrender at Santa Teresa—his "preferring the voice of humanity to the horrible roar of cannon." In such a case, a bang-up sham battle would allow him to quit California gracefully, with honor and with no real loss of face.

Captain John Sutter was, unfortunately in this case, a genuinely simple man. For all the picaresque scrapes of his younger years, he took the civil war entirely at its face value and wrote Hartnell, excitedly, on December 13, 1844, "Right here, I am still in a state of war. Every day, drilling is going on. I have a strong garrison and several thousand Indians who have all been notified and are ready for service in a moment." According to Vallejo, Sutter made two "attacks" on his property, his men killing and eating one of Vallejo's beeves and confiscating some of his horses when they could not find the government herd there. But Sutter did not really begin his offensive until the governor sent him the promised general land title, empowering him to grant lands to immigrants in the name of the governor.

Sutter's first move was to send his schooner, heavily armed, to Yerba Buena. The naval operation sounded just the right note for his campaign. It was a fiasco. The *alcalde* of Yerba Buena

159

led a comic-opera commando raid on the craft, captured it, seized its armament and smuggled it to Castro in the customs house launch. Castro's reaction was incomprehensible, even in such an *opéra bouffe* war: he restored the guns to Sutter's schooner!

If *Californios* were confused by the double- and triple-crosses of the plotters in both factions, Americans in California were completely in the dark. Most of them simply threw up their hands in disgust. But the lingering resentment over the Isaac Graham affair of 1840 led some to join Sutter and Micheltorena against Alvarado. Even Isaac Graham himself rushed to join Sutter, with vengeance in mind. Larkin predicted that Sutter's riflemen would zealously pursue the rebel leaders with knife, pistol and rifle in order to gain revenge on their oppressors of 1840. Also, the rumor that British interests were backing Castro and Alvarado worked on the natural Anglophobia of the Americans and swung them to the Loyalist side. There were some foreigners who favored neither neutrality nor Micheltorena. One was Charles M. Weber, Sutter's former employee, who had led the foreign legion in the non-battle of Laguna Seca which, presumably, frightened Micheltorena into the Santa Teresa capitulation. He made his way with the Hernández brothers to New Helvetia to persuade Sutter not to back the governor. The Swiss consulted with a council of war, consisting of Bidwell, the vengeful Graham and five others, arrested Weber and theoretically threw him and his companions into the fort's *calabozo* for plotting against the government. Actually, their confinement was in comfortable quarters.

As Sutter's strength swelled, rumors increased in volume and variety. Fear seized many Californians other than Castro and Vallejo that Sutter intended to conquer all of northern California —and for himself or the United States, not for Micheltorena. The facts of Sutter's general title were garbled, too, making it into a license to *confiscate* established ranches in California in order to give them to his followers. Worst was the propaganda that Sutter had armed 2,000 of his Indians and was planning to loose them on the settlements. Powerless to stop this propaganda Sutter saw support for Castro deepening in northern California. He did not yet know it, but southern California was persuaded by these predictions of Indian atrocities to support the rebels, too.

CHAPTER X

———⟨∿∿⟩———

THE SOLDIER

THE turning of popular opinion in favor of Castro should not have worried Sutter. On paper—and on the Fort Sutter parade ground—he had assembled the most powerful force ever seen in California. They drilled smartly, they were well armed and they were supported by artillery. Sutter's march southward started out as a triumphal one, and he recalled it with pride as the high point of his career: "The whole country stood in awe of me. Such a military force had never before been seen in this part of the world."

Sutter's triumph was short-lived. First, the weather altered. Skies darkened and rain began to drench his army. His men were not amenable to discipline, except for his doggedly loyal Indians. To his dawning dismay, he found that he could not exert the personal kind of leadership in warfare which came easily to his lieutenant, John Gantt, or even to the rough irregular, Isaac Graham. His long letters back to Reading, holding the fort, soon began to betray his lack of confidence in himself and his cause. In the main, these communications reminded Reading of chores to be done and emphasized the importance of keeping a sharp

163

watch on Vallejo. But they also revealed his fear of death in the civil war. On January 3, 1845, he counseled Reading about the Kanaka girl of whom he was so fond: "In case I should be killed, you will see that Manuiki receives well her wages coming to her, until the last day of her being in the establishment."

Another worry was the fate of the courier, his old New Mexico friend, Pablo Gutiérrez, whom he had sent to Micheltorena. Sutter learned that he had crossed the San Joaquin River safely, but soon distressing news reached him. He wrote Reading, "Pablo was caught near the Positos, close by our camp, and probably killed. Many reports come about him. So much is certain, that his clothes are found." For once, the rumors were correct. Gutiérrez had been captured by a rebel party near San José. Sutter's message, though hidden between the double soles of one of his boots, was discovered. They hanged Gutiérrez as a spy, to the nearest tree.

Antonio Suñol, William Gulnac and British Vice Consul Forbes intercepted Sutter and tried to dissuade him from joining what they considered a lost cause. Sutter was unswervable, but their arguments, passed on to the ranks, did grave damage to the morale of his men. Sutter sensed the ardor of some of his riflemen cooling. A few of the Englishmen who had attached themselves to him drifted away upon Forbes' urgings. Sutter admitted, "I am very sorry Captain Gantt was all the time in their camp. In our camp, all are in good spirits and I hope, when I see the camp of riflemen, I can bring them all in good spirits again. Perhaps some of the British subjects will return."

As commander, he found himself incapable of dealing severely with his officers and could only complain to Reading when Gantt's men committed some outrage. "Captain Gantt's camp killed two cows and one yoke of working bullocks of Mr. Gulnac's. When they did tell him, he [Gulnac] said he wished that God would sink his farm and make a lake of it. Certainly, it is not right to kill his oxen. I don't know how Captain Gantt could allow such things." Instead of hustling Forbes and Suñol out of camp, or arresting them as he had Weber, an indecisive Sutter simply called for a meeting to discuss the situation. The result was a further erosion of morale. He wrote Reading, "I am determined to give Mr. Forbes and Don Antonio very short answers and proceed to San José, by all means. They have a document of Castro's that the foreigners have a note to elect another governor, and many other things, but they will see that all is useless to persuade us. We just had a meeting of the committee and, at present, we are determined to act in favor of the general and according to his orders. They will try all that lays in their power to turn us in favor of the other party. I don't know what interest Mr. Forbes may have, to be in favor of this faction. One reason is that he is in relationship with a good many of the country people and, perhaps, has some political view, also."

The next incident in Sutter's march was the capture of a Castro scout. He almost bungled this, too. His cavalry squadron overran the man as he was observing the movements of the small army. Sutter recalled, "I had the man brought before me but he gave me evasive answers to my questions. Although I had him put under guard, he succeeded in making his escape. My corporal jumped upon an unsaddled horse, caught the spy with a lasso, and brought him back. I then put handcuffs on him but told him that I should release him as soon as he reached his home near San José."

The soft-hearted conqueror followed a vanguard of twenty-five mounted riflemen to Mission San José, where the *padre* received him warmly, informing him that Castro had fled upon the approach of Sutter's scouts, after beginning to fortify himself. Most of the Mexican-Californians at the mission were friendly to Sutter's side of the conflict. In fact, they were altogether too friendly. Without mentioning his own inadequacy as a commander and disciplinarian, Sutter wrote Reading, "We had ample refreshments served to us but some of the men could not resist drinking too much of the wine which the major-domo placed before them and they became intoxicated." Somehow, in order to keep dogging Castro's steps, Sutter managed to get his weaving troopers on the road to the pueblo of San José. This time, he was careful to camp short of the settlement, well away from the wineshops. Next morning, he demanded eighty horses of the *alcalde* and peremptorily ordered him to close all *cantinas*. Sutter was determined to dry out his recalcitrant army. ("I knew that I had some bad customers among my riflemen.")

Toward noon, he entered the town with a twenty-five-man escort, to find it nearly deserted. Who should greet him but Suñol. The Spaniard reported that the *alcalde* had fled along with most of the male population, but that he had himself attended to the closing of the *cantinas* for Sutter. According to Suñol, it was not Sutter's approach which had drawn off Castro, but rather the rebel leader's desire to blockade the governor in Monterey. Sutter immediately marched his sobering force through the pueblo and along El Camino Real toward Monterey. But when he encamped at San Juan Bautista, he learned that the insurgents were really fleeing from him now, for they could muster no more than 90 to oppose his 200 men. When Castro lifted his siege, Micheltorena marched out to meet his victorious (but untried) marshal from New Helvetia. The governor left an aide in command of the capital and combined his 150 *cholos* and 25 to 30 militiamen with Sutter's force on January 9, 1845, at the Salinas River.

Sutter was uncertain of the actual strength of Castro's force but consistently overestimated it. Thus, he reported to Reading:

> The enemy we could not find. Castro and Alvarado, with their party, about 200 to 250 men, were flying before us and took as many horses as they could find on the road, about 600 or 700, so that we had a poor chance to get some fresh horses. The general is determined to finish the revolution and get hold of the rebels. It may cost what it will. So he concludes to follow them below, to Santa Barbara and the pueblo [of Los Angeles], where Castro's party is gone in hope of getting assistance there. . . . Don Andrés Pico raised 125 men in favor of the general but when they meet they may join the rebels and leave

Pico, because they will tell them that we are coming to kill, burn, plunder, etc. If Castro doesn't stand and fight below, he may probably escape and return through the *Tular* [i.e., the San Joaquin Valley] to San José and there would be some danger for New Helvetia. However, we will follow them very fast, because we will find plenty of good horses below.

Sutter, gullible as ever, was taken in completely by Micheltorena's fervent vows of pursuit and punishment of the insurgents. Actually, the one thing the governor did *not* intend to do was follow Castro with any speed. Instead, he dawdled and delayed. Sutter was so caught up in the excitement and glory of campaigning at last that he entirely failed to detect Micheltorena's malingering. As he dictated to Bancroft in his memoir, "Every evening after our day's march, the quartermaster [Jasper O'Farrell] laid out the camp; the tents were pitched, the necessary orders and the watchword for the night were given. The Mexican soldiers often wanted to tear down the fences for firewood, but I forbade them to do that and sent them to the distant forests for firewood. They obeyed me, and Micheltorena's officers marveled that the men executed my orders so well. The two divisions always camped near to one another and Micheltorena and I exchanged visits. This showed that he held me on terms of equality with himself."

While Micheltorena camped, recamped and camped again, Alvarado displayed some of the leadership of which he was not entirely bereft. He persuaded Castro not to make a stand anywhere in the north but to retreat all the way to Los Angeles. There, he so skilfully nurtured anti-Sutter and anti-Micheltorena feeling that the entire south went over to the rebel side. Meanwhile, Castro was denouncing Micheltorena in a communiqué for allying himself with Sutter, whom he described as an enemy of the country. "We will shed our blood rather than permit our country to endure this infamous aggression," he wrote. "Do not flatter yourself that our lives will be destroyed by those bandits to whom you have promised our ranches and property!" After

167

this bit of bombast, Castro spurred his men south and occupied Los Angeles a day after his scouts attacked and seized the government barracks. Among those captured was Don Andrés Pico, the most competent soldier in the south, and the one man upon whom both Sutter and Micheltorena were counting to hold the region loyal to the government.

Not a battle; not a skirmish. It was a war of movement and pronouncements, so far. Micheltorena was careful not to close within 100 miles of Castro in his "pursuit." The only victory for Sutter—hungry for them—was the capture by one of his scouting parties of no less a rebel leader than Manuel Castro. He, of course, was the very originator of the revolt by his raid on Micheltorena's government horse herd, which had led to the governor's capitulation. Sutter's men seized him at La Lomita de Linares, between modern Watsonville and Gilroy. On his person they found important documents of the rebel "government." Some of the *gringos* were for hanging him on the spot but the more pacific men prevailed over the lynchers. Castro was taken along as a prisoner when the scouts united with a larger force of Sutter's, commanded by two veterans of the Isaac Graham affair of 1840.

Word of Castro's capture reached the little rebel army camped at Rancho La Brea, near Gilroy. José Castro immediately planned the rescue of his namesake. He organized a scouting party of a dozen men commanded by a Yankee, Charles Brown, who was married to a Mexican girl and sympathetic to the Castro cause. Sutter's lieutenants now proved themselves to be as militarily inept as their commanding officer. According to Sutter, they were surprised by a superior force and obliged to surrender Castro in exchange for Brown. In later reminiscences, Sutter usually brushed over the incident quickly, pointing out that despite the exchange, his men had held on to the prized rebel documents and that he had handed them over to the governor himself.

The truth of the matter would seem to be that Sutter's unit was completely outfoxed by Brown and his handful of men. Toward midnight, Brown reached Sutter's camp, on La Cuesta de San Luís Gonzaga, lying in the middle of Pacheco Pass, the route through the Coast Range from San José to the San Joaquin Valley. In an account which he dictated for historian H. H. Bancroft, Brown summarized the commando-like exploit which embarrassed Sutter so intensely:

> We surprised them, tho', I must confess, that if they had known how few there were of us, and the condition our stock was in, so fagged-out that we couldn't have gone on two miles more, they could have killed us all if they chose. . . . I halloed out to the enemy to surrender Manuel Castro or we would, forthwith, attack and destroy them. I talked as loud as I could and the echoes of the mountains helped me to make them believe that I had an overwhelming force with me.

Castro shouted back to his friends not to fire and one of Sutter's lieutenants asked Brown who he was. When he answered, they proposed that if Brown would agree to join them, they would release Castro. Brown consulted with his men and agreed to the exchange. Then, he recalled, "As I was going up, I felt very shaky for, if the other party had the slightest knowledge of how weak the Californian party was, they could have kept me and Castro, too, and another Californian [prisoner] whose name was Juan Elizalde. However, all turned out well. Castro was released." (According to Sutter, Elizalde was no prisoner but his cavalry chief.)

As if Sutter's aides had not bungled enough, they now let their other prisoner slip away. Brown reported:

> The other fellow escaped down the bluff. How he did it, unperceived, I never could comprehend. The fact is that the man was not even missed till we were on the point of starting, for, be it remembered, the party wouldn't stop there the rest of the night, fearing the Californians were very strong and might come back upon them. Their force was of about 73 or 74 men and their position was almost impregnable. After I got among them, I realized how foolhardy my conduct had been.

Brown tagged along with the detachment of Sutter's army. When he finally revealed how few men he had commanded, Sutter's lieutenants ruefully admitted that he had outgeneraled them. For a while, too, they were very angry and, in Brown's words, "inclined to eat away their nails." They marched into the San Joaquin Valley and then back to San José again, via Livermore Pass. There, Sutter's men proved that bungles come in threes. They let their erstwhile enemy go to the pueblo alone. "Several of the party handed me different sums of money to buy things for them, like whisky, tobacco, etc.," explained Brown. "I took good care to have the best horse in the country saddled to go after the things and I started—and have not been back since."

Alvarado claimed that there was also a skirmish in which a unit of Sutter's force was mauled by one under *Alcalde* Francisco Guerrero of Yerba Buena and Romualdo Pacheco, later governor of California during the American period. But Sutter was silent on the matter.

On the eleventh, Sutter again wrote to Reading. He reminded him, as usual, of a myriad of chores to perform in managing Fort Sutter. But again his innermost thoughts strayed to Manuiki, whom he had had to leave behind and whom he wanted to keep safe during his absence. "Some guns have to be repaired," he reminded Reading, "and some locks. Among the locks is one which I wish to get repaired on Manuiki's outside door. . . . Where the ladies live, the locks are not in order. Harry, he knows where the keys are. . . ." After more small talk and advice on sowing wheat, Sutter again returned to the subject of his female companions at the fort: "I wish that Peter Lyons don't neglect his duties by waiting on the ladies."

Unlike his captain, Gantt, Sutter considered himself a gentleman-soldier and did not choose to live off the land like a guerrilla. When he ran low on coffee or sugar, he simply ordered more from Larkin in a strictly businesslike fashion. When he needed beeves he did not send out a raiding party but formally requisitioned the animals from uncooperative Dr. Marsh with a document signed "J. A. Sutter, Commander in Chief of the Forces of the River Sacramento." Sutter was badly advised by the Forbes-Suñol peace commissioners, who told him Marsh favored Micheltorena and would march with him. Sutter had finally to force his neighbor to join his unit, and then it was as a common soldier who proceeded immediately to spread the infection of dissension throughout the ranks. Sutter finally realized, fifty miles out of San José, that Marsh was plotting to ruin his expedition. And yet he took no real action to stop him. The Doctor had a gift of gab worthy of an Irishman and won a number of men's allegiance away from Sutter.

Ostensibly a private, Marsh used his glibness to insinuate himself into the very councils of war between Sutter and Micheltorena. He made trouble at the highest as well as the lowest level. All that Sutter, inadequate as a commander, could do was to complain in letters to Reading: "We have Dr. Marsh amongst us, who uses all his influence to act against me. The council was dissolved, another elected, dissolved again. Now there exists a committee of three, Captain Gantt, William Dickey and MacIntosh, and Marsh as secretary. They say they will act with me but it is not true. They are just contrary and want to use me only for a tool because the general agrees to everything I propose." Instead of clapping Private Marsh into confinement, like Weber, Sutter did nothing but brood: "Dr. Marsh is opposed to us. . . . He remains a traitor. . . . Never would I have thought that certain persons could act so against me. Besides the committee, there are some more secret councillors, like Mr. Hensley, Mr. O'Farrell, etc., but they cannot do me much harm."

With the expedition going badly so soon, Sutter still hid from himself the obvious fact that he was not cut out for military leadership. His governing by committee was no way to run even a peacetime army, and on campaign it was the sheerest folly. He was still proud of the close harmony he enjoyed with Governor Micheltorena, whose flattery found its mark in Sutter's vanity: "I am in great favor by the general," wrote the self-styled military

171

commander of the north to Reading. "He gives me every proof of friendship and many marks of high esteem, which causes some jealousy in our camp particularly since we have Dr. Marsh amongst us. . . . The general distinguishes me very much. He treats me as a friend and like a brother. . . . Everything goes pretty well now, but for a great deal of grumbling and growling in the camp about some comforts which cannot be procured."

Sutter's Indians were still loyal and well disciplined, and to keep them that way he appointed one of his lieutenants to command and exercise the second platoon of his redskin grenadiers. But the *gringos* of the rifle company were growing increasingly disgruntled and anxious to return home. Sutter managed to quiet their mutinous grumbling for a while by calling upon Governor Micheltorena to address a speech to them on January 14. "It made a good effect amongst them," he reported. "An angel from Heaven could not speak better. He requested them to remain a month or two in service and [promised] he will reward them well. It is very inconvenient for me to make such a long campaign but we have to finish, by all means."

Micheltorena sent two couriers in an attempt to get the Los Angeles authorities to prevent the rebels' seizing the schooner *California,* expected daily from Mexico with government money and supplies. Sutter had little success with his own runners. He sent one to Mission San José to order William Johnson to join him, but Johnson ignored his command. Sutter dashed off an angry note to Reading, "I am afraid the rascal is gone up to you, to play his tricks with the [government] horses." Vallejo, too, was still on Sutter's mind. He did not write him but did send a warning note to Reading: "Of the Vallejos, I think there is not much to fear but it is good to be on your guard. . . . This morning I received a courier from Capt. William A. Richardson. He fears that some danger will be for the establishment [Sutter's Fort]. You have watchful friends on the other side, Captain Richardson and Mr. Murphy. If you could be united and having the launch, it would be very good to take Sonoma and take the cannons and military stores up to Sacramento."

Reading was unable to act upon Sutter's brazen suggestion that he attack Vallejo. With barely enough men to defend New Helvetia, a campaign against Sonoma was the furthest thing from his mind. Alvarado's friend, Antonio M. Osío, in fact, predicted that Reading would soon have his hands full, at the fort, for a party of warlike "Valsavales" (Walla Walla Indians) was wandering ominously about the plain. Sutter had run across them on the San Joaquin River the previous October. They had wanted to winter on the Feather River, but he had forbidden it. He had told them that game was more plentiful on the west side of the Sacramento, which was true enough, but his real concern was their proximity to New Helvetia and Hock Farm. Now they were lurking about the neighborhood of Sutter's Fort, leading Osío to write Vallejo, "Several persons assure me that there is no point in greater danger than New Helvetia, on account of the Valsavales Indians, and that they will have to take great care."

Sutter apparently told Micheltorena that the traitor, Charles Weber, was lying in chains in the Sutter's Fort dungeon. In fact, he had merely placed Weber under house arrest, giving him comfortable quarters although under Reading's guard. He had even written Reading, "Please tell Mr. Weber that I could not find him when I left, to bid him goodbye." Now, at Rancho de Espinosa, Sutter magnanimously interceded with Micheltorena in behalf of Weber, an old employee, after all, and the other prisoners at the fort, Pedro and Mariano Hernández. "I asked the general about Mr. Weber and represented his situation, that he is very necessary in his business, etc., and did for him what I could. But the order of His Excellency is that Mr. Weber shall remain as a prisoner in the fort till we return from the campaign. His punishment will consist in this. The two Hernández have to remain prisoners, also, until we return."

Sutter demonstrated his kindness in another quarter. While his expeditionary force was fragmenting around him, he took time to make one of the kind gestures which made him so well liked sometimes even in spite of himself. He tried to persuade Micheltorena to give Mission San Miguel to an immigrant family, along with its neglected vineyard and orchard. The roof tiles alone, he estimated, were worth $10,000. The governor's willingness to consider the matter was excellent proof of Sutter's influence with him.

This influence was weakest, however, in military matters. When he promoted him to colonel, Micheltorena gave Sutter a trumpeter and a squadron of cavalry as an escort. But he did not relinquish command, even when painful hemorrhoids prevented him from mounting his horse. Instead, he threw away another week by waiting for his carriage to be brought up. Thomas Larkin, a perceptive observer of the progress—or lack of it—of the Sutter-Micheltorena campaign, observed: "The general has, at the present, all means and power to put down any disturbance in California. . . . [But] he travels 4 or 5 leagues a day, some days none. He has now sent for his four-wheel coach to chase enemies over mountains. Over some of these mountains this coach, I think, must be carried on soldiers' backs. By the time he arrives at Santa Barbara, Castro may be in Monterey!" Of Sutter's riflemen, Larkin ventured: "The foreigners now are very anxious to meet the Californians. In a few weeks, they will become tired and will, perhaps, leave the general and go home to their farms. In this case, Castro may gain the day." Larkin proved to be an excellent prophet.

While Sutter fumed at the maddening delays, Micheltorena led him slowly to Mission San Luis Obispo and thence to Mission Santa Ynez, where he settled himself into quarters for a few days. At Santa Ynez, Sutter and his rifle company, plus a captain of dragoons, asked to be allowed to attack the insurgents, by way of the Cañon de los Prietos, while the governor continued with the main force to Santa Barbara on El Camino Real. Micheltorena vetoed the idea as too rash. At all costs, he was determined to avoid bloodshed. The governor, almost as compulsive a letter-

writer as Sutter, preferred bombast to bombardment. From Santa
Ynez, he sent a communiqué to the bishop, to the *alcalde,* and to
the port captain of Santa Barbara. He swore that he had never
taken anything from anyone without payment; he promised that
he would molest no one except those who bore arms against him.
And even for these rebels he held the best of feelings, he assured
his correspondents, *if* they would lay down their weapons.

The southward march was slowed by more than Micheltorena's
infirmity and double-dealing. The coastal shelf all but pinched
out, and natural obstacles threw themselves in Sutter's path. From
Santa Ynez, his men had to build a road along the beach to bring
his cannon to bear on Santa Barbara. But there were no rebels
lurking, only citizens who urged a suspension of hostilities. During his stay of several days at Santa Barbara, Sutter enjoyed good
quarters and excellent meals, sometimes dining with the bishop.
Micheltorena conferred all one afternoon with the bishop's secretary, and after the long interview, the governor's behavior became, if possible, even less militant.

A witness reported, "He did not want to meet the rebel force.
It was apparent that his ardor had cooled." Micheltorena insisted
that he did not want to lose fifty of his men while killing perhaps
twice as many of the enemy. He repeated—not in Sutter's hearing
—that he would use every means and exhaust every resource to
prevent the shedding of blood.

During the palsied pursuit, there was little that Sutter could do
except send letters ahead to friends in southern California, asking them to prevent the *California* and her cargo falling into
rebel hands. To his adjutant, Charles Flügge, he wrote, "The general told me there was nobody down below in whom he could
put faith but Andrés Pico. I told him he could depend on you.
For that reason, he charged me to write you." He ordered another of his men, to "in the name of legitimate government, take
10 to 12 well-armed foreigners aboard and direct [Captain Juan
Bautista] Cooper to sail [the *California*] to Monterey at once."
Sutter also protested his innocence of the wild charges which had

accumulated in the south against him, his "mercenaries," and his "savages."

There was only one scare during Sutter's Santa Barbara stay. As he recalled, "Captain [John] Wilson invited me and a few of my officers to have supper with him. While we were eating, the captain of cavalry, Santiago Estrada, came in and called me to one side. He told me that Governor Micheltorena had sent him with a guard of 25 men for my protection, as he had received information which made him fearful lest I should be seized and made prisoner. I told Estrada that I would make some excuse and go with him as soon as possible. A short time later, we all left Captain Wilson's hospitable house and were escorted by Estrada to headquarters. Micheltorena was then sick with piles. He could not mount his horse but was obliged to travel in a kind of buggy in which he could stretch himself at full length. I found him in bed when I returned from Captain Wilson's, and he said that he believed I was in danger." But all was quiet. Sutter and the governor had breakfast with the priests next day, and the bishop gave them his blessing. While the army marched out, Sutter remained in Santa Barbara with a twenty-five-man escort to order supplies. He went first to Wilson's store. There, the captain's stepson, seventeen-year-old Romualdo Pacheco, was clerking. From him, Sutter ordered 100 pairs of duck trousers for his soldiers but had to be content with the entire stock, 70 pairs. He also bought shirts, tobacco and other merchandise. Sutter was sensitive about the tales of his force being a band of plunderers. He not only forbade looting by his troopers, but was very careful to procure supplies in a legal fashion, issuing government orders even for horses.

The camp at El Rincón, where he rejoined the governor, was unpleasant. The weather was wet and dreary, and the army ran out of meat. Sutter's grenadiers gathered mussels and clams on the beach, but the riflemen did not have the same appetite for them as his Indians. Morale among his *gringos* plummeted to a new low.

Meanwhile, in Los Angeles, Andrés Pico, José Carrillo and Pío Pico, all prominent leaders of southern California, had been won over to the rebels. Even Yankee community leaders in the south such as Abel Stearns and Don Benito Wilson were convinced that they had to rid California of the *cholo* pests and their master, who had carried war to southern California. Pío Pico chaired a quorum of the departmental *junta,* or provisional assembly. Suspicious of Sutter's role in the war, he denounced the governor not only for breaking the Treaty of Santa Teresa but for arming foreigners and Indians and giving a high command to a man known to have made threats against Mexico. The *junta* took over the governing of California and indicated that it wanted a native Californian to succeed Micheltorena. At first, the governor refused to treat with the *junta* at all, but after conferring with Sutter on the matter, he gave them an answer. It was an ultimatum of sorts, but he promised to pardon the rebels, even their leaders, if they would surrender. Again, the governor was talking out of both sides of his mouth. He was out-machiavelliing the Florentine himself. For, while he bluffed Pico and fooled Sutter, he was dickering secretly with Antonio Coronel of the *junta* to end the affair so that he could get out of California, honorably, before (as he put it) the province should fall into American hands.

Few foes so reluctant to fight as Micheltorena and Castro have ever crossed the pages of history. Don Augustín Janssens, the prominent Southern California *ranchero,* interviewed them both. "I had a long conference with Don José Castro," he recorded, "about his *padrino* [godfather], as he called Micheltorena. He said that since Mexican days, he owed many favors to the general and that he would do everything possible to avoid having any conflict with his forces—that they, the Californians, were going forward and if he and the general should meet, he would salute him." At Santa Ynez, Janssens met Micheltorena. "I talked with the general, alone. I reported what José Castro had told me and he replied that he had not expected Castro to take part against him,

177

because of his services to him in Mexico. . . . He had thought that, in case of his retiring from California, he would recommend that Castro be placed in his position. I reported to him the words of Castro—'I hope that the two sides will not exchange shots.' "

Unaware of Micheltorena's duplicity, Pío Pico and the *junta* declared him deposed. Pico was named the new governor. Alvarado and Castro immediately pledged their loyalty to him. He then called on all citizens to arm themselves, and he and his brother, Andrés, raised reinforcements for Castro's 150 men, preparing—finally—to make a stand at Mission San Buenaventura.

Even Sutter now began to see that the situation was deteriorating beyond repair. He persuaded Micheltorena to sign his land grant by stressing how much of his personal fortune, $8,000, had gone into His Excellency's service already. Handing him the document, the governor observed that it was poor pay for all Sutter's sacrifices and services. Secretly, Sutter was inclined to agree, although he graciously kept such thoughts to himself: "Indeed it was so. . . . At the time, nobody would have given me 10 cents for an acre." But, he thought, "In case I should be killed, my family would have the benefit of this grant." It was well that he attended to the matter. The preponderance of power was shifting quickly to Castro. A fear of property confiscation and personal exile threw some forty to sixty hard-bitten Yankees, including many ex-mountain men, in with the rebels. Some estimates ran as high as 100 men. As fighters, they were the equal of Sutter's riflemen, and their morale was immeasurably higher. Their leaders were Abel Stearns, Benito Wilson, James McKinley and William Workman. Most were volunteers, though some were drafted into service. Among these new rebels were such sharpshooting frontiersmen as Nathaniel Pryor, John Rowland, Jim Beckwourth, Louis Vignes, and the redoubtable trapper, Big Bill (*Le Gros*) O'Fallon, whom Sutter labeled a mercenary, pure and simple— "O'Fallon marched against us with his gang for the sake of getting horses."

Someone—Sutter, Micheltorena or Gantt—sent Lt. James

Coates with a small party to reconnoiter along the beach toward Mission San Buenaventura, some twenty miles from Sutter's camp. This scouting mission would prove to be the turning point of the halfhearted war. The patrol blundered into an ambush at Los Pitos and was captured, wholesale. There was little or no resistance by the rain-drenched, hungry *gringos,* and the rebels treated them more like brothers than captives. Their captor was none other than the ubiquitous Manuel Castro, who immediately began propagandizing and sent for José Castro. When the general arrived, he told them that he had nothing against them, even trying to convince them that the whole responsibility for Graham's exile in 1840 lay at the feet of Thomas Larkin and David Spence, who, he claimed, had wanted to be rid of business competition. Whether the captives were ready to swallow this elephantine fib or not, they were fed up with the discomforts of marching and bivouacking in the rain and were delighted to give Castro their parole in exchange for their release. Coates led them back to camp where, Sutter later recalled, "he told us that they were treated well and had been released upon their word not to take up arms again against the Californians. I had my doubts that everything about it was straightforward but we were obliged to let them go."

Slender as it was, there was still, Sutter knew, a chance of whipping Castro. If his two legions would only hold together, it could be done. "It was now decided to attack the enemy," he told H. H. Bancroft, "and I was elected to lead the attack. With my entire command, enforced by the Mexican dragoons and by two companies of Mexican infantry, I started, about sundown, to cross the mountain range. Micheltorena, with the artillery and the remainder of the army, waited until the next morning to continue the march along the beach. During the night it rained very hard. The hills became slippery; men and horses fell and rolled down into the ravines. When day broke, I found myself in the forest in sight of the Mission Buenaventura, but not more than half of my command had come up."

More than the weather and sloppy footing was decimating Sutter's force. Coates and his parolees were inducing their comrades to desert. Another saboteur, William A. Streeter, who had served as an interpreter between Castro and Coates, had accompanied the paroled men back to Sutter's camp specifically in order to exaggerate the dangers of attacking Castro. By the time Marsh, Coates and Streeter were through, Sutter's once-crack legion had shrunk to only fifty demoralized men.

Sutter pictured that unbearably tense moment: "A council of war was held. Captain Gantt believed that not half of the guns would go off. Lt. Félix Váldez did not think that we were strong enough to make the attack. Estrada said he considered it no longer a night attack, for it was now daylight. Only the captain of the Indian company, Ernest Rufus, was confident and said that the muskets of his company were in order, for his Indians had taken good care of them." Proof that Sutter was equally nagged by doubts appeared in the quick note which he dashed off to Reading on the eve of combat: "The situation of the enemy is very favorable and for this account our riflemen will not go into battle. Twice we were under way to attack him [Castro] and after one whole night's hard work we were obliged to return on account of the rain. The general persists in attacking them and I am in a very bad situation. Fourteen men who were taken prisoner returned, besides six deserters; some were sick, and only a few will go with the general. The forces of the enemy are nearly the double of ours. . . . I can hardly describe to you how bad I feel on account of the behaviour of the men of the camp." A gloomy Sutter looked beyond Buenaventura to the fate of New Helvetia, cautioning Reading, "I recommend to you all vigilance possible and to get as many people for defense as you can. Even the trapping party would be of great service. I believe Castro will pay you a visit before we are able to return."

While he waited for permission to strike the enemy, with his army melting in the rain, Sutter took time to write another letter to Reading, a long and rambling one which again betrayed his anxiety.

180

We are about one half-mile from the fires of the advanced guard. A good many of our company left us this morning, also, without giving notice, and with the greatest trouble in the world I could get about forty men here. About half of them were determined to remain with the general; the others wanted to return. But I believe that nearly all will remain except a few exceptions. Amongst them is Mr. Sinclair, by whom I send this letter. Who could believe when we left my establishment and when we joined with the general, about 200 men strong, how reduced we are now! The general was greatly deceived, but he will fight the battle and tomorrow morning it will be done. We are, with the Indians, about 300 men and the enemy has nearly or about double that strength.

If I have the luck to survive the day, I shall endeavour to return as quick as possible. . . . Everything that will have to be done I leave entirely to your good judgment. In all cases, it is good that you get as strong as you can for defense. It will also be good if Sonoma could be taken; it is a pity that the launch has had to lay so long at Yerba Buena. I don't know who will take care of her now since Mr. Rae is dead. I think Captain Hinckley, Perry [McCoon] and [Gardner] Wyman, with a whole gang, left yesterday without leave. It is very necessary that you look sharp for them because it is believed that they will take some of the national horses, colts, etc., having the intention to go to the Columbia River. Two corporals deserted, also. I believe they are with them. Our trapping business will have to be postponed when I come (not very soon) home. But, in all cases, we can build the little fort up there. The trappers will be wanted to continue the war and for the protection of the establishment.

The other party gained through their flattery and kind treatment and lies a good many of the fourteen men who were taken prisoners, particularly Mr. Coates. I believe he would rather take up arms in favor of the other party. I hope the other party of Captain Stevens will have safely returned from the mountains. What a pity that the general was a little slow in his movements. We could have prevented that they could take positions in San Buenaventura. I think you are very glad to get rid of some of the ladies, soon. I hope you neglect not to protect

181

poor Manuiki, which I recommend to you very much in case I should die. . . . The foreigners in Santa Barbara and vicinity are more in favor of Castro than of the general, because the most influential persons (merchants and owners of vessels) are in their favor. But I hope it will be changed when we gain the day tomorrow. In the pueblo of Los Angeles, it is the same but in case we come there, a great many newcomers would join us. So few as we are now, here, we have by all means to save the honor of the foreigners. The general would never have gone so far if he would not have depended on us. And now, two-thirds of the men leave him. He told me that it would have been better that they had never come to join him. They told the prisoners in the enemy's camp that the Vallejos have taken New Helvetia. But I cannot believe it. I wish they would be taken prisoners, and all cannons, guns, military stores, etc. I shall do it very quick when I return if it is not done before. You can depend on Merritt. Tomorrow morning, I will ask the general if Mr. Weber and the two Hernández can be set at liberty and will tell it to Mr. Sinclair verbally, because there will be no time to write. Every year, Manuiki makes a garden of her own to plant melons, etc. Please let her choose a piece where she likes in the garden. She has always the best and largest melons and watermelons. You will just tell it to Harry. Also assist Makaena that he can plant like usual.

The *alcalde,* who was with us, left yesterday with my permission. I told him to raise 25 or 30 good Christian Indians near San José, or more, and come up to you as quick as he possibly can to assist you to protect the fort. I hope all the old muskets are now in good order to arm some men with them. The Indians are pretty good soldiers now. . . . They do their duty well and I think they will show themselves.

The arrival of some stragglers increased Sutter's force somewhat and served also to bolster his courage. He recalled this short-lived moment of triumph: "I told my officers that an immediate attack might have good results, since the enemy would hardly expect us in such weather. I had been informed that they had

had a *fandango* the night before and were probably still half drunk and asleep. At all events, I was determined to make the attack. Taking with me as many men as I could gather, I made a charge upon the town. The merry-makers of yesterday were panic-stricken and fled in every direction. Since we came out of the woods, they could not tell how strong we were; hence, they did not stop running until they came to an open place about three-quarters of a mile away, where they tried to form ranks. They began to swear at us, as was their fashion, calling us thieves and all kinds of bad names." Sutter was elated; he had struck the rebels and they were on the run!

John Coffin Jones, however, believed that the "patriots" retreated so quickly before Sutter's charge not because he was another George Washington at Trenton but because of the false rumor, which had swept the camp earlier, that Andrés Pico was marching to join not Castro but Micheltorena. Castro blamed his defeat at Buenaventura on the fact that his powder had become damaged by the rains, rather than on Sutter's dashing attack. But, of course, Sutter's powder was in even worse condition from rain-soaked bivouacs.

In his brief, delirious, moment of victory—the high point of his career—Sutter sent Bidwell to the governor for permission to pursue Castro. To his astonishment, Micheltorena refused, advising him that it would be better if they continued the advance more slowly, and together. According to Alvarado and Vallejo, Micheltorena next held a secret interview with Castro to arrange for a final sham battle—a victory for Castro—and a peace treaty which would save face for the governor. Sutter was still not in on the secret or even, apparently, suspicious. But he was devastated by what he took to be Micheltorena's timidity or indolence. "If we had followed up our advantage, we could easily have routed them, but this was not the Mexican fashion."

While Micheltorena stalled, possibly embarrassed by Sutter's modest, bloodless victory at San Buenaventura, the Swiss, acting on the governor's orders, occupied the town. "I demanded wine,

aguardiente, and meat from the major-domo. While the priest of
the mission was on our side, the major-domo favored the enemy.
He protested against my requisitions, pretending that Castro and
his men had taken away everything. Since I was convinced that
this was not true, I threatened to break open his cellar if he would
not produce the provisions which I required. When he saw me
determined, he yielded at length, and provided plenty of everything. We spent all next day at the mission, eating and drinking
well and enjoying the dances of the long-haired and short-shirted
Indians from the Mission San Antonio, who had come to play
for us. The Indians had a regular band with them." The one
jarring note in Sutter's victory celebration was the hatred of the
southerners, now revealed to him: "The inhabitants of the mission
informed me that the Californians had threatened to nail me to a
large cross at the mission if they could catch me."

A messenger from Castro, under a white flag, delivered an
invitation to Micheltorena to fight. The governor answered by
promising his godchild bayonets at first light. During the night,
the rebels successfully raided the governor's corral, but Sutter
was still able to move his men forward the next morning. As
he passed Rancho Santa Clara, a beautiful woman who, he believed, was Alvarado's ex-mistress, came out with her son by her
side. The boy carried a stack of tortillas wrapped in a cloth. The
woman asked one of Sutter's riflemen where his captain was.
The soldier pointed to John Gantt and the boy presented him with
the tortillas. When he opened the bundle, he found a letter inside
from Castro and Alvarado, calling on him and his men to abandon Micheltorena and Sutter and to go over to the insurgents.
Gantt showed it to Sutter, who passed it on to the governor. Another disconcerting incident occurred that evening when a mother
of thirteen children came to Sutter to beg him not to be hard
on her nine sons, all in Castro's service. That night, Sutter encamped in a large vineyard, surrounded by a stone wall, which
protected his horses from rebel raiders. Micheltorena was sick

in bed and the entire responsibility of the government cause fell upon Sutter's shoulders.

The next night, Sutter camped at the old Cahuenga adobe, headquarters for the ranch belonging to Mission San Fernando. Easily visible across the otherwise empty, arid plain was the enemy's hilltop camp. The Swiss mounted a heavy guard because he knew that Castro had been reinforced by the Picos. But the only attack he suffered that night was from the wind which blew down his soldiers' tents and sent stinging sand into their faces in the darkness. Few of the men slept that night. At dawn, Sutter prepared to attack.

The New Helvetia fifer, a bass drummer, and Sutter's three snare drummers signaled his men forward. The drumrolls were soon drowned out by cannon fire. Sutter put three pieces into action against Castro's two. Alvarado personally touched off the first round before surrendering the artillery to his cannoneers. But Sutter's gun crew scored first, their first shot shattering the wheel of one of the rebel field pieces. Firing then became general. During the battle, Sutter's gunners delivered 100 rounds of grapeshot and cannister, while Castro's men replied with solid shot. When they ran out of cannonballs, they used round boulders. Despite the bombardment, the soldiers—who took cover under the banks of the Los Angeles River and the arroyos tributary to it—escaped injury. Although Pío Pico claimed that three or four *cholos* were killed and John Coffin Jones upped the estimate to twelve casualties, all in Micheltorena's camp, most observers reported the only dead to be a rebel mule, decapitated by a cannonball.

Sutter's old skipper of 1839, William Heath Davis, who was in the Cahuenga-Los Angeles area at the time, believed that the virtually nonexistent casualty rate was due to Micheltorena's ordering his men to fire over the heads of their adversaries, supposedly out of feelings of humanity. If so, their compassionate aim was reciprocated by the Castroites. British Vice Consul James A. Forbes reported that the rebel foreign legion was ordered to fire at the

Mexican artillerymen only, and never at Sutter's American riflemen. But again their striking inaccuracy suggests that the frontiersmen were merely going through the motions. In the confusion of the battle, so painstakingly delayed by Micheltorena until he could not possibly win, Pío Pico encountered José Castro skulking in disguise and out of danger—or, at least, out of what little danger there was at Cahuenga. Doubtless, he was waiting for Micheltorena to end the comedy. Pico, no more privy to the Castro-Micheltorena double-dealing than Sutter, also had to reprimand two of his men when he found them contacting Sutter's Americans. He need not have worried; they were selling desertion, not buying it.

In his recapitulation of the Battle of Cahuenga, Sutter understated the gravity of his situation. "The enemy became frightened and those in charge of the cannon took to their heels. Had we rushed upon them immediately, we might have secured the victory. But we had bad luck. Some of the Mexican dragoons who were with us began to waver and a number of them deserted. The order to charge was not obeyed by the riflemen. I saw treachery lurking behind guns and said to Micheltorena, 'I shall go and see why Gantt does not advance.' "

Moving over to his lieutenant, Sutter was aghast to find that Gantt's riflemen were casting a ballot to decide whether to stay on his side or to go over to the enemy! They told him that they would not fight their fellow Americans. (Reflected Sutter, "Dr. Marsh was a good talker and knew how to stir up mutiny.") When Sutter spoke sharply to Gantt—"What are you doing here, not obeying orders? Why do you not advance?"—Gantt's matter-of-fact answer was, "We are voting which want to go with one side and which with the other." An appalled Sutter could only glare at his lieutenant and reply angrily, "This is the time to fight, not to vote!" But the battle, such as it was, broke down into utter chaos.

Sutter wandered off, never lonelier. Gantt joined the other deserters, accepting Pío Pico's guarantees that they would not be punished. One of Gantt's men even claimed that Pico, besides promising them kind treatment, offered to join them in declaring California independent of Mexico then and there. Perhaps Pico and Micheltorena both were looking ahead only sixteen months to the Bear Flag Republic, the next act of the drama whose finale would be the Mexican War. Isaac Graham may have intended to show fight, like Sutter, but when he went out to palaver, he was captured by Joaquín de la Torre, probably to his great relief. Crushed by the failure of his prestige and eloquence to sway the deserters, Sutter determined to return to the governor's side and make a stand. He was, at least, pleased that his deserting men did not join the enemy force.

On February 20, 1845, Captain John A. Sutter's brief, vainglorious, military career came crashing down around his epaulettes. He explained the end of the affair to Bancroft: "On my way back to Micheltorena, I suddenly found myself surrounded by thirty Californians. Had they known who I was, they would, doubtless, have cut me to pieces. Luckily, Antonio Castro came up and, recognizing me, said to the men, 'I shall take over your prisoner.' He then saluted me and said, 'I am very glad that you are here.' " All that Sutter could think to say, with defeat bitter in his mouth, was "Yes, but I am not."

Castro sent a *vaquero* hurrying off to summon Alvarado. The former governor rode up, dismounted, and embraced Sutter like a close friend. He ordered a bottle of *aguardiente* and poured drinks for Sutter and himself. Then he sent the cowboy to bring Don José Castro. When the general appeared, Alvarado called to him, "Castro, dismount and salute Captain Sutter." He did so and clasped Sutter in the customary California *abrazo*. All three then mounted up and rode to the Cahuenga adobe. Despite the courtesy of his captors, Sutter was frightened for his life. He could not forget the rebel threat, to nail him to a cross: "I rode between Castro and Alvarado, and the mounted Californians, who looked as though they would like to eat me up, formed a hollow square around us."

187

CHAPTER XI

THE PACIFIER

SOME Mexican-Californians accused Sutter of surrendering all too willingly at Cahuenga. Antonio M. Osío charged that he waved a white flag and begged Alvarado's favor. Jealous John Laufkotter could not even bring himself to believe that his old roommate was anywhere near the engagement. He wrote, "It seems Mr. Sutter kept away from the scene of action and regaled himself with whisky in a saloon in town." In truth, Sutter was forcibly removed from the scene of battle but not to a *cantina;* his temporary residence was a dark, cell-like room of the Cahuenga adobe. No sooner was he locked in than someone stole his fine double-barreled rifle, which he was obliged to leave outside the door. Although he detailed Bidwell to search for it, he never saw it again.

Crowds of Angeleños occupied the hilltops around the field of Cahuenga. The men observed the action intently while the children played and the women told their rosaries. Many of them had family or close friends involved in the conflict. Some of the people got wind of Sutter's capture and clustered curiously around the window of the adobe to peer in at Castro's prize catch of the

189

campaign. Shortly afterward, an officer, accompanied by a strong guard, pushed his way through the throng and demanded Sutter's sword. Years later, Sutter described the scene in the gloomy house: "As I gave it to him, I thought to myself, 'this looks bad.' Fortunately, I saw an officer by the name of Eugenio Montenegro, a captain of cavalry whom I knew very well. I beckoned to him and said, 'You can do me a great favor. Tell your superiors that they know nothing of the usages of war if they put an officer of my rank under a common guard.' This had the desired effect. My sword was given back to me."

But to the crestfallen Sutter his career seemed finished and his life in precarious balance. His spirits were raised somewhat by Castro's officers inviting him into the adjoining room for a drink. There, they asked him for his parole, since they needed all their men to do battle and would prefer not to have to post a guard over him. He promised not to try to escape and John Rowland, one of the first Yankee *rancheros* to settle in southern California, spoke up to offer himself as security against any attempt by Sutter to flee. That evening, Sutter made the twelve-mile journey to the pueblo of Los Angeles in the company of Rowland and the local *alcalde*. He was quartered in the house of Don Abel Stearns. All the officers of the new government but Pío Pico were there to celebrate with a slightly premature victory banquet. Micheltorena had not quite yet run up his white flag. Juan Bandini, Secretary of State, invited Sutter to join them at table, but he politely declined, explaining that he had just come from the battlefield and was dirty and jaded. Indeed, Sutter was so thick with dust that Stearns did not recognize him at first. When his captors insisted, Sutter joined them for a drink, but soon excused himself, pleading fatigue, and let Stearns show him the way to a comfortable bedroom where he fell immediately into an exhausted sleep.

During the night, Stearns knocked loudly and repeatedly on Sutter's door to arouse him. ("I was so worn out that I could shake off the sleep only with great difficulty.") The American told him that two visitors insisted upon seeing him. Sutter dressed hurriedly and found James McKinley and Andrés Pico, the Los Angeles militia captain, awaiting him. To hurry Micheltorena's surrender, they sought Sutter's help. They wanted him to write a letter advising the governor that further resistance was hopeless. Sutter needed no convincing that Micheltorena was whipped. But he considered such an act incompatible with his honor as a loyal officer of the government. When the two men asked him to write Rufus not to resist further with Sutter's well-trained Indians, he lied his way out of the difficulty. He said that he could not write Spanish well enough and that Rufus could not understand it in any case. He did agree, however, to write to Micheltorena in French. "But we can neither read French nor German," chorused Pico and McKinley. Sutter countered, "You surely have someone who can." He was banking on the lateness of the hour to save him. Pico would not be able to find a French translator at midnight. He was right. They let him pencil a note to Micheltorena in French. "I was satisfied that they would not examine too closely what I said, so I wrote to Micheltorena in French in such a manner that he would understand my position and would know that I was forced to write."

Whether Sutter's note was an influence or not, Micheltorena surrendered. (Perhaps he did so right on schedule.) Word of his collapse was given Sutter along with a warning: "There is much discussion as to what should be done with you. Some are for shooting you, others for deportation and confiscation of all your property." Sutter could think of nothing to say but, "I am in their power. They can do with me as they please."

Jim Beckwourth, the Negro mountain man who had been recruited to Castro's army with his twelve followers, thought that the *gringos* who loudly demanded Sutter's death intended only to give their prisoner a good scare in return for his pompous pronouncements of "No quarter!" on the day before the battle. Beckwourth and some of the Americans and foreigners in the rebel army had at that time sent a letter to Sutter and Gantt, offering to withdraw from the battle if Sutter would let his *gringos* do like-

191

wise. Sutter had snapped furiously, "Unless the Americans withdraw from the insurgent army immediately, I will shoot every one by ten o'clock tomorrow morning."

Castro and Alvarado were anything but harsh on Micheltorena. It appeared that their prisoner had dictated the terms of the Treaty of Campo de San Fernando. To make the best possible impression on Mexico City, he was allowed to march his *cholos* through Los Angeles, with music and flying colors, to a camp at Palos Verdes. Sutter mourned, "This music was like a dead march to me. I was really the greatest sufferer. Defeat meant much more to me than to the governor." He was particularly troubled by the plight of his Indians. "In the capitulation, they had been given every advantage which the Mexican soldiers had received but they were treated badly while I was held prisoner. They were obliged to carry burdens from Los Angeles to San Pedro, like pack animals, to supply provisions for the vessels on which the Mexican soldiers were to be sent home. For this, they received no pay and scarcely enough food to keep them alive."

The white prisoners, on the other hand, were treated well. Gantt and Marsh were offered not merely their liberty by Governor Pico but a contract to capture horse-thieving Indians. Sutter, although uncertain about his ultimate fate, was comfortable enough in detention. He was given a razor and a clean shirt, and a breakfast with Bidwell (who brought him a present of some oranges) cheered him considerably. He secured permission, as well, to visit a friend whose house was only a few hundred yards from Stearns' home.

There Sutter met Secretary of State Don Juan Bandini and some other officers. Bandini asked him to join him in a walk in the garden, gave Sutter a cigar, and invited him to play billiards. Although this was a real treat—Bandini's billiard table was probably the only one in California—Sutter, still badly depressed, declined. He excused himself by saying that his present state of mind did not allow him to play billiards. "Yes, I can believe you," sympathized Bandini. Then he abruptly changed the subject.

"Now, please tell me how it was that you came with Micheltorena. Did you come of your own free will, or did you receive orders to march with him?" Aware that his fortune and perhaps his very life hung in the balance, Sutter worded his answer carefully. "I received orders from Governor Micheltorena to march." Bandini came back, "Have you these orders? Can you show them to me?" "No," answered Sutter. "I had them with me and I believe that they are with my baggage at San Fernando. I believe that I could get the papers if I had horses to send to my servants at San Fernando." Bandini allowed him to send a messenger to pick up the documents. Among the papers was the critical marching order from Micheltorena. When Sutter handed it over, Bandini cried, "Now you are saved!"

The friendly Peruvian took the orders to Pico and Castro. He also spoke in Sutter's behalf. Next day, after breakfast, he called for the prisoner and escorted him to a meeting with Pico, Castro and Alvarado. Had Castro been vindictive, he could have loopholed Article Four of the treaty, which allowed Loyalist officers like Sutter to remain in government service, and which guaranteed their lives and property. But he informed his apprehensive captive that he was convinced that he was guilty of nothing more than carrying out his duty to the former legal executive. He promised to recognize his position and to reinstate all his former rights, property and offices. Pica and Alvarado concurred.

Sutter's despair began to dissolve when they asked him to swear allegiance to the new government. By the time Pico and Castro confirmed him as *Comandante Militar de las Fronteras del Norte y Encargado de la Justicia,* Sutter was once again the optimist. He retained his composure although inwardly he exulted. "This office gave me much more power than the one conferred on me by Alvarado! Formerly, I was obliged to notify the government first and wait for instructions. Now, I had executive power. I could do what I thought was proper and inform the government of my acts afterward." Naturally, Sutter had not the slightest objection to swearing an oath of allegiance to the Pío Pico government. He received, in return, a document confirming him in the position which Micheltorena had originally granted him. The meeting then adjourned to the rattle of glasses and bottles of *aguardiente.*

Sutter was only forty-two years old. He was still tough and resilient, though the defeat left its mark on his pride. (As late as 1879, just before he died, he complained to the Sacramento *Record-Union,* "We were defeated by treachery and desertion!") From the wreckage of his politico-military career, Sutter began to rebuild. His first concern was getting back to New Helvetia to set his own house in order. It was not easy. Bidwell was helpful and bold enough to request that the government replace the 150 horses which Sutter had lost in the campaign. He was told that they were scattered all over southern California and could not be rounded up. Luckily for the now penniless Sutter, one of his past kindnesses paid off. He ran into a German cooper, named Mumm, for whom he had shipped barrel staves, gratis, on his launch. The German now showed his gratitude by rounding up a number of horses and presenting them to his old *patrón.* Sutter promised to pay for them after returning to his fort. Some of his men had been able to hang on to their mounts; others were able to borrow money to buy horses. After numberless delays, Sutter was ready to start for home. Bidwell tested Pío Pico a last time, asking that the New Helvetian soldiery be sent home at government expense. As he and Sutter expected, Pico refused. Pico offered to give him credit, but Sutter realized it would cost him too much to get his small army home. Some of his old spunk returned and he gave the governor a tart answer: "No, we will live on horseflesh first." Still, he was grateful when Pico gave him an order on Mission San Fernando for porridge for his Indians.

Sutter led his once-proud army back toward the Sacramento River. The *padre* at San Fernando treated him more like a conquering hero than a defeated partisan. While his officers sat at one table, Sutter dined with the priest at a place of honor at his table. The mission cellars produced a supply of good wine, too.

Leaving San Fernando, the Swiss struck across a semi-desert area of stunted vegetation and Joshua trees, which he termed "dwarf palm trees." He had no guide, so when the horses were on the verge of collapse from lack of water, he simply headed them for the nearest spur of the mountains. There he found a stream and ordered the tents pitched. The next day, he reached San Francisquito ranch, where he halted and sent some scouts forward to find Tejon Pass. He long remembered the moment when he reached the summit: "What a magnificent view we had from the pass and how beautifully green the Tejon Valley looked. We passed through snow in places and, on our way down, it seemed like going into Italy."

Sutter rested his men and animals an entire day in the Tejon Valley, although he did not like the looks of the natives: "The Indians looked sour; not very friendly." He was sure that he would find plenty of horses in the *Tulares,* or San Joaquin Valley; enough to ride and to eat, if need be. When his Indian troopers asked him for permission to go ahead, Sutter reluctantly assented. He knew that they could travel much faster, foraging for roots, herbs, grasses and seeds. But he was worried over the "sour-looking" natives through whose lands they had to pass almost unarmed.

From his Tejon camp, Sutter and his dozen whites and Kanakas followed the trail of the Indian grenadiers northward. The horses were frequently on the point of giving out and progress was inevitably slow. Every stream in Sutter's path was transformed by the spring run-off into a moat to impede him. The Kings River was particularly difficult to negotiate. Sutter offered Indians of the area what little money he had, but they were very "saucy" and refused to help him. Where he would have taken a bull whip to them a few months earlier, he now had to swallow his pride and continue without their help. At Tulare Lake, he found an Indian village of considerable size. Again, the redmen refused to aid him in any way. All he could do was swear in German and French (and possibly Spanish and English) and wish that he had been able to persuade Pico to let him have his brass cannon back. He had stretched to the very limit the scant supply of rations which he had brought from San Fernando and San Francisquito. Luckily, one of his men fashioned a bit of wire into a hook and was able to catch a number of fish for the mess.

At the Merced River, where he had his men build a raft, to cross, he found that most of his horses were done in. On the far side, he could see four Indians, driving 125 or so animals. Sutter guessed that they were rustlers, stealing Santa Clara Valley stock. He told his men that they would have to walk to New Helvetia if they did not help him capture the herd. The worn party followed him in a clumsy charge which routed the horse thieves. Sutter seized the entire herd. With fresh mounts, his party felt much stronger. Although the Stanislaus River crossing proved even more perilous than the Merced, morale was rising. He had to build a raft there without a hatchet or any tool more sophisticated than a bowie knife, but he was undaunted. He later explained his technique as an amateur boatwright when faced by a raging torrent: "We helped ourselves by lassoing the dry branches from trees and made a raft by tying the branches together with strings. The Kanaka swam across the river with a line which he tied to a tree on the opposite shore. Only one man, with a little luggage, could cross the river on the raft at a time; he had to lie flat and to ferry himself across by pulling the rope. The raft was pulled back by a rope and, gradually, we all crossed safely. The horses, of course, had to swim across and since the riverbank was very steep, we had no little difficulty in getting them to the shore. The horse thieves had, in the meantime, mobilized their whole village and kept on molesting us. We had to keep up a constant fire while we were building the raft and crossing the river." The night after fording the Stanislaus, Sutter did not dare pitch camp because of the presence of hostile Indians. There was no path to follow, but he led the men toward the North Star. All his provisions were gone now, but a hunter killed an antelope, so he did not yet have to put his men on a diet of horsemeat.

The Indian grenadiers reached the fort several days ahead of him. Reading immediately sent horses and provisions to meet his employer at the Mokelumne River. Three months earlier, Sutter had boasted and threatened that he would seize Sonoma. Now he slunk meekly into his fort, hoping to be unnoticed by the Vallejos. There he holed up, licking his psychological wounds while his jealous rivals crowed over his failure. The turncoat John Gantt described Sutter and his woebegone army: "With their hearts on the ground, down tumbled all the air-built castles, and most dreadful was the crash." John Coffin Jones chortled, "Sutter had fallen and, I think, like Lucifer, never to rise again." Thomas O. Larkin was not only kindlier but a better prophet than Jones. He wrote Abel Stearns that he was sure Sutter would shake off the hostility that the Mexican government felt toward him. Still, Fate played a bitter little joke on the would-be conquering *Comandante*. The date of his humbled return was April 1, 1845—All Fools' Day.

But Sutter's psyche recovered rapidly. First he threw the cook, Bill Daylor, into the *calabozo* for tampering with Manuiki's affections. Then, just two days after his return, he was back in the field on a punitive expedition against Indian raiders, who, emboldened by his long absence, had raided the neighboring ranches of Thomas Lindsay and William Gulnac. They drove off all the cattle and killed Lindsay. Though Sutter was no friend of Gulnac, whom he usually lumped with Marsh and Weber as "undependable," he had his drummer roll off a call to arms. He then led a flying squad of twenty-two picked men in pursuit. After a fast march, he caught the Indians, defeated them and killed (according to some accounts) at least fifty warriors. But it proved a costly campaign; his close friend, Juan Vaca, was shot and killed at his side, and a number of his men were wounded.

Indian troubles continued. Some men whispered that Castro was behind the rash of outbreaks, using them to weaken and harass Sutter, perhaps to drive him from California. It was rumored that Castro hired Chief Raphero to turn his Mokelumnes against their protector. This was a total error for the chief. Sutter did not intend to sit tight in his fortress, awaiting Raphero's attack. Instead, he tracked the enemy down and defeated them. He captured the chief and court-martialed him. Soon the Mokelumne's head was impaled on a spike above the main gate of Sutter's Fort. The grinning skull with its windblown hair was a macabre warning to those who threatened New Helvetia. Sutter had then to deal with another Indian threat—one that hurt him because it involved Chief Rufino, whom he had considered one of his most devoted followers. He had so trusted him as to give him a commission in his grenadier guards. Rufino, in revenge for Raphero's execution, killed his own brother-in-law, a loyal soldier and Indian *alcalde*. It took Sutter considerable time—several months, in fact—but his dogged pursuit eventually brought Rufino to bay. Sutter tried him for murder and had him executed on September 16, 1845.

From time to time, the inhabitants of Sutter's Fort were unnerved by tales of the roaming parties of Walla Wallas in the Sacramento Valley. Supposedly they were war parties, intent on avenging the murder of Chief Piopiomoxmox's (Yellow Serpent) son, Elijah, by Grove Cook in the summer of 1844. Because the incident occurred at New Helvetia and Sutter had been unwilling to punish Cook, rumors identified him as the Walla Wallas' main target. But they never struck. Sutter was ready for them in any case. Much of his time in 1845 was spent in Indian pacification, and he returned to his callous practice of "adopting" the children of Indians killed in his punitive campaigns. He distributed them to friends as servants. If not slaves, they were serfs. He did not sell them to bidders but used them instead to earn what would today be called good will and the extension of credit, forgiveness for unpaid debts, and so forth. He wrote San Francisco merchant William Leidesdorff, "I will send two Indian girls, of which you will take which you like the best. The other is for Mr. Rid-

ley, whom I promised one longer than two years ago. As this
shall never be considered as an article of trade, I make you a
present with this girl." When he delivered another Indian girl to
the wife of a friend, he promised the woman another servant
girl: "As I have to go shortly on several campaigns against hostile
Indians . . . I will send another who is a little larger. Since my
absence, the Indians are becoming like they were before. I ought
not to be a single week from home." In May 1845 he wrote to
Suñol, "I shall send you some young Indians after our campaign
against the Horsethieves, which will take place after the wheat
harvest." He continued to hire out adult Indians, sending thirty
to Suñol on a single occasion. He cautioned the Spaniard to keep
them away from Christian Indians so that they would not pick
up vices. Suñol was to keep them as long as he liked; Sutter would
return them to their families, when he was through with them,
with his launch.

Sutter wanted Reading to help him restore peace on the
Feather River Indian frontier, near Hock Farm. He asked him
to send "the Old Man" of the Hock *ranchería* to the Willo tribe,
since he spoke their language. Sutter wanted the Willo chiefs to
come to Hock for a pow-wow. Should they refuse, said Sutter,
"I think it would be good to pay them a visit. I will come up
and join you. I see now how it is. If they are not kept strictly
under fear, it will be no good." He told Reading that he needed
more Indian men and boys to get his fields back into full pro-
ductivity. A short time later, he asked him to demand the surrender of the Butte Creek *ranchería* braves who had killed some
of his hogs and cattle. "Give them a severe punishment, to make
them understand that they shall do this no more in future. . . .
I think it is a great deal better, for all who have land there, that
the people are saved as much as possible for labor. . . . I wonder
if [Chief] Saleanack will come or not. I wish he would, and save
us a campaign. All the tribes which should show hostility, of
course, you will use arms against them, that the whole valley
respects in future the white men, more and more."

However ineffective Sutter had been in the Mexican-California war and in politics, he was in his element when disciplining Indians. In June he negotiated a treaty with the Horsethief Indians to put an end to their rustling, even persuading them to settle down near his fort, where he could keep an eye on them. He wrote Suñol:

> They have sent me an express that they will come here if I pardon them, which I have promised to do. I expect them in a short time. You may rest assured, sir, that my manner of treating with these Indians will have good consequences for the good of the country and much better than the costly and pretentious campaigns that never meet with success. Marsh and Gantt have promised much to the government, but they will not be able to fulfill their promises because they haven't a man who will go with them. "Poor Sutter," who is treated with such contempt in this country, will show that he can eradicate horse stealing, little by little. I have always, with great sacrifices, worked and acted for the best interests of the country, but it has never been appreciated and I am always paid with ingratitude.

By the fall of 1845, even with Walla Walla war scares, Sutter had the northern California Indian situation very much in hand. When Larkin worried over reports that the tribes were on the warpath against Sutter, the latter laughed off the story:

> I don't know who could have told such a story. The Indians, all, are very friendly and obedient. . . . When I arrived from the campaign, I had to regulate a few disorders among some of the tribes but, in general, they behaved themselves very well. When the report of my death came here, on the whole Feather River and Sacramento River, there was an awful mourning for me and all was very sorrowful, as they looked upon me as their father and benefactor and protector. When I arrived here, a great many chiefs and people visited me to convince themselves that I was alive, yet. This affection and gratitude of the poor Indians was very satisfactory to me, particularly when I learned how some ungrateful white men were on the point of acting here and wished very much that I would be dead, to have a chance to rob and plunder. It was high time I arrived here!

Indians were not Sutter's only troubles in 1845. Reading, although a solid man, had let many of his enterprises run down during Sutter's absence on campaign. When he inspected his tannery, fields, and trappers, Sutter was appalled at the results of Reading's laxness. He quickly posted stringent new rules for Sutter's Fort and secured a new major-domo to execute them. When a lad named Sullivan, in John Sinclair's employ, stole a butcher knife, the usually easy-going Sutter responded harshly. He gave the boy twenty-five lashes and wrote Reading, "Everybody had a pleasure to see it . . . . He says he is very glad that he got the 25 —and that he will steal no more."

Next, Sutter had to send Reading to Hock Farm to get Sam Neal to shape up. In a note to Reading, he grumbled, "It is so inconvenient that Neal cannot read or write. I wish you would be so good as to tell him to be very careful to save the tallow, as we have the soap factory going, and to be saving of the meat, the bones, heads, feet, etc., of the cattle." Reading was too good a man to spare at Hock for very long. Soon, Sutter had him heading his trapping parties again. In 1845 his fur brigade totalled thirty-two men, a few boys, with 100 horses and mules and some canoes. Sutter, at this time, placed William Benitz in charge of his Fort Ross properties, replacing an old employee, Jack Rainsford, but he was chiefly concerned over the property that was becoming his favorite, Hock Farm: "I wish very much that I could get a trusty man to take charge of the farm."

As the population and sophistication of his settlement grew, so, too, did its problems. Settlers haggled so over their accounts with him that Sutter had to order Reading and Bidwell to keep the most careful and accurate account books possible. A new problem was desertion. Augustín, a cowboy and Indian soldier, ran away with his woman and two Indian boys. They stole several horses, including the one trained to operate the tanbark mill. Sutter sent a party of his men in pursuit. Although Augustín was caught and returned from Marsh's ranch, the old doctor appropriated the two boys. Sutter had to write him to ask for their return.

201

He took the opportunity to extend a peace feeler: "If you like to have a good neighbor, I am perfectly willing to be one. It depends entirely on you."

An attempted rape case distressed Sutter. An Oregon immigrant, James Houck, tried to attack George Davis' wife. Sutter could not catch the culprit but he rushed a note to Larkin: "I sincerely trust that you will use every exertion, as far as is consistent with the duties of your office, to bring such base and unprincipled men to a sense of justice by a punctual and rigorous execution of the laws." Then Theodore Cordua stole Thomas Hardy's squaw. "It makes Hardy nearly crazy. I gave Cordua orders to send her immediately back."

Sutter did his best to make peace with everyone as he scrambled back to his old position of power. He confessed to Suñol, however, that Weber still held a grudge against him. Looking ahead, confidently, to a Yankee take-over of California, he predicted about Weber, Gantt and Marsh: "These men will pay, one day, for their chicanery and insolence, because of the great change which is taking place in California." He added Flügge to the Weber-Marsh crowd, too, accusing him of trying to ruin his straitened credit. In a postscript of a letter to Reading, he wrote, "I am sorry that the news of Flügge's death was false." Writing to Victor Prudón, General Vallejo's aide, he was even more blunt. "It was with the greatest displeasure that I heard from Mr. Wolfskill of that bad rascal, Flügge, not being dead." (Flügge did go to paradise in 1845, but it was an earthly one, Hawaii.) In October 1845, Sutter was writing to Reading: "Gantt, Coates and the pirates are on their way down here. They caught only a few beaver and were not at all successful. Hicks is apoplexed so that the half side of his body is like dead. They had to wait once for him in camp 15 days. God, the Almighty, punished this rascal. I wish He would continue and punish a few others!"

Sutter planned to pay off his creditors in full, with wheat, in 1846. He asked James A. Forbes, the British Vice Consul, to get the Bernal brothers to give him more time. He was supremely confident. His secret weapon against debt was irrigation. He was confident of securing bumper crops in 1846 because he was digging a canal from a dam on the American River to water his fields. "Employing all the experience which I have now with the soil and climate, a very large and good crop must be raised. If I have success this time, then I will be out of all my trouble. To conduct this business well occupies me often whole nights. Nothing shall, this time, be neglected that I am once liberated from all my troubles. . . . I shall not rest until I shall be able to furnish them [his Russian creditors] every year about 15 or 20,000 *fanegas,* and this will be sure when I water my fields." He told Larkin that he planned to sow 6,000 *fanegas* of wheat on his irrigated land, to locate a grist mill and a sawmill on the canal, and to ditch the whole *rincón* to keep cattle and horses from trampling his crops. One good crop and he would be in the clear. "I am tired of laboring in vain!" he exclaimed.

Although all his wheat was promised to the Russians, Sutter saw a bright agricultural future ahead for California and had not the slightest doubt that he could also pay off Suñol, the Hudson's Bay Company and all his other creditors. A true visionary, he saw the coming change from a pastoral economy to an agricultural one. (Unfortunately, like everyone else, he did not dream of the cataclysmic mining period that would intervene.) Besides his 6,000 *fanegas* at New Helvetia, he sowed 200 more at Hock Farm.

He hoped to reimburse one of his creditors, Leidesdorff, in furs. But his 1844–45 trapping parties failed him because of bad management in the field. He assured Leidesdorff that there were plenty of beaver and otter but a great shortage of good trappers to take them. Reading had kept his men at home to garrison the fortress, and the few furs destined for Sutter's storerooms had fallen into the hands of John Sinclair and Theodore Cordua. Peter Lassen, too, Sutter's neighbor and former employee, had helped to ruin his season. He had detained two of Sutter's trappers, one of whom, Mast, was also his brewmaster. With Sutter's beer bringing $35 a barrel at Yerba Buena, Mast's absence was costing his employer a lot of money, and Sutter was furious.

Worst of the lot, in Sutter's opinion, was Dr. John Marsh. "It is not right for my neighbors to act in this manner, knowing that these boys are hired by me, furnished with complete equipment, and all of them in debt to me. Dr. Marsh is the baddest of all. He gave them grog for furs and robbed me in this manner of a large amount. But I shall take other measures about this," he promised Larkin. One such measure was Sutter's setting up a sort of modified rendezvous system, such as he had become familiar with in the Rockies. He kept the trappers away from the fort—and the temptation of the ranches of Sinclair, Cordua, Marsh and Lassen. He sent flour, dried meat, grog, medicine and blankets to Reading's field camp at Hannishaw, advising him, "It is, in all cases, better that the furs remain in your camp so that the people here on the place don't know that we have some. They would torment me for it, even those who are in debt. When I need some, it will be the best way to send the person with an order to receive it from you." Sutter sent Reading a locked chest for the catch, too. "Nobody will see it and so we can keep it a little secret. If not, the people here would trouble me for furs." Sutter also managed to hire the able Michel Laframboise away from the Hudson's Bay Company. In a gesture designed to cement his loyalty, Sutter sent Laframboise his own shotgun, urging him, however, to take very good care of it. Asking Leidesdorff for musket and rifle flints, percussion caps and duck shot for the canoes he would send out in October for the fall hunt, he reassured the merchant about his trappers: "Now I shall watch them, next season, and make them move."

From Leidesdorff, Sutter ordered the popular striped cloth (*manta*) to cover his 100 Indian boys and girls. He was ashamed to admit it, but they were nearly naked or in rags and would be until he could get his blanket factory into operation. "When strangers come here, it looks very bad," he confessed to the merchant. He promised to pay, as always, but added, "After having

204

received this favor of you, I will no more trouble you until I have made a good remittance."

Another creditor, Eugenio de Celís, proved more troublesome. He had long before attached Sutter's schooner for debt. Sutter had considered reclaiming it by force with the many volunteers who came eagerly forward. But on further thought he decided to mind his manners and depend on the intervention of his English friend, James Forbes. In various letters, he complained bitterly of the disruption of his trade by the seizure of his schooner. He wrote Reading, "How inconvenient it is here to be without a launch. Never I felt it so hard as at present." It was just like old times. He found himself firing off a drum barrage of promises and excuses to keep creditors at bay, while he worked from dawn till dark to patch up his agricultural empire. He asked Larkin for cotton to plant. Almost a century ahead of his time, he found that the plant grew beautifully in the Central Valley. Not for a moment did he lose faith either in himself or in California's rich soil—"One good year more and then I shall be clear of debt." And he was devoted to Larkin: "I look upon you as the only person in this country who assists and encourages enterprise."

Long before the close of 1845, Sutter's prodigious energy had begun to pay off. His hat factory was blocking headgear; a loom was weaving blankets; his distillery was turning out barrels of wild-grape pisco. In an immigrant named Bonney he found an excellent tanner. Sam Hensley and the Hawaiian, Maintop, kept his surviving fleet at sea, although its flagship, had been seized. Three blacksmiths kept up a steady din, and two gunsmiths joined them around the forge. Two coopers, a German wagonmaker, a millwright and several carpenters were now in his employ. One of the carpenters was a man he could have done without—James Marshall, a simple man who would make history but who would ruin himself and Sutter in the process. Sutter was manufacturing his own bird shot from Russian lead and buying fine rifle powder from the French (who refused it to the Californians). His saddler was kept busy making harness for twenty plow mules; his me-

chanics were shaping plows equal to those of Boston in quality—
some of them the huge prairie plows required to break the virgin
sod for his widening wheat fields. Sutter estimated that he needed
twenty more and he begged Larkin to find him some iron. "It
is like gold to me," he wrote. All the while, the practical dreamer
was planning a city in the wilderness.

Sutter's entire future, ironically, was staked on American immigration. Completely disillusioned with Mexico, he was also recovered from his flirtation with France. So sure was he that
California would become American territory, and soon, that he
wrote Larkin that he would never have to pay the high Mexican
duty on the farm machinery he was expecting in about a year.
Larkin, in fact, felt forced to criticize his friend in an evaluation
of him which he sent to Washington, because of his identification
with American interests: "Sutter is . . . active, well informed, but
too sanguine. He lives in expectation of this country belonging to
the United States." Larkin might have added how unbounded
was Sutter's faith in the future of California agriculture. He had
written the American consul: "You will have a good many of
the newcomers down in Monterey. Some of them have a great
deal to say against the country before they have seen anything,
and run her down. I think they are very poor judges. . . . If I
have a little luck next year, the people will be astonished at my
farming business."

Sutter strongly believed that the Mexican government should
encourage American immigration and settlement, rather than attempt to block it. "I advise now the government to give all these
immigrants the unoccupied land of the San Joaquin, Stanislaus,
Merced, etc., and the other part of the *Tulares,* and no more than
about two leagues to a person or a family. When the government
agrees to this, no longer will even one horse be stolen by Indians
in the whole country. This would save the government great and
useless expense. I traveled now for a whole month through the
Tular, coming from Los Angeles, and was observing and thinking

a great deal about the Horse Thieves. I found that there are so many difficulties that, even if several thousand dollars would be spent and thousands of Indians killed, it would not be much better. The only remedy will be to send all these emigrants there, which will be a great benefit and acquisition for California. All those who are coming with their families are an industrious and peaceable people." Sutter even succeeded in converting Larkin to his way of thinking and soon had him expressing such sentiments as, "If the government does not settle some of these newcomers on the other side of the San Joaquin, this country will soon be ruined."

Despite the American promoter Lansford Hasting's fiasco—the promised 1,000 immigrants that dwindled down to just 10 —Sutter was delighted by the overwhelming turn of the tide of immigration. He sent Caleb Greenwood to Fort Hall to divert some of the Oregon-bound travelers to the Bear River Road to Sutter's Fort. Caleb did a good job. Oregon pioneer Joel Palmer reported that "Mr. Greenwood, an old mountaineer, well stocked with falsehoods, had been dispatched from California to pilot the immigrants through." Before the season was over, Caleb persuaded from thirty-five to fifty wagons to alter their destination from the Willamette to the Sacramento. The first party which reached Sutter's Fort was that of William Swasey and W. L. Todd. Sutter reported the dozen or so men to be farmers and mechanics, with some money and 500 cattle, and in better condition than any party which had ever arrived. They were followed by a fifteen-man party led by Solomon P. Sublette, youngest brother in the Sublette clan of mountain men. Sutter, overenthusiastic as usual, told Larkin that they were men of property, some of them wealthy. "Not one company has arrived before in this country which looked so respectable," he added. He was much impressed with Sublette, but was notoriously inaccurate as a judge of men. Leidesdorff called Sublette a blackguard.

Sure that the immigrants' chances of receiving Mexican grants were slim, Sutter took the lead in offering them portions of his own land. He urged Larkin, Reading, and others to follow his example. He expected to welcome 10,000 Mormons to his fort by October 1846. Sutter was not alone in predicting the great wave of Mormon immigration to California. Boston papers looked ahead to the 10,000 in a wagon train twenty-five miles long, and a New Englander friend of Larkin's wrote him to warn, "Look out for the avalanche!"

Sutter could not have dreamed that Brigham Young would prefer an isolated valley in the basin and range country, at Salt Lake, to fertile California. But, aside from that, he was a pretty fair prophet. "Nothing can stop this immigration. In case of opposition, they would fight like lions. They are well armed, better than all the former immigrants. They all have superior rifles and pistols. . . . The best the Government could do would be to give these immigrants the San Joaquin and the whole *Tular* Valley. They would lose their horses no longer by the Horsethieves." All this he predicted to Larkin, while at the same time he promised Reading, "I use all my influence to keep them all up in the valley."

Sutter had thrown his fate in with the Americans but he had not yet given up the idea of bolstering his farming empire by colonizing Swiss and Germans in the Sacramento Valley. In 1845 he advised Germans to come to California and promised to use his influence with the Mexican government to help them. He mentioned the plan of the German immigration promoter, Capt. B. Schmölder, too: "At the present time, a resident of the country has projected a plan for direct immigration from Germany and is about departing for Europe to organize an association for that object." To attract Teutons, Sutter assured them that a good tailor would make his fortune in just three years in California. Day laborers would get from $20 to $75 a month. As for doctors, he cited the example of Dr. John Townsend, who was offered a bonus of $200 just to settle in Los Angeles, adding "I have it in contemplation to build a hospital, myself, and to place over it a skilled physician, as cases needing his assistance occur daily." He never built the hospital but shortly afterward hired a physician and dentist, Dr. William Gildea, and gave him a Sutter's Fort outbuilding for a clinic. Sutter put him on salary to treat the Indians, but white settlers had to pay for his services. After checking his diploma, Sutter wrote Larkin, "Dr. Gildea is a very good doctor and has his documents from the universities. He is a gentleman of intelligence and is in his charges very moderate, not like our quacks who pretend to be doctors, like Marsh."

Although Sutter clung to a stubborn personal loyalty to Micheltorena, he was wise enough to steer clear of any further involvement in Mexican-California politics after the debacle of Cahuenga. Political squabbling was constant during Pío Pico's governorship and it led Sutter to observe:

> For the political future of the country, great uncertainty, of course, prevails. Its great distance precludes the idea of a duration of Mexican sway, however desirable that might be if entrusted to so excellent a chief as Micheltorena, with his enlarged views upon the protection of foreigners and the fostering of immigration. The United States, as well as England, have fixed their gaze upon this country, so fertile and favorable for trade, while France, on the contrary, would willingly see it an independent domain. In union with Oregon, a great and powerful "Pacific Republic" might be created, with the most magnificent prospects. Whatever may be the final destiny of the country, so much appears certain—as the natural result of immigration, it will, within a few years, gain strength for a complete declaration of its independence.

Agriculture and immigration remained his twin talismans. He wrote Marsh: "My wheat crop looks very well, thank God in Heaven! After a low calculation, I will get about 6,000 *fanegas*. I would have more but after I was gone from here, they stopped sowing." Sutter expected to double his harvest with irrigation in 1846 and to bring in huge crops of barley, peas and beans. The Russians were consuming four times as much wheat in Alaska as when he had been there only six years before. He bragged to Marsh of his negotiations with France for another fine wheat market—the Marquesas Islands and Tahiti. Wheat trade with Hawaii was also likely. "Through our excellent water communications, the sale of our products has facilities unsurpassed in the world . . . Captains have often assured me that this harbor [San Francisco] is the finest in the whole Pacific Ocean." When he repeated the Russian wheat tale to Larkin, Sutter added extra embellishments:

> Don Pedro Kostromitinoff told me that if I could give him a full cargo for four 400-ton ships, they would take it. In a few years, their contract with the Hudson's Bay Company is expired. He promised also to give me the preference of this contract. It is 7,000 *fanegas* of wheat every year. The demand will be stronger this year because the Russian American Company made a contract with the Emperor to supply Kamschatka with wheat. . . . And what good pay, in notes or bills of St. Petersburg! I am certain that, in two years from now, I will be able to make a fortune, because everything is now arranged and prepared.

By the twilight of 1845, the wheat king of California was also the master of 4,000 cattle, 1,500 mares, 200 tame horses and mules, 3,000 sheep, and many hogs on his snowless and virtually winterless ranges. The beasts needed almost no care other than a little shepherding by his Indian hands. He mused, "It is particularly a great assistance to us—one, indeed, which we could hardly dispense with—that we can hire the Indians as laborers very cheaply. They make slavery wholly unnecessary here and may be employed for all field and house work. In harvest, I have frequently employed at least 400 Indians."

Sutter had made an amazing recovery from the disaster of Cahuenga. But it was nothing in comparison with the success of the Sutter of legend. Increasingly, travelers were spreading over the world wild tales of the *Kaiser von Kalifornien*. Eliot Warburton's fancy was perhaps typical. In his 1846 book, titled

Hochelaga, or England in the New World, the English author wrote: "An adventurous German, a Captain Sutter, raised an army of five hundred Indians, drilled them with words of command in his own language, equipped them, besieged the Mexican governor in his capital of Monterey, and drove him out with shame."

CHAPTER XII

THE VISIONARY

THE long last act in the drama of Sutter's California career began on December 10, 1845, with the return of John C. Frémont to Sutter's Fort. Unfortunately, Sutter was away at the time, but his surrogate, John Bidwell, did his best to satisfy the Pathfinder's rather peremptory requests. Frémont wanted sixteen mules, six pack saddles, some flour and other foodstuffs. Besides, he wanted the use of Sutter's smithy to shoe all the mules. The zealous Bidwell tried to be as helpful as his employer would have been, but he had to tell the captain that there were no mules to be had, only horses. Also, he regretfully reported that there was no coal for the smith's forge. Frémont's manner did not improve with this news. He became even more reticent and spoke only to Kit Carson, and then in low tones which Bidwell could not catch and which he was obviously not meant to hear. As they rode off, one of Sutter's men heard Frémont remark to Carson that Sutter was obviously reluctant to help them.

After learning of Frémont's displeasure, Bidwell rode out to the American camp with Dr. William B. Gildea, Sutter's physician. Frémont did not deny the uncalled-for remark but, steering a course between hauteur and contempt, informed the young major-domo that he was an officer of the United States government and Sutter of the Mexican government, that there were difficulties between the two countries, and that he therefore understood the "unwillingness of Sutter to help him." He shrugged off Bidwell's explanation of the altered circumstances since 1844, when Sutter had had a herd of 100 of Peter Lassen's mules at the fort.

Bidwell did his best to mollify Frémont but he had little success, although he managed to round up fourteen mules for him, besides cattle and food. He also let him have Sam Neal, the smith, to shoe the animals. On the fourteenth, Frémont led his men south to join up with the main party, under Joe Walker.

Sutter did not return to the fort until the seventeenth. Frémont was long gone. There was nothing to be done to heal the breach. He was careful to report Frémont's coming to Vallejo, but he made the mistake of dating his letter December 10, when he did not even arrive back at the fort until a week later. This appeared to delay his report an unconscionable time. When he passed on Frémont's official excuse for being in California—to pass the winter in a temperate climate before going to Oregon— an angry Vallejo scribbled a note on the back of Sutter's letter and threw it across his desk to his secretary. It read, "Inform him it was received after twenty days' delay and charge him, in the quickest way possible, to send detailed information about the new immigrants, a thing which has always been done in similar circumstances, even in the case of small parties, and which he inopportunely failed to do when it was most necessary and, even, urgent." Actually, for all his pro-American sympathies, Sutter was much more prompt in reporting on Frémont to Vallejo than he was to his good friend, U.S. Consul Larkin. He did not write him until December 22. Unperturbed, Larkin simply thanked his unofficial aide and asked him to forward to Frémont his offers of assistance, both as consul and countryman.

By the beginning of 1846, a rumor was circulating in California that Sutter had sold New Helvetia to the Mexican government. Possibly, the story grew out of an information leak at Sonoma. Vallejo had written to President Bustamante of Mexico to point out the desirability of acquiring the bastion in order to close the door communicating with the United States. He admitted that the fort, cannon, and adobe buildings were not worth $100,000 but added "the security of the country is what is to be paid for, and that is priceless."

Sutter was surprised but hardly nonplussed. He wrote Vallejo's aide, Victor Prudón, on New Year's Day, 1846, "Do you think the government will buy it? I would like to be certain of that so that I might take the necessary measures. In case the government decides to make the purchase, do you believe it will be possible to obtain some part of the sum on account, sufficient to pay a part of my debts?" He was ready to sell, now—once the wheat was in. If not bound to the American cause enough to refuse offers, he was honest enough to feel himself obliged to pay off the Russian debt. "I could give possession of the establishment after the harvest. I believe the government will do well not to neglect this affair, for next autumn there will be very many emigrants from the United States. . . . A respectable government post here in this place will be very necessary." Again, Sutter was trying to assume an uncomfortable—if not impossible—posture of standing simultaneously on both sides of the fence. The protector of Americans was willing to sell his fort to the Mexicans if the price and timing of the offer were right.

Perhaps in hopes that Prudón would use his influence to persuade the government to buy the fort, Sutter advertised its future with information given him by Lansford Hastings and Frémont (via Bidwell). He told Prudón that many immigrants were expected, that two steamers were bound for California, a coastal trader and a Sacramento riverboat. He passed on the rumor that Dr. John McLoughlin of the Hudson's Bay Company planned to retire in California. "He will make matters move," promised Sutter, "he is a great protector of agriculture." He also predicted the arrival of a printing press by ship, claiming that he would soon be publishing a paper at New Helvetia, half in English and half in Spanish. Mentioning that even isolated Tahiti had a paper, *L'Oceanie Française,* he said, "Such progress is made throughout civilization, and here we are so much behind."

Sutter's foresight was keen. But he could not size up Frémont correctly, or guess the havoc the discovery of gold would wreak with his two mainstays—agriculture and immigration. Nor could he see that Mexico was not going to pay him $100,000 when it could assume and pay off his debt to the Russians—standing at $31,000 in 1845, after his wheat shipments—in exchange for the mortgage on New Helvetia. Sutter was entirely unaware of this stratagem, but it was never approved, in any case, for the Mexican War broke out and swallowed it up.

Sutter was mellowing as well as growing honest as prosperity continued to agree with him. But occasionally he lapsed into his old arrogance. Via Prudón, he brazenly attempted to bribe the officers of the Monterey customs house. He asked him if he could not get his farm machinery imported, duty free, if the men in the *aduana* were to receive from $4,000 to $6,000 from the American shippers. Sutter described them as "very rich, and from one of the first houses in New York and London." Such an arrangement would make the customs officials immensely popular in and around New Helvetia, he reminded Prudón. He then reported that his traders were going to set up warehouses on San Francisco Bay and on the Sacramento River, where they would sell goods on credit for wheat and salted salmon. Chided Sutter, "The other merchants who do business in this unhappy country want nothing but hides and tallow, the ruin of the country." He advised his friend to make use of the Vallejos. "If you know how to exploit them to good purpose, you can quickly become rich." Small wonder that Vallejo was exasperated by Sutter's high-handedness.

By 1845 his horizons were once again as boundless as his ego. He spoke of his conversations with Captain Bonnet, master of the *Lion.* The French troops in the Marquesas and Society islands, not counting the natives, consumed 650 *arrobas* of flour per day and their government would prefer Sutter's wheat if it could be obtained at the Chilean price of $4 the *quintal*. Concluded Sutter, "We could very well compete at that price if the cursed customs house ceased to exist. If this country derived anything from the customs house, one would not complain so much. But it is only good to provide for a lot of useless officers who devour the very marrow of the country. Once a newspaper is published, it will unseal the eyes of the blind. I trust that you may take a part, and an interest, in this affair of a press."

Before he closed out his communiqué to Prudón, he passed on word of Frémont's discovery of a practicable Sierra crossing. (On Christmas Day, Hastings had arrived at the fort to crow—"A road through the Stony Mountains 400 miles shorter than has ever been traveled!") This led Sutter to prophesy: "I can assure you that, in five years more, there will be a railroad from the United States to here. I can actually see it, for the Rocky Mountains are already beginning to be peopled. There are settlements where I saw nothing but deserts. . . . The mass of the immigrants come from the United States and increases the population to such an extent that one more mass will extend it even as far as the Pacific. A year or two more and no force will be able to stop the migration."

As the oaks and cottonwoods dropped their leaves into the eddies of the Sacramento River in 1845, relations between the United States and Mexico sagged to a new low. Sutter was aware of this deterioration, caused largely by the issue of annexation of Texas, and was not surprised by a September proclamation by Governor Pico. This edict, instigated by orders from Mexico City, called a halt to the admission of Americans to California unless they carried valid passports. Although Sutter took his official position seriously enough to go along with the governor, he was so pro-American by now that he opposed the policy in principle. He received the document on October 21, along with erroneous news of war between Mexico and the United States, and called

217

the settlers to a meeting. He read them the ordinance, discussed it with his audience, then adjourned his neighbors until a meeting which he scheduled for Monday, October 27.

There was no need to take violent action; he knew that the proclamation was a dead letter the moment it was issued. When he wrote Reading about it, he observed: "The *bando* which has been published here contains beautiful ordinances. I wonder if they will use force, as all foreigners I have seen since don't like to leave the country. . . . Here, the people hardly take notice of it. I think when it comes to the point that the United States should declare war, Mexico would be willing to comply with everything that the United States demands from them." Bidwell was more alarmed than Sutter, warning him of a rumor of 500 to 600 Mexican troops en route to California to put a stop to American immigration and to drive out the Yankees. "I think they are too late for that now," observed Sutter calmly, "because these newcomers are determined to fight. When all are here, we will hold a public meeting, principally to advise all of the families to remain and settle in the valley."

Still, Sutter was relieved when the government made no attempt to have him enforce the immigration ban. He became uneasy again, however, when he heard that a government delegation was at Sonoma on its way to New Helvetia to visit him. As early as May, he had picked up rumors that José Castro wanted to see him. Larkin advised the American Secretary of State that Castro undoubtedly wanted to determine how well Sutter had strengthened himself in his adobe stronghold. A gloomy Sutter wrote Reading that he was well aware of the Mexican government's bad intentions: "But," he vowed, "they shall not catch me in their snare. If they come on the other side of the *embarcadero,* I will let them know that they and their officers may come here, but that the soldiers and the other mob will have to remain on the other side. Perhaps they will be offended but I don't care. We are determined not to let them go into the fort. I will be on a sharp lookout and will inform you of everything that may happen."

Sutter expected Castro to make a wide swing from Sonoma to disarm American immigrants who had settled west of the fort. Ominous news reached him that the wives of two Americans had been put into jail and that several settlers had been ordered to report to Sonoma. All of them refused to comply and came to Sutter for advice and protection. "They told me," noted Sutter, "that the people on the other side [of the Sacramento] would be ready to fight. I wish they would leave us alone a year longer. But when they begin, we must drive them from the Sonoma side and take possession here. We will be on the defensive until succour comes from the Columbia and the United States." Once more, Sutter looked to the security of his fortress. He mustered a night guard of twelve whites, three of whom patroled the plain outside the walls. He kept a canoe ready for swift launching, to recall Reading's trappers, should he need reinforcements.

Just before his visitors arrived, Sutter advised Larkin: "Messrs. Castro and Alvarado, etc., are welcome here when they come not with soldiers. I hope they will be prudent enough to leave them at Sonoma because it would create bad feelings and mistrust amongst all the foreigners here and of the citizens as well. . . . We are very numerous, at present, and would suffer nothing which would not be right. Why did they make such a proclamation against peaceable immigrants? As if the whole country would be in danger."

It was a nervous and fearful Sutter who awaited the visitation. He considered all Mexican officialdom aligned against him and was afraid even to visit Yerba Buena since friends had convinced him that he would be seized. Should it prove necessary to meet Sitka's Russian representative at the bay, Sutter planned to stay aboard ship the whole time. He had been warned that guards, at the entrances to San Francisco Bay, were looking for him. Sutter's worrying drove him to rash thoughts, if not acts: "If only 1,000 more immigrants would have arrived! I think it would be just the proper time now to give them a blow, when troops are coming. I think we have to begin the row." He dispatched a strong, theatrical message to Larkin, largely on the plight of American immigrants, which ended: "If it would not be in your power, or in the power of a man-of-war, to protect them, *I will do it!* All are protected here and before I suffer an injustice done them, I die first!" But he betrayed his uneasiness on the very eve of Castro's arrival by complaining to Reading about how little support he found in his settlers. "I can assure you that I don't like, at all, the behaviour of many a foreigner. They are wavering and undecided. . . . I believe, really, that Castro has no good intentions. Leese had a hand in the affair. He wrote a letter, and told the bearer to tell me nothing of it. But the letter, written to the immigrants, was shown to everybody. It appears that they do blame me, that I allow the immigrants to come in the country, and I had received positive orders to prevent it. . . . Leese is coming with Castro to play his intrigues."

When the Mexicans arrived, they apologized profusely, if lamely, for not having announced their coming. It was sheer carelessness, they said. They need not have bothered. Sutter had been well aware of their every movement through his Indian scouts. He had expected them on the tenth, but it was not till the eleventh that they presented themselves to his Indian ferry-man across the Sacramento from his *embarcadero*. He sent Bidwell to greet them formally. Watching them approach over the riverine prairie, he ran up the eagle-and-serpent standard of Mexico, smartly, and gave the signal to his cannoneers to fire a crashing seven-gun salute.

At the main gate, Sutter welcomed General José Castro, Colonel Victor Prudón, Jacob P. Leese, and Andrés Castillero, a deputy to the Mexican congress who had come to California to make peace with Pico after Micheltorena's defeat—and to investigate Sutter's Fort. To his relief, Sutter found that his visitors came in peace. He quartered the officers in the main building of his compound but kept their escort of soldiers in his outbuildings.

Exactly what took place during the visit is not known. As the years rolled on, Sutter liked to suggest that Castro and Castillero begged him to sell New Helvetia to the Mexican government, in order to stop the influx of Americans. "They said, all the time, that I was holding the key to California." Even if they made an offer, it may not have been the $100,000 which Sutter later chose to recall as the sum mentioned in November 1845. Sutter called Bidwell, Reading and a clerk to a conference in his office. He asked their opinion of the transfer. They were of one mind in opposing the sale, no matter how princely the offer. Their worry over their fate, should their protector desert them, was reflected on their faces as they asked, "What shall we do? What will the settlers do if you abandon us to the Mexicans?"

Sutter always insisted in later years that his three associates made up his mind for him. He would not sell. He told the historian, Bancroft, thirty years later, "I was bound they should have protection. But for this, I should have accepted the offer." This was not quite true. He knew that his future was tied tightly to American settlement of California, no matter what flag might be flying over the country. But he was willing to sell his New Helvetia settlement—only not until the harvest was in and his debts paid in wheat. In the bitterness of later financial ruin, he forgot this and constantly lamented, "Often have I regretted that I did not accept. . . . For this sacrifice, I have been paid with nothing but ingratitude."

The image of Sutter as a father-protector of American immigrants was born early and widely believed. One of his early associates, William Swasey, laid the continued existence of New Helvetia as a refuge for Americans solely to Sutter's desire to protect Yankees. Out of an oversimplification of Sutter's motives grew a legend of his selflessness and self-sacrifice. A case in point might be Castro's command of November 11, issued at Sutter's Fort and probably at John Sutter's urging. By it, he commanded the Swiss to assign immigrants a place where they might work and maintain themselves, subject to final approval of their residence in California by him or someone else high in the government. This in effect relaxed the anti-immigration order of September. But Castro and Sutter were of one mind on this matter for widely differing reasons. The general wanted potential troublemakers concentrated in one spot, remote from most Mexican settlements. Sutter hungered for a large, trained work force to make his dream of agricultural plenty come true. He needed artisans to help run his establishment, and he needed neighboring American settlers as a convenient market.

Castro, of course, prefaced his edict with references to the onset of winter, the hospitable sentiments that animated all Californians, the sufferings of past parties of immigrants, etc., etc. This was sheer window dressing. But he did allow Sutter to issue passports to American artisans already in California. They could settle in Sonoma or San Juan Bautista as well as New Helvetia. Any American who arrived in the future, however, would have to wait for passports until Sutter could consult with the government. Castro ordered him to make frequent reports to Vallejo and himself on the number and place of origin of immigrants, their trades and skills. He also ordered Sutter to translate his decisions into English and to communicate them to the Americans at and around the fort. Finally, he commanded Sutter to use his political authority to inspire in the immigrants submission to the Mexican government and confidence in himself as commanding general.

The emissaries started homeward on November 12. As his battery boomed out a farewell salute, Sutter decided to escort his visitors as far as the Cosumnes River, some twenty miles distant. He took Bidwell and two or three of his Indian cowboys as an escort but carelessly neglected to tell anyone else of his plan. When he was only a mile on his way, he and Castro saw fifty men galloping toward them from the fort. "What is all that?" asked a worried Castro. "Oh," lied Sutter, as bewildered as his guest, "only some of my men who would have followed us sooner as an escort in your honor, had they been able to get their horses together in time." When his visitors left him to continue southward, Sutter asked his horsemen the real reason for their frantic pursuit, only to discover that they had feared treachery by Castro and, to prevent the kidnaping of Sutter and seizure of the fort, had formed up a large posse with which to rescue their *patrón*. "Neither Bidwell nor I had any such apprehensions," remarked Sutter. "We knew these people better than the others."

In truth, Sutter had been surprised and greatly pleased by the cordiality of his guests. He told Larkin that he thought that their visit would benefit everyone and that he was now on the best of terms with the authorities. To Suñol he said, "I think these gentlemen do not regret having visited this settlement. People talk a great deal but when we meet one another, things are quite different."

The evening after bidding Castro goodbye, Sutter was surprised by a return visit from Prudón. The colonel apologized for his unexpected reappearance but (according to Sutter) asked him to reconsider Castillero's offer to buy New Helvetia. As Sutter remembered, Prudón said, "Consider our offer. But we will do still better. I am authorized by General Castro to offer you for New Helvetia, in addition to the $100,000, all the lands and cattle belonging to the Mission San José." Prudón assured his old friend that he would be paid in full. He admitted that the government's coffers were yawning empty, but he guaranteed Sutter a large cash down payment and the balance from the lucrative customs house receipts. Again, Sutter claimed that he gave the matter considerable thought only to turn it down.

Sutter wrote to Reading, who was gradually replacing Bidwell as the loyal confidant he needed, psychologically as well as practically, to report that "All is right, now, and nobody will be disturbed. The visit will be to great advantage to me because the Commissioner of Mexico said that my war expenses must be paid and Bodega must be returned to me. He called this a fraudulent act of the government. I am, like before, military commander, with more power than before!" Finally, writing in confidence to

Reading, Sutter revealed that he had decided not to sell the fort, yet. "Castro and Castillero were very pleased with the establishment. They asked me if I would not sell it, for a very high price. I told them that I could not, on account of my engagements for wheat, etc. Castillero told me, after having seen all, that he conceived very well that I could hardly part with it."

Castro's visit was an interesting interlude. When it was over Sutter had to return to the many demands of a growing economy. His whimsically named launch, the *Lady Drinkwater,* and his fleet of canoes were always out on the water and his wagons and carts were busy hauling lumber and shingles to the fort from the Pine Woods up the American Fork. From the fort, they then transported wheat to the *embarcadero* to load on vessels lying in the Sacramento. As more and more Americans flocked into California, Sutter was called upon not only to issue them passports but to perform marriages, which he did, knowing full well that the Mexican government did not recognize civil marriages and although Larkin chided him about it.

No immigrant was ever turned away from the gates of Sutter's Fort. He welcomed them all, the good and the bad. To Reading he commented, "I don't know how all can live here. A good many wagons (82 or 83) are behind, so they say. If it is true or not, I don't know. I wish it were." But few of Sutter's neighbors matched his vision. Some resented the newcomers as potential rivals. Others among the established Yankees and foreigners feared another Graham affair. Sutter observed, "Some of our people are frightened to death. John Sinclair would not have an immigrant in his house and he thinks to go to the Columbia River next spring." Although it was a time of tension, Sutter wasted no time in worrying. He was too busy, putting 800 *fanegas* of seed wheat into the Sacramento Plain and making offers on American wagons to add to his fleet of five vehicles. "What an advantage they will be, to get the wheat from the fields," he enthused.

Sutter encouraged Larkin more than ever now to visit him at

the fort. Many Americans were arriving in distress and some were actually destitute. "The snow is on top of the mountains," Sutter warned him; "their animals are worn out; some of them have spent all of their property. . . . It is a pity to see them in such a situation as they are in, now." Larkin replied that he wanted to help his fellow Americans, but that he could not get to the Sacramento as yet. Instead, he sent Sutter an open letter which he asked him to distribute, in multiple copies, to the immigrants. Dated November 12, 1845, it invited the Americans to send a committee to see him in Monterey. With it he sent a note to congratulate Sutter for his efforts in behalf of the arriving Americans. "I am aware that you and Dr. Marsh have had much difference of opinion in many important points, yet both have the same intent in the all-engrossing subject of this country, *viz.* immigration."

Sutter took advantage of his improved relationship with Castro to issue a statement which was intended to put Sub-Prefect Francisco Guerrero of Yerba Buena in his place. It explained in no uncertain terms that New Helvetia was unique and not under Guerrero's jurisdiction: "This establishment, being a military post destined for the defense of the frontier, the reduction of the heathen, and vigilance over the immigrants who come by way of the Rocky Mountains, and not an organized town, there are no civil authorities nor can there be any, because the individuals who are actually here are generally composed of transient strangers without residence and subject to the military. Those who live in the establishment are artisans, also foreigners, and paid a salary by me. The rest live on the ranches which have been given them by the departmental government." Before signing off like a good Mexican officer with a flourishing "God and Liberty!" Sutter told Guerrero, point blank, that he took orders only from the commander-in-chief himself. "I am informing you," he continued, "to save you the annoyance of sending me more communications, in future, with reference to the administration of this point in my charge."

CHAPTER XIII

THE OPTIMIST

IN 1846, Sutter gave himself just two years to get himself clear of debt. This was in no sense wishful daydreaming. By continual, frenetic activity, he was at last closing in on his goal. He personally supervised his field hands now—even on Sundays—sowing his wheat acreage. He had twelve plows and six harrows at work at New Helvetia and four more plows and a harrow at Hock Farm. He was increasing his salmon fishery, putting the catch up in barrels to sell for $20 each, and planning his floating grist mill. In January and March his notes to Larkin brimmed over with optimism:

> We have the best prospects for a good and rich harvest. I am plowing and sowing every day. If I had only six plows more! The English iron is not good to make American plows. . . . If you could procure me some good iron of all dimensions, it would be not only a great service for me but for the whole Sacramento Valley. I could supply them all with plows, as I have the best kind of mechanics to make them. . . . In the seven winters which I have passed here, only two was so good as this. . . . 1,200 acres are sowed in wheat . . . 100 acres in barley, smooth and pointed.

Now I am sowing peas, potatoes, preparing for corn and cotton. Vegetables I will, likewise, have a great quantity. Onions at least for about $1,000. . . . The next fall will be a powerful immigration here. It is stated from 10 to 20,000, which I hardly can believe. I think if 2 or 3,000 would come, it would be a great many. It is good when I have plenty to eat for them. Therefore, I am building a floating mill in the American Fork to furnish plenty of flour.

Sutter was delighted to see California becoming civilized before his very eyes. When a Mrs. Allen Montgomery put on a quilting bee—unheard-of in California before this time—he held the fort, practically alone, giving all his men permission to attend the social event of the season, indeed, of the decade. His townsite on the Sacramento at the sheep and hog farm was being surveyed by Lansford Hastings and Bidwell. He had even chosen a name for the city which he saw there in his dreams— Montezuma. (Unfortunately, Lansford Hastings chose the same name for his own settlement, planned for Carquinez Straits, and Sutter had to settle for Sutterville.) Sutter could almost hear the rumble of carriage wheels through the busy streets of his metropolis. He wrote Reading at the trappers' camp that he was giving him one of the 200 lots being laid out, rambled on about his choice of the hilly site, where the river banks never overflowed, and told him of a small lake which he hoped to use in making adobe bricks. Hastings, he said, planned a big dwelling and storehouse there, and he rattled off the names of a host of others who were almost as enthusiastic over Sutterville as he was. Sutterville, *née* Montezuma, threatened to become the apple of Sutter's eye, taking over from Hock Farm.

On January 14, Sutter welcomed Yerba Buena's port captain, William S. Hinckley, and its U.S. Vice Consul, William Leidesdorff, to his fortress. Since both men were in uniform, Sutter donned his own before riding out with them to inspect the Leidesdorff grant on the American River, where a hired man was putting in wheat for his employer. Only a mile or so from the fort,

Sutter spied a camp. While he was still wondering who the strangers might be, a familiar-looking figure approached on horseback: Kit Carson.

"Where is Captain Frémont?" asked Sutter. "Over there," gestured the scout, "in his tent. He is tired and not yet up." Sutter learned from Carson that Frémont had arrived during the night. He asked the mountaineer to call his commander, and when Frémont appeared at the flap of his tent, Sutter introduced him to his guests and invited him to join them for supper at the fort. Frémont agreed, telling Sutter he would move his camp down the river to the fort during the day.

When Sutter returned to the fort, he saluted Frémont with a salvo from seven pieces of ordnance. He then treated him to a sumptuous dinner, which was as ineffective as his geniality in thawing Frémont's coldness. Puzzled, Sutter wondered, "Frémont acted strangely toward me, as if he were guilty of some crime. . . . I had always been friendly . . . and had assisted him in every way possible. When he was at the fort, the first time, Micheltorena had sent a military commission . . . to inquire what Frémont was doing at New Helvetia. I had expected the soldiers and had hurried Frémont off before they came. When they arrived, I told them that he had gone, already, and simply sent a colorless report to the government."

Throughout the Pathfinder's visit, Sutter failed to suspect what lay behind his barely veiled hostility. "It never occurred to me that Frémont was after the country for the United States." Perhaps the gullible Swiss swallowed Frémont's story that he was simply surveying a route from the States to the Pacific. (This was the reason he had given for his presence when Prefect Manuel Castro had demanded an explanation on January 29.) Doubtless, Frémont told Sutter exactly what he told the cousins Castro, that his men were not soldiers but hired hands, packers, hunters and the like, and that he intended to winter his party in the Central Valley until the weather might let him make his way to Oregon.

The story was soon garbled and he was said to be surveying the boundary between the United States and Mexico.*

Dubious as he was about just where Sutter's loyalty lay, Frémont nevertheless readily accepted his lavish hospitality. Sutter gave him supplies and provided him with passage to Yerba Buena. One of Frémont's fellow passengers on the schooner was the Bear Flag plotter, William Ide. The two men undoubtedly had an interesting conversation on the downriver run. When the *Sacramento* returned to Sutter's *embarcadero* at the end of January, it brought rumors of war between the United States and Mexico. This explained Frémont's rudeness to Sutter, but did not excuse it. There was also a story current that a Mexican expeditionary force was being mounted at Mazatlán to sail for California. Two weeks later, Sutter noted in his diary that he felt California would soon be delivered up to the United States. As on so many occasions, he was a good seer.

Part of Frémont's hostility toward him was justified by Sutter's political ambivalence. He was still misconstruing his role of a neutral, precariously fence-straddling. This was now patently impossible, with a confrontation in California between the United States and Mexico only weeks away at best. Sutter was increasingly disillusioned with the American immigrants who flocked to his fort. He had placed great hope and confidence in them as sturdy ranchers and farmers who would transform the Sacramento Valley into an agricultural paradise. Instead, they turned out to be largely arrogant riff-raff. Incredibly, as early as January 1846, they were threatening his control of his fort, causing Sutter to slip back briefly into a pro-Mexican posture, whether he really meant it or not. Openly, he expressed his delight at the news of a Mexican army coming to California. Mexican troops might mean order, at least, and a chance for him to enjoy the kind of stability to which he had grown accustomed during Micheltorena's governorship. He wrote Marsh, "Here, no doubt, I will get a good

* In his later court-martial, Frémont claimed that he intended to explore south from Sutter's Fort to the Gila River.

supply of them and I am very glad of it, as some of the foreigners in the valley are committing depradations and I have no force to prevent them." While he did not tell Marsh why he could not use his trappers and Indian grenadiers, he was considerably more candid in his note to Reading. He revealed his theory that Great Britain was behind the movement of Mexican troops. Although he felt that the soldiers would not be able to handle the Americans, should as many as 3,000 to 5,000 immigrants arrive, he said, "If these troops come here under my command, it is well enough. . . . If I am in favor, it will be good for the whole valley." His mind drifted back to the good old days: "So it would have been if we had gained the day in the last revolution. But the miserable jealousy of Marsh and Gantt ruined the whole. They could not bear that I would earn a little honor and power, which would have been entirely to the benefit of the foreigners. For one reason, I am very happy that troops are coming here, because the laws and my authority are very little respected here. A respectable garrison here will make a great alteration."

Events in March revealed how powerless Sutter had become, even in his own fortress. During the previous month, there were several Indian runaways, and one of his servants broke into the stores to steal liquor. But the crisis came when three of his Indians reported that their blankets had been stolen, in the very compound of the fort. Recalled Sutter, "The boys told me that *Ingleses* must have done it." When Sutter established that the thieves were Granville P. Swift and Franklin Sears, the latter a braggart and notorious Indian-killer, he confronted and tried to lecture them. To his alarm, they insulted him, threatening to seize and burn the fort. With Bidwell away at the moment, Sutter had no one around upon whom he could really depend, aside from a clerk or two. Faced by the lawless Americans, Sutter was plain scared. He confessed later, "I was waiting every moment for a ball or a knife. . . . We had not one man who spoke in our favor and the whole mob assembled before the house." Sutter had forgotten that his New Helvetia had become an American community, and

231

he had dared to take the side of Indians against white men. Bidwell joined him, but had to hide with Sutter and a few loyal employees in his room throughout the night of March 5, 1846, while the rabble took over the fort. Sutter was virtually a prisoner. Swift stabbed an Indian, and one of his confederates threatened to cut Sutter's belly open. Bidwell managed to pacify the troublemakers with a plug of fine Cavendish tobacco. Deeply humiliated, Sutter made no mention of the affair in his logbook. The only full statement for March 5 had to do with the hatter; the subsequent entry was broken off, thus: "Sent *baquero* . . ." and never completed. The day after the night of terror, he wrote in his diary, "Nothing of importance occurred." But, thoroughly discouraged, he wrote to his confidant, Reading: "What a pity to be under the necessity to be governed by the rabble. . . . If better people are not coming with the next immigration, it would be better to leave the country entirely."

While Sutter's empire tottered, Frémont was bullying his way through the San Joaquin Valley and into the Coast Range, a settled area where he was decidedly unwelcome. His action forced Castro's hand—which may have been Frémont's intention. On the very day that Swift and his cronies bullied and intimidated Sutter, José Castro addressed a brusque note to Frémont, ordering him to retire from California. If Frémont would not do so, Castro promised to throw him out. When the Pathfinder made no move to comply, Castro issued a call to arms on March 8. He asked his fellow citizens to place themselves under his orders to cure what he called "the ulcer of Frémont's presence." He accused the American followers of committing "depradations and scandalous skirmishes." The very same day, Manuel Castro suggested to Larkin that he advise Frémont to leave. Otherwise, he would come to an unfortunate end. The consul's reaction was to warn Frémont that Castro had 100 men in the field and perhaps an equal number coming to join him. But he did not advise him to withdraw. Frémont forted up on the top of Gabilán Peak. When Larkin's courier returned, he told the consul that 2,000 of his countrymen could not dislodge the Americans from the peak over which floated the Stars and Stripes. But Frémont was bluffing. He did not want a fight—yet. He abandoned his position and slipped away to the north.

It was on March 14, 1846, the very day on which President Polk declared war on Mexico, that Sutter learned of the Gabilán Peak affair from Marsh. He was sure that Frémont in his "growling" retreat would fall back on the fort. Sure enough, the Americans set up camp, a week later, directly across the American from the fortress. Sutter recognized that Frémont not only had two moats—the Sacramento and the American rivers—between himself and any pursuit but also had taken the precaution of keeping the American River between his camp and New Helvetia. Frémont need not have worried. Sutter's peculiar, partisan neutrality was in full flower. He had learned his lesson well in the Micheltorena debacle. He was playing a game of wait-and-see while betting on the Americans. Sutter would take no part in any *coup d'état,* even though he agreed with John Coffin Jones that the government of California was on the verge of collapsing from within.

During this nervous period, many men expected Sutter to declare himself. But he was resolved to stand pat. Unaware, however, that power in California was shifting from Sutter to Frémont, many agreed with Waddy Thompson, former U.S. minister to Mexico: "California is literally a waif and belongs to the first occupant. . . . Captain Sutter is the real sovereign of the country, if anyone is. I have no doubt his force would be more than a match for any Mexican force which will ever be sent against him."

Frémont's explanation of his retreat was glib. He told Sutter that he had waited for Castro on the peak for three days but, since he had not come to California to make war, he had then withdrawn. Sutter found Frémont less confident than before. In an unguarded moment, he complained that not a single immigrant had volunteered as a reinforcement for his company, although he

233

had made it known that he needed men, supposedly to protect the U.S. government horses and other federal property. Of one thing Sutter was certain: after Cahuenga, *he* was not going to volunteer to anyone for anything. This time he sat tight, and watched Frémont put farther distance between himself and Castro.

A minor difference between Sutter and Frémont was eventually to widen into a complete break. Camped at Peter Lassen's ranch on April 11–14, Frémont bought stolen horses from the Indians. This infuriated Sutter, who was trying hard to eradicate horse thieving in California and was having considerable success in his campaign. "I wrote him," recalled Sutter, "demanding that he should leave the stolen horses and not drive away property belonging to others. He made no reply to my letter. I was an officer of the government at the time, and a magistrate, and I deemed it my duty to enter the protest. This act Frémont never forgave me." How right Sutter was! The haughty Frémont, in his days of glory in California, treated Sutter abominably. When Sutter came all the way over to the side of the United States, throwing open the gates of his fort to Frémont, he expected appreciation. He got none. When he asked Kit Carson why his commander was so unfriendly to him, the scout told Sutter, "Remember that letter."

With Frémont gone to the north, events settled down to the usual routine at New Helvetia. Sutter was busy securing fruit trees from Father José Real and 2,000 grapevines from Sonoma. He joined more couples in unholy wedlock, over Larkin's (mild) protests that such civil marriages were not recognized in Catholic California, and he approved the ditch which two of his men planned to dig around his pasture for irrigation. He had again to discipline Daylor, the cook, fining him for assault on a man named Hess. But, once more, the shakiness of his once-autocratic rule was demonstrated to Sutter. Daylor asked for and was granted a jury trial. To Sutter's consternation, he also got a reversal from the veniremen and a $35 fine levied against Hess. On April 13, to Sutter's immense relief, Reading brought in the trappers from

Camp Hannishaw. They had been out since October 3, 1845, and without them Sutter's power had waned drastically. Sutter still had faith in California, but he did not like the drift of events. In contrast to the militancy of some immigrants, others were showing the white feather and clearing out for Oregon before the political storm lowering on the horizon should break.

Sutter had one major success that spring of 1846. He persuaded two of the principal chiefs of the Horsethief Indians to submit themselves to his authority, with all their warriors. More than that, they promised to support him against the other Sierra tribes of horse stealers. Sutter exulted, "I hope to put an end to the robberies which are being committed daily on the families of the San Joaquin!" He granted the two chiefs *cartas de seguridad* (passports vouching for their good conduct) and reported the good news to the government. Despite this temporary elation, Sutter was so acutely aware of the precariousness of his position that he considered, for the one time in his career, asking Vallejo for help. As he told Marsh, "I must have assistance. It cannot be expected that I do everything on my own expense. I have already expended many thousands of dollars about Indian affairs and have received not even thanks." He did not mention the fringe benefits of his Indian campaigns—children to be distributed as serfs, virtual slaves. When he could not deliver a promised servant to a friend in April he assured him, "But if I can get some when I make the campaign against the Horsethieves, I shall not forget you."

On April 28, 1846, a mysterious visitor was Sutter's guest at the fort—a Mr. Gillespie who claimed to be traveling for his health. He did not for a minute fool his host. Gillespie's name struck a chord in Sutter's memory, and he recalled him as an officer aboard the U.S.S. *Brandywine* at Honolulu. Worse for his visitor's disguise, Sutter's clerk knew him by sight, having seen him many times, as U.S. Marine Lt. Archibald Gillespie, around the Washington Navy Yard. Although, when confronted, Gillespie admitted to Sutter that he was an officer, he still insisted that he was in California only to deliver some family letters to Frémont. Sutter was too polite to call any of his guests a liar, but he wrote to Leidesdorff in regard to Gillespie's visit. "I suppose it is of more importance. Without this, Mr. Gillespie would not go so far."

Sutter dutifully reported Gillespie's arrival to Castro. The reason for Sutter's zeal and sense of duty was obvious. Time—in which to sell his fort—was running out. In his communiqué about the mysterious Gillespie, he reminded Castro of the potential value of his fortress to the Mexican government. "I recommend you to station a respectable garrison at this post before the arrival of immigrants from the United States, which will be about the middle of September. According to reports, they may number some thousands, though not ten thousand as has been said. Believing that the government will buy my establishment, I shall put everything in the best order. I am putting a new story on the large new building, which you have seen, and will make it ready as soon as possible, containing quarters for two or three hundred soldiers, with sufficient parade ground within the fort for the troops."

If Sutter was sincere, he was clutching at a straw as he saw his empire on the point of crumbling. On the other hand, he may very well have been dissembling. In either case, he still tried to maintain his peculiar neutrality. While he made such a point of doing his duty to the Mexican government, he fed and rested Gillespie and provided him with guides to Lassen's place. Sutter even loaned Gillespie his pet mule. (Since he had paid $300 for the gentle animal, his subsequent anger was justified—"He returned it windbroken, and that was the only profit that I got out of this affair.") Gillespie, who found Frémont in time to join him in a scrape with raiding Klamaths, passed on confidential orders to him—orders that remain unknown to this day. But whatever their substance, they made Frémont reverse his route of march and he led his expeditionaries slowly southward, camping finally at Sutter's Buttes. Frémont's explanation for his return to the

Sutter's Fort area was that he had found the Siskiyous blocked by snow.

Sutter's services to Frémont and Gillespie won him no friends among the troublemakers who now hung about the fort. Friends warned him that two of the Americans had bad intentions toward him. Even his Indians turned ugly. When he tried to send ten of them to Leidesdorff to make adobes, they refused to go to Yerba Buena. Others would not work even at New Helvetia. When Sutter asked one of the Americans to pay a $200 debt, the fellow cleared out instead. A rifle was stolen (an act unheard of only a year or two before) and, worse, the crowd of Americans refused to give Sutter the slightest help in capturing the thief. Even when the rifle's owner offered two men $8 each to track him down, they declined. Sutter saw his power draining away like sand in an hourglass. But he was strangely benumbed, paralyzed. He could only lament to Leidesdorff: "Formerly, it was better. Under Micheltorena, the people were very obedient and turned out if I did request them, but not now. . . . Everybody says now there is no law in the country. . . . I wish the government would assist me. We are much exposed, at present. A good many rascals feel themselves very independent. I shall write to Señor Castro about this affair." So alienated was Sutter from the American cause by the action of the roughnecks at New Helvetia that he was once again flirting with Mexican authority.

He was even more depressed when he wrote Dr. Marsh:

It looks, everywhere, very gloomy and I can assure you that, if I could, I would leave the country. If the government would purchase the establishment, and pay in gold and silver, I would sell it, pay all my debts, and go somewhere else. I am, indeed, very tired and wearied because a great many foreigners behave very bad. Your property is no more safe like it was 6 months ago. No more obedience to the laws.They march with their feet on Authority. Lately, by defending my rights and property, three, at once, fell over me, right enraged, touched me and I was, every minute, waiting for a merciful knife or a ball. When, with the next immigration, we get no better people, I don't know what to do. Always, I kept up my good spirits, but now I am entirely discouraged.

Sutter had banked on American immigration. It was his secret weapon, the factor that would guarantee his agricultural empire. Now he felt betrayed. Yet characteristically he was soon in good spirits again at the receipt of a letter from Switzerland, bearing the happy news that his eldest son was coming to the fort to join him. John August Sutter, Jr., was due to arrive in about six months' time. Still the *poseur,* Sutter bragged of his son's fluency in several languages, his counting-house experience, his sister's education, and of his younger brothers, one in a military academy and the other in a "celebrated agricultural institute." Sutter planned to shift some of the heavy responsibilities, which now staggered him, to young August's shoulders as his chief clerk. He would keep the rest of the family in Switzerland until the younger children finished their education.

The heartening news from Switzerland returned Sutter to his role of dedicated gentleman farmer. He wrote Reading in May, in great delight, "God the Almighty did send us a most splendid rain. . . . During the whole night, I could not sleep at all, so much pleasure it was for me to hear it rain. How beautiful looks, now, the wheat field south of the fort."

But the rain did not improve the field of politics south of the fort. Francisco Guerrero, Sub-Prefect in Yerba Buena, signed an order forbidding the purchase of land by foreigners and ordering them to leave the territory. If they did not leave, he threatened to expel them. Sutter noted that Guerrero had left himself an out: he would expel them—whenever the country found it expedient. The truth was that Guerrero had even less force to call upon than Sutter. The settlers paid little or no attention to the order. But Sutter misgauged its effect on hotheads like Granville Swift and Ezekiel Merritt. It alone was not aggravation enough to cause another Isaac Graham affair, but it was one of several final, decisive catalysts to direct action. The American malcontents prepared to counteract and even to anticipate punitive measures by either of the Castros or by Guerrero.

But first Sutter, unwittingly, had his role to play in the crisis, bringing to bear one more ounce of pressure on the men who would soon call themselves Bear Flaggers. On May 30, he told Gillespie that he was convinced that not only was Castro planning to attack Frémont but that he had turned on New Helvetia. According to Sutter's informants, probably friendly Indians, the general was inciting the Indians to revolt and to burn the nearly dried wheat standing in the Sacramento Valley fields. For his own part, Gillespie reported to Sutter that he found the Indian *rancherías* strangely deserted and told stories of Indian servants of the whites killed by warriors. Soon, Frémont's aide, Edward Kern, contributed a rumor that the wheat fields were due to be fired to keep food supplies from the American immigrants expected by fall. Finally, an overt act of Castro's shoved Sutter rudely off his cherished fence and right into the Americans' camp, although they were far from ready to welcome or trust him. Someone in Castro's following presented a fine new rifle to an Indian chief, Eusebio—for the express purpose of assassinating Sutter. Whether or not he believed the wild new tale that Castro was also behind the Klamaths' attack on Frémont, Sutter was convinced of Castro's part in the Eusebio plot. "I am positively sure that General Castro has excited the Indians to revolt and join the Californians in exterminating the settlers."

The next act of the unfolding drama involved a group of Mokelumne Indians. Well dressed and well armed, they came to the fort one day and were soon deep in mysterious conversations with Sutter's Indians. That night, a group of them slipped into Sutter's corral to drive away his horses. One of the guards detected them and gave the alarm. Sutter himself led six armed men in an immediate pursuit, but the rustlers fled to safety in the woods. Sutter stated flatly, "The Mokelumne Indians were engaged by Castro to revolutionize all the Indians against me, to

massacre the farmers, and to burn the houses and wheat fields."
He repaired immediately to his old Indian strategy of hitting war
parties hard and fast, before they could strike at him, and on
June 3, 1846, Sutter led a force out of the gates of the fort, with
Reading his second in command.

Sutter's luck was really beginning to desert him now. During
the crossing of the Mokelumne River, one of his rafts capsized.
No one was killed, but Reading and another man barely escaped
drowning. Lost in the river were precious rifles, pistols and much
ammunition, besides the clothes of twenty-four of his men. Sutter
left them behind and hurried on with his diminished company
toward the Calaveras River. Long afterward, he gave a brief account of the disappointing campaign:

> At sunrise, we took a little rest and dispatched a reconnoitering
> party. Suddenly, a dog appeared at our camp, which led us to
> believe that the enemy could not be very far away. A little later,
> a messenger came galloping with the news that the advance guard
> was engaged with the enemy. We immediately rushed to the aid
> of our men, some of whom had already been wounded, and were
> unable to continue the fight. Upon our arrival, the enemy retired
> and fled to a large cellar-like hole in the bank of the Calaveras.
> Protected by brush and trees, they continued shooting their
> arrows at us, although we had them blockaded and killed a good
> many of them. When, however, our ammunition gave out, we
> thought it prudent to leave the scene slowly, making the Indians
> believe we intended to camp, but as soon as we were out of their
> sight, we started on a forced march, crossed the Mokelumne and
> reached the fort on June 7.

Although the campaign had been inconclusive, Sutter did not
forget his one-time ally who had sold himself to Castro for a rifle.
He put a price on Eusebio's head. Chief Pollo collected the
renegade's scalp eventually, and delivered it to Sutter, who paid
him his share of the $100 reward and then, in businesslike fash-
ion, dunned five of his associates, who together contributed the
remaining $75. By August, Sutter could write to Leidesdorff,

"The Mokelumnes are all now at Amador's. So soon as the war is over, I shall get them punished."

But August seemed a long way off on June 7, when Sutter returned to the fort. He had no time to rest up. The very day after his arrival, Lt. Francisco Arce rode up with 6 or 8 soldiers and 150 government horses. He was driving them from Sonoma to Santa Clara via Sutter's ferry. Arce was an old friend who had once commented to Sutter, "California is like a pretty girl; everybody wants her." Among those lusting for California were some of the hard cases who were hanging about the fort. They now gravitated to Frémont, secured his secret blessing, and decided to prevent Castro's mounting a force of cavalry with which he could carry out his threats of expulsion. On the tenth, Sutter noted in his diary, "This morning a party of Americans took from Arce and his party all their horses." The Bear Flag Revolt had begun.

CHAPTER XIV

THE PATRIOT

FORCES that would dramatically affect Sutter's destiny were at work in the early summer of 1846, although far away from New Helvetia. James K. Polk, the Tennessean who symbolized the spirit of aggressive "manifest destiny," had been elected President of the United States largely on the strength of his pledge to annex Texas. He did just that—over Mexico's strong protests—in March 1845. But an invisible plank in his political platform was his plan to add California to the Union, too, and he quickly set to work to realize his dream of empire. Polk made efficient use of the services of Consul Thomas O. Larkin as a secret agent, hoping to persuade the native Californians—whose ties to Mexico were never strong—to join the Union voluntarily. Progress toward this end was being made, but it was frustrated by the bullying moves of Frémont and the adventurers who would shortly be calling themselves the Bear Flag Republicans. The Bear Flaggers intended to emulate Texas by declaring an independent California.

When a cavalry clash on the Texas-Mexico border led to a declaration of war by Congress, on May 13, 1846, Commander-in-Chief Polk made sure that California was not left out of his military's plans for conquest. He sent General Stephen W. Kearny overland from Fort Leavenworth to California, to back up the Pacific Fleet of Commodore John D. Sloat, who now had orders to seize California's seaports.

But before either Kearny or Sloat could take effective action, the Bear Flaggers made their play.

Zeke Merritt—except for his stuttering, a fair copy of Isaac Graham—ignited the Bear Flag Revolt (originally called the Popular Movement), on June 10, 1846, by seizing the government's horses on the Cosumnes River, not far from Sutter's Fort. Merritt's force was composed of only seven men, including the enormous Robert Semple (*Oso Bueno,* or Good Bear) and the knife-wielder who had earlier terrorized Sutter, Granville Swift. Merritt allowed Lt. Francisco Arce to keep his sword and, when he released him and his companions, asked him to tell Castro to come and get his horses—if he dared. The raiders, still under Merritt's command, then descended upon Sonoma. There, on the fourteenth, they captured Gen. Mariano Vallejo, his brother Salvador, Col. Victor Prudón, and the general's brother-in-law, Jacob P. Leese. Merritt then escorted the prisoners to Sutter's Fort, leaving William B. Ide in command at Sonoma. One of the garrison, William L. Todd, kin of Abraham Lincoln's wife, whiled away the hot hours in the plaza by creating a flag based on Lt. Henry L. Ford's design. The banner of what would be a brief, comic-opera fatherland, the California Republic, bore a single star and a grizzly bear, the latter symbolizing strength and courage. Unfortunately, Todd's artistic ability fell rather disastrously short of his target, and his symbol appeared (especially to the disdainful Mexicans) more porcine than ursine.

Sutter learned of Sonoma's fall when Merritt brought in his prisoners, expecting the Swiss to be his turnkey. Frémont had, meanwhile, moved his force (ostensibly independent of the Bear Flaggers) to New Helvetia. He was now as hostile to his host as he was doting to his Bear Flaggers. Sutter was not to be forgiven his protest over Frémont's buying stolen horses. Nor did he now appreciate Sutter's denunciation of the seizure of Arce's herd. He may even have learned the contents of a too-outspoken letter which Sutter wrote Prudón after some of his horses, and Cordua's, were stolen by Americans. "It is necessary to make prisoners of the principal ones. I hope Captain Frémont will assist me with these people, for he has the power to arrest his own compatriots. If this is allowed to pass, it will be very bad in the future. In case Mons. Frémont does not wish to assist in the arrest of some of the worst of his countrymen, I will attempt to do it alone and, if my forces are not sufficient, I will write to Mons. Vallejo for aid." But, during the brief twilight of Mexican power, Frémont made no attempt to challenge Sutter's authority. Perhaps the farcical outcome of Thomas ap Catesby Jones's precipitous move in 1842 inhibited him. In any case, Frémont did not yet consider it the moment for overt action, and he only told Sutter that, if he did not like what the Americans were doing, he could cross the San Joaquin River and join the Mexicans.

It was Frémont, really, not Merritt who turned the Sonoma prisoners over to Sutter; but he was swiftly disenchanted by Sutter as warden. He refused to mount a guard over them, shared meals with them in his quarters, and enjoyed their company on long evening strolls. From Leidesdorff, he even ordered a demijohn of brandy, some sugar and tumblers for them. The extra barrel of brandy, ordered at about the same time, was doubtless for his own consumption. As Sutter's troubles proliferated, he slipped into a continual craving for strong spirits. Now bald fraternization made his role of pro-American "neutral" an absurdity. In rendering the prisoners' imprisonment as painless as possible, Sutter risked—and took—Frémont's wrath. It was a courageous act by a man not overendowed with that sort of grit. On the other hand, he cooperated completely with the American officer in defense matters, and sent Bidwell to the Cosumnes to get his Indian allies to warn him of any approach of the 200 to

300 men rumored to be on the march toward Sutter's Fort under Castro's command.

When Frémont finally exploded and confronted Sutter, he demanded, "Don't you know how to treat prisoners of war?" Sutter replied, "Indeed, I do, Captain Frémont; I have been a prisoner, myself. Take charge of these men, yourself. I don't want to have anything further to do with them." Frémont then asked him how trustworthy his clerk might be, as warden/jailer. "Mr. Loker is a gentleman," answered Sutter. "You can trust him." But Loker did not like the job and shortly joined the volunteers forming up Frémont's California Battalion, which was growing out of the Bear Flaggers plus many of Sutter's trappers and other locals. Frémont then turned the prisoners over to John Bidwell. But Bidwell was equally lenient, ignoring Frémont's orders that no fraternization be allowed, that a close guard be kept over them, and that the few letters allowed them be censored. Instead, Bidwell gave Prudón English lessons in exchange for tips on how to improve his Spanish. Frémont was aghast and his disciple, Lt. Edward Kern, artist on his expedition, protested Bidwell's friendly relations with the prisoners. It was not long before Kern, backed by Frémont, was claiming all responsibility for the captives. Bidwell gave up the unequal fight, left the prisoners in Kern's hands, and joined the California Battalion's nucleus, although he detested many of the Bear Flaggers and other rootless vagabonds, looking for nothing more than a fast *peso*.

Frémont then formally turned custody of all prisoners over to Kern. Sutter was warned that Frémont intended to arrest him if he continued his visits to the prisoners, whom Frémont's guards referred to as "the damned greasers." Sutter turned cautious and did not again visit them until the Stars and Stripes waved over New Helvetia. One of Sutter's employees heard that Frémont intended to hang the Swiss should a single prisoner escape, and U.S. Navy Lt. Joseph Warren Revere (a descendant of Paul Revere), visiting the fort, warned Sutter of threats by the guards to shoot him—for the crime of compassion for the unfortunate

Vallejo and his comrades. But a number of men like Bidwell, Charles (Philosopher) Pickett and even Ned Kern himself, later, took courage from Sutter's example. They sympathized with Vallejo's plight. Kern paid little attention to Frémont's orders to throw into jail, in irons, anyone—Sutter included—who refused to obey his orders and to shoot anyone who might endanger the security of what he now termed Fort Sacramento. In fact, Kern treated Vallejo so well that the general, once he was freed sent the twenty-three-year-old lieutenant a present of books and other articles.

For years, Sutter insisted that he was never replaced in command of the fort. He stubbornly denied the facts documented by dispatches, rosters and payrolls. His humiliation rankled. However, at the time, he admitted his true situation to Leidesdorff: "I can assure you it is not very pleasant to have another as commander in his own house and establishment." He sought to save face by adding, "I accepted this in the hope that when Mr. Kern [shall] have to join Captain Frémont again, I shall be his successor." Sutter made the best of a bad situation and, after a time, became a warm friend to Kern. He invited the lieutenant to take his meals with him in his quarters, where his fine china and silver contrasted elegantly with the rough deal table and benches. He tried to fatten up the tubercular Kern with rich soups, roasts, cheeses, onions, butter and melons. But the lieutenant was not only plagued by the fort's fleas and by attacks of black fever, he was also an epileptic. At first, it was not always easy for Sutter to admire the amateur soldier. For one thing, Kern despised all Indians, including Sutter's. For another, he sneered at Sutter's fifty-man force—Kanakas, Indians, Mexican *vaqueros* and runaway sailors—which he took over, vowing, "I would not march through Coventry with them."

Sutter's compassion won out over his jealousy and humbled pride. He felt genuinely sorry for the young man, wracked by chills and fever. Too, he was amused by Kern's clumsy infatuation with the wife of his blacksmith. And he was particularly

247

delighted by the low opinion which Kern shared with him of the Bear Flaggers. Sutter did not enjoy having an upstart officer order him to keep detailed records of the garrison, but he was grateful for the pay Kern gave his white soldiers, ten of them, and the $4-a-month clothing allowance he gave Sutter's Indian troopers, plus a little petty cash. The longer Sutter was confined in the fort with Kern, the better he liked him. In 1852, when he looked back, it was to good old days and he wrote Kern, "How many hearty laughs we had and enjoyed ourselves in our poor old times."

Even while Sutter was still in nominal command of Fort Sacramento, Frémont was ranging the countryside in an undeclared war of maneuver. There was not a single battle, for the Pathfinder had not yet received word of the outbreak of war between the United States and Mexico. But the *opéra-bouffe* war turned cruelly real with the torture and murder of two Bear Flaggers, Thomas Cowie and William Fowler, near Santa Rosa. Lt. Henry Ford, like Merritt a veteran of Sutter's Micheltorena War legion, struck back savagely, thrashing Joaquín de la Torre's force at Rancho Olompali, near San Rafael, on June 24. But real retribution came from Frémont and Kit Carson. By their orders, peaceful old José Berryessa and the DeHaro twins, Ramón and Francisco, were shot to death near San Rafael. It was cold-blooded murder, revenge for the earlier atrocity. De la Torre then led Frémont on a wild-guerrilla chase by feinting at Sonoma. While the Pathfinder rushed there with his expeditionaries, plus some of Sutter's trappers, de la Torre slipped away to Santa Clara to join forces with José Castro. Frémont woke up at last, and crossed the Golden Gate (which he named) from Sausalito to the *presidio* of San Francisco. There, he put the fort's ancient guns out of commission by driving rat-tailed files into the touch-holes. His strategy was more political than military; he wanted to bag more prisoners—hostages—to jail at Sutter's Fort. But his chief prey, William S. Hinckley, *alcalde* of Yerba Buena, eluded him (by dying a few days before he arrived), so he had to arrest a substitute, Harbormaster Robert T. Ridley. The latter, like Hinckley, was one of Sutter's old associates, and thus in Frémont's eyes more Mexican than the Mexicans themselves. He sent Ridley under guard to Fort Sacramento to join the Sonomans along with three other Mexican-Californians caught up in his sweep.

Although he detested the worst element among the Bear Flaggers—bullies who had even stolen the blankets of his Indian boys—Sutter again demonstrated his characteristic ambivalence. He wrote Leidesdorff, near the end of June, that he counted on 200 Oregonians dropping down to serve under the grizzly standard after news of the California Republic should reach the Northwest via the Hudson's Bay ship. And when seven Oregon homesteaders appeared, Sutter was delighted to recruit them for "our forces." Yet, he would write of Merritt and his gang, "The Bear Flag was raised at Sonoma by a band of robbers under Frémont's command."

On July 4, 1846, Frémont abandoned circumspection and took a bold step. He gave an Independence Day speech at Sonoma which led Bidwell to write a declaration of independence for the Bear Flag Republic, now presided over by William B. Ide in place of Merritt. At the same time, Frémont began to form an army of battalion strength from the Flaggers and other immigrants. Sutter wanted no part of the Bear Flag mob. To him, they were little better than horse thieves. He determined to bide his time until the United States flag would again ride the wind above his bastions. His stake in California's future was too great to trust it to the rabble.

As soon as Sutter received word of John D. Sloat's July 7, 1846, seizure of Monterey and annexation of California, he ran up the twenty-seven-star flag of the Union which the commander at Sonoma had sent him. He never forgot that great day: "A long time before daybreak, I had the whole fort alarmed and my guns ready. When the Star Spangled Banner slowly rose on the flag-staff, the cannon began to fire and continued until nearly all

249

the windows were broken. Some of the people around the fort made long faces, because they thought that they would have had a better chance to rob and to plunder if we had remained under the Bear Flag. The Sonoma prisoners, not knowing what was going on, were greatly surprised. I went to them and said: 'Now, gentlemen, we are under the protection of this great flag, and we shall henceforth not be afraid to talk to one another.' Frémont has acted like a tyrant." (Thirty years later, recalling the day, he claimed, "Had Sloat been a day later, California would, undoubtedly, in my opinion, be English today.") Shortly afterward, a lieutenant on the *Portsmouth* sent him a piece of muslin to fashion into a twenty-eighth star, for Texas, to bring his Stars and Stripes up to date.

But Sutter had prolonged his wait-and-see neutrality too long. On the twelfth of the month, the very day after Sutter dropped the crude Bear Flag and hoisted the Stars and Stripes, Frémont shoved him rudely aside and gave command of Sutter's Fort to his surrogate, Ned Kern, who further humiliated Sutter by officially renaming his command Fort Sacramento.

On July 12, answering Sloat's call for aid, Frémont hurried south with his California Battalion and a cannon supplied him by Sutter. The initial conquest of southern California would be overturned; Gillespie's garrison would be driven from Los Angeles; General Kearny would be defeated at San Pascual before victory would come to American arms. But when it finally arrived, on January 13, 1847, Frémont was there to receive the capitulation of the Mexican-Californians, now led by Andrés Pico. Ironically, their surrender took place at the battlefield site where Sutter had been defeated and captured almost two years before—Cahuenga.

With Frémont gone, tension relaxed at Sutter's Fort. About two weeks after his departure, Commodore Stockton ordered Vallejo and the others to be set free on their paroles of honor not to take up arms against the United States. Sutter had meanwhile made their "Prison of the Sacramento" as pleasant as possible, largely by an endless series of chess games with them. While the monomaniacal Frémont campaigned toward his destiny, Sutter endured the ordeal of waiting, for the Mexican War did not further involve the fort. He did so by throwing himself into his farming and other chores. The Indians no longer wished to work in the fields, and Sutter lacked his old power to persuade them to change their minds. Most of his white laborers had vanished. Only two of his old-timers, Sam Neal and Edmund Bray, were still with him, and he thought so little of the pair that he quipped to a friend about his work force, "It would be better entirely new." Six of his twelve wagons were broken down and his smiths and wagonmaker had all gone to war. With six to eight of his plows lying unstocked around his yard Sutter wrote to Larkin, "When Mr. Williams can start four plows, it is a great deal." Sutter blamed many of his reverses on his lack of good plows and, thus, his inability to get all his grain into the ground by January 1. Late sowing, he realized, would not even pay expenses.

The launches were constantly under way, hauling wheat not only from his own fields but from Leidesdorff's as well, for Sutter had taken over there when Leidesdorff's hired men bungled the harvest. He also ordered Philosopher Pickett and some cowboys to round up about 140 head of Leidesdorff's horses, and promised the mulatto merchant an honest Swiss cheese- and butter-maker from among the immigrants he expected. Sutter's intensive cultivation of Leidesdorff's friendship was partly because he was the agent of the Russian American Company, which was becoming restless about payment. Although a grasshopper plague took his onions, and a November 1845 drought halved his grain crop, still he harvested 4,000 *fanegas* of wheat. His boats also picked up redwood lumber and delivered to Yerba Buena, for transshipment to Los Angeles, thousands of barrel staves. From Leidesdorff, Sutter secured lampblack, seal oil and right whale oil for his tannery. Sutter believed in business-as-usual, and, war or no war, he intended to turn out leather which would please even a fastidious bookbinder.

251

Yet the ambivalent Sutter was simultaneously working, through Leidesdorff and Larkin, to interest the United States government in buying New Helvetia, to protect the American-born settlers of the Sacramento and San Joaquin valleys. He wanted to pull out, now, with a profit, clear himself of debt, and fall back on Hock Farm. He saw his Feather River farm as the natural supply point for a garrison of U.S. troops at New Helvetia. His Kanakas, Harry Owens and Maintop, had kept Hock Farm in good repair after a disappointing succession of white overseers had neglected their duties.

On the first day of September, Sutter was told by one of his Indians that an immigrant wished to see him. Going to the gate of the fort, he met Edwin Bryant standing beside two Indian sentries and an insolent corporal who had lectured the traveler on the changed circumstances of Fort Sacramento. The non-com told Bryant flatly that Sutter had no control over the post, but the visitor insisted upon seeing the fort's founder. Sutter greeted him cordially, of course, and apologized profusely for the bad manners of the "Bear" on guard. He confessed that he did not have the authority to invite Bryant to remain inside. When he replied that he was well aware of Sutter's hospitality under normal circumstances, and needed only a little meat, salt and vegetables, Sutter sent a servant for the provisions plus onions, tomatoes and melons, to give to the Yankee. He refused compensation, as he almost always did.

Sutter invited Bryant to dinner on September 3. There, like so many visitors before and after him, Bryant was struck not only by his host's cordiality but by his urbanity, good manners, dress and deportment. In contrast with the rude frontiersmen surrounding him, Bryant found Sutter an "old school gentleman." Sutter regaled his guests with tales of Switzerland, the French army, and the founding of New Helvetia. Perhaps tiring of Charles X and Napoleon, he trotted out a new yarn about his being so hemmed in with Indian assailants, several times, that he had had to subsist for many days on nothing but grass! As usual, he showed off his wheat fields, his technique of "fencing" them with ditches, and his horse-mill. Among his agricultural experiments was an unirrigated plot which impressed Bryant no end. Said he, "I never saw a ranker growth of hemp in Kentucky."

On September 7, Sutter was finally able to secure a room in the fort for Bryant, who moved in just in time to participate in an Indian scare. Chief Piopiomoxmox brought a band of Walla Wallas back to New Helvetia. Rumor numbered the braves at 250 and their intentions an old revenge for the murder of the chief's son. Kern sent couriers for reinforcements. Com. John B. Montgomery ordered aid to be rushed to Sutter's Fort, and Lt. John S. Misroon was dispatched to Sonoma to head up a relief expedition. There was even talk of Purser Daingerfield Fauntleroy's Leather-Ass Dragoons—so called because of the leather patches reinforcing the seats of their trousers—galloping to the rescue from San Juan Bautista. But Lt. Joseph Revere got there first, joining Kern and Sutter with his Sonoma force. When he rode in, he found them drilling soldiers and enlisting civilians. At the gate hung the by-now weathered head of the renegade Indian, Raphero, as a warning to the Walla Wallas. Both Kern and Revere were eager for a fight. For once, Sutter's was the coolest head. He talked with Yellow Serpent when the chief reached the fort and learned that he had only forty warriors with him, was accompanied by women and children, and came in peace. (At least, he opted for peace, whatever his earlier attentions, when he saw 150 armed whites and nearly 300 of Sutter's Indian allies waiting for him at the American River.)

Sutter won back precious prestige by his handling of the Walla Walla threat, of which he wrote, "Exaggerated reports caused such a panic throughout California that a massacre of the Walla Wallas was just barely avoided." First, he had been able to call in his old Indian allies; second, he had managed to parley with Yellow Serpent and avoid bloodshed. Third, he had signed up a number of the Walla Walla warriors as reinforcements for Frémont's California Battalion! Recalled Sutter, "I knew that they were good fighters, so I asked them if they would go to Frémont's assistance and told them that they would be paid for their services. Being a warlike people, many of them were glad to go. François Gendron [Gendreau], a Canadian who had a Walla Walla woman for a wife, I made captain of the detachment. From among the natives on the Stanislaus and Mokelumne, old horse thieves who had reformed, I formed another company and placed it in charge of José Jesús, a Christianized Indian. In addition to these, I dispatched about twenty white men. An American by the name of Charles Burroughs I made commander of the whole force."

To awe any hostile Indians, Kern marched his powerful force up the Valley to Sutter Buttes, leaving Sutter briefly in charge of the fort once again. After his return, he and Sutter worked well together, recruiting men to rush to the aid of the American forces in the south, where the *gringos* were suffering reversals. Sutter's morale was much improved by Kern's trust. On August 8 he signed enlistment papers and on the 16th, Lieutenant Misroon confirmed Kern's appointment of Sutter as a lieutenant in the volunteer dragoons of the U.S. Army and as second in command at Fort Sacramento. He was to carry out all Kern's orders, to drill the soldiers, to take command in the commander's absence. Although Sutter was not given a proper uniform allowance, he was advanced $10–$15 for clothing from ship's stores, given $50 in pay and rations, and a tobacco allowance. Lieutenant Misroon also restored him to his position as magistrate of the Sacramento area.

Walla Walla war scares could not distract Sutter entirely from farming. He was counting heavily on the arrival of 15,000 Mormon immigrants in the West. Thus, when he learned in September that only 2,000 to 3,000 were on the road, Sutter was greatly disappointed. He had expected the population influx to double wheat prices, to $4 the *fanega*. He was tired of working so hard for such little profit. Labor costs were high, even though his workers were paid in drill, calico and *manta, rebozos,* butcher knives, beads combs and (for the sick) rice.

Small wonder Sutter more than toyed with the idea of selling out. He put so much faith in rumors that Com. Robert F. Stockton was coming to New Helvetia to buy it that he ordered more tumblers and a couple of good tablecloths from Yerba Buena so that he could entertain him in style. Sutter was willing to go to the bay to see Stockton, too. "I will do all my best to sell it and pay my debts," he told his friends. He also hoped to get a good lawyer who would get his Fort Ross and Bodega properties back, with the United States government's help. Foolishly, he tried to pressure the Russians into helping him, asking for a document in his support and threatening to pay them $10,000 less than agreed upon, in wheat, if they refused. His stratagem back-fired. The irritated Russians sought an attachment of his mortgaged New Helvetia property in order to secure payment in full of their old account. Prematurely confident of success, the perennial optimist exclaimed, "I thank God in Heaven now that we are under such a good, protecting, government!"

Sutter's enthusiasm should have flagged during September when he had to hire Col. William H. Russell as his attorney to fight the Russian American Company's attachment proceedings. But, strangely, the new difficulty, rather than depressing him, sparked his fighting spirit. He demanded, by what right did *Alcalde* Washington A. Bartlett of Yerba Buena exercise his jurisdiction in *Alcalde* John Sinclair's district? He labeled the action unwarranted, improper; a usurpation of Sinclair's duties. And, he added, by what right did Bartlett issue an attachment without affidavits to the effect that he intended to either abscond or fraudulently convey the property? "What's the matter with the ordinary process of law?" thundered the adventurer who had skirted the nether edge of legality for years. "I have always understood that an attachment was an extraordinary remedy. . . . Where does he find authority to issue an attachment without an attendant suit for the recovery of the debt?" Not as cocky as he appeared to be, Sutter tried feverishly to unload New Helvetia on Uncle Sam. Impatient of rumored visits by Stockton, he now wrote the commodore directly to offer the fort to the government. To avoid a quick refusal, he quoted no selling price (though he hoped to get $80,000) but offered to rent it for $1,000 a month —the sum he considered that the United States owed him, since the raising of the flag on July 11, for housing soldiers, volunteers, emigrants, and Walla Walla and Nez Perce wards of the government.

Sutter used the negotiations, most of which existed only in his mind, to put off creditors like Suñol. "It is very probable that the government will buy my settlement and if the war had not begun, I believe the bargain would already have been completed." Sutter was confident that the government would honor its obligations and with his rationing costs, as lieutenant and commissary for Kern, running to $600 and $700 per month, he boasted, "It is the first time I have done so good a business." To Reading the hopeful Swiss wrote, "I have a large amount to receive of Lt. Colonel Frémont," and to Suñol, "As soon as the commodore returns, everything will be settled and I shall not delay paying you."

Sutter's relations with Mariano Vallejo were so much improved that the latter's brother, Salvador, complained that he could not fathom what "Masonic bonds" tied together two men so diametrically opposite in their views. Salvador could never bring himself to trust Sutter. With matters going so well in so many quarters, at least in his hyperactive imagination, Sutter again turned his fury upon Bartlett: "The foregoing inquiries or suggestions have conducted me to a firm determination (unless you, in a reasonable time, fully and satisfactorily explain your conduct), to lay the whole matter before Commodore Stockton and Colonel Frémont and, at the same time, to institute suit for damages both against the Russian Company and yourself, for damages on account of the injury I have sustained by what I consider your illegal, unjust and improper conduct."

In November, Sutter was once again in the depths. He poured out his grievances to Reading: "It cost me a great deal and I have sacrificed myself for the welfare of the public and, particularly, to foreigners who immigrated into the country. I need not tell you what I have done. You know all. At this day, there would not be a farm in the Sacramento Valley if I had not established myself here and not so many immigrants would be here yet. I know very well that my enemies, like Marsh, etc., work against it. But their influence will be of no account."

On December 9, he again turned on *Alcalde* Bartlett. Refusing to open new correspondence with him on the Russian matter, which he termed a malicious suit, he promised: "As soon as the United States government establishes courts for this country, with judges of legal attainments, I shall bring suit for damages against all engaged in the affair." Because the *alcalde* had made a dig at Sutter's "high legal counsel," the Swiss leaped to Colonel Russell's defense. "I have all confidence in him as a gentleman and as a lawyer from one of the most responsible offices [U.S. marshal for Missouri] in the gift of the President." He brushed aside Russell's lack of Spanish by saying, "If we are to be governed by the Spanish law, I should suppose this district was out of the jurisdiction of the justice of the peace of Yerba Buena." Sutter ended his letter with an abrupt dismissal of Bartlett: "Wishing no further unpleasant correspondence, I am your obedient servant."

CHAPTER XV

THE RESCUER

I N January 1847, the Mexican War was still dragging on, its denouement a year away, when suddenly the war was temporarily forgotten by the New Helvetians. Seven gaunt and harrowed men staggered into Johnson's ranch, on the Bear River north of Sutter's Fort. These surviviors of a sixteen-man party dispatched on snowshoes for help from Sutter, reported sixty-odd men, women and children doomed to death by starvation at Truckee Lake (now Donner Lake) unless Sutter could get aid to them.

Sutter was more familiar with the Donner party's plight than any other Californian. In September of 1846, he had received Charles T. Stanton and William McCutchen, sent ahead by the Donners for assistance. Even then, they were the very rear guard of the season's immigration and dangerously behind schedule because the Donners had elected to try the 300- to 400-mile Salt Desert shortcut which Lansford Hastings was promoting. With the Donners low on food and losing their animals while still in the Nevada desert, Sutter had rushed seven mule-loads of dried beef and flour to them. He turned the pack train over to Stanton, and

259

gave him two of his Indians, as mule drivers. McCutchen had been so badly used up that the hospital was the only place for him.

Sutter had not heard another word of the Donner party until October 28 when James F. Reed came into the fort on a mission similar to Stanton's. He had been banished for manslaughter on the Humboldt River, but was determined to return eastward to rescue his trapped family. Sutter had outfitted him and a by-then rested McCutchen with a mule and twenty-six pack horses loaded with jerky and flour. They had set out on November 1, but a heavy rain had begun on the very night of Reed's arrival and they were turned back by deep snow in the mountains. Sutter had then advised Reed to go to Yerba Buena to get help from the United States Navy, since the task was too big for New Helvetia's resources, especially with so many of Sutter's men gone south to reinforce Frémont's California Battalion.

The frostbitten leaders of the snowshoe party, William M. Foster and William H. Eddy, sent word to Kern and Sutter of the now-desperate plight of their snow-trapped comrades. Kern asked for volunteers but got only three men because of serious doubts that the government would make good on its promises to pay. Sutter and John Sinclair then offered to hold themselves personally responsible for expenses, and six men followed Aquila Glover out of the fort on January 1. Seven more, including Eddy, joined him at Johnson's ranch. Sutter and Sinclair furnished the relief party with horses, loaded with supplies, and the Swiss dispatched his launch to San Francisco Bay to recruit more rescuers. Citizens there petitioned the military governor for aid, and Reed and others managed to raise $1,300 at Yerba Buena to bolster Sutter's already hard-taxed resources. Lt. Selim Woodworth, USN, noisily assumed command of all rescue operations but then proceeded to sit on his hands in a camp on Bear River, while braver and quieter men headed into the deadly white mountains. Caleb Greenwood, the old mountain man, volunteered his services, but his eighty-four years finally told on him, forcing him to fall back short of the snow-covered cabins of Truckee Lake.

James Reed tried again with another relief expedition in February. This time he was able to get through. He brought back some of the emaciated sufferers in March. Finally, on April 13, *Le Gros* O'Fallon led a final expedition which brought out the last survivor, the so-called "ogre," Lewis Keseberg, said to have enjoyed his diet of human flesh. All the rescuers were shocked by the grisly evidence of starvation and cannibalism in the filthy campsites. The snowbound immigrants had eaten up their supplies; then what little game they could catch; next, their stock; their dogs; bits of leather; and, finally, one another. In all, forty-two persons died; forty-seven survived. Sutter's two Indian muleteers froze to death, along with brave Stanton, and were eaten. Sutter was shaken when he heard the news. But he was really horrified by the callousness of some of the women, who told Cordua that they preferred the flesh of Indians to that of whites, with the heart and liver tastiest of all. To neighbor Edward E. Dunbar, he could only say, in shock, "They eat my fine Indians up!" Years later he told the historian, Bancroft, "The provisions not satisfying the starving sufferers, they killed and ate, first, the mules, then the horses, and, finally, they killed and ate my good Indians."

Yet Sutter let his compassion overrule his horror. He hired the pariah Keseberg as supercargo of his launch when everyone else despised him as a monster who had probably murdered Tamsen Donner to add her to his larder. (Sutter was accused, as ever, by those who were jealous of him and shamed by his compassion, of having other motives than Christian charity. Some said that Keseberg had known him a few years earlier and had some sort of hold over him. This was very unlikely, since Keseberg did not even arrive in the United States until 1844.) William A. Trubody, a child of eight years at the time, recalled the feeling against Keseberg at Sutter's Fort: "When we landed at Sutter's in '47, I remember them accusin' Keseberg, the Donner party man, of killin' people at Truckee Lake and saltin' 'em down. We kids were so afraid of Keseberg that we always ran away when we saw him." Sutter, however, was aware of the German's terrible mental anguish and felt sorry for him. He knew that Keseberg suffered from agonizing, screaming nightmares as a result of his bestial experiences in the Sierra. But finally, in December, Sutter tired of the "cannibal" and replaced him on the launch. Even Sutter could not resist joking that he had been forced to get rid of Keseberg as supercargo because the boat was so slow when he was in command, that its passengers were afraid that they would run out of food on the river and be eaten by their "captain."

Many made Sutter the hero of the relief expeditions, instead of the more deserving Stanton, Reed, Glover and Eddy. J. Wesley Jones wrote, for example, in 1853, that "the old hero led the way." But although he had a part in all five of the attempts made to rescue the Donner party and bragged, "Often it was necessary for me to go with my men and cattle to drag them [the immigrants] in to safety, out of the snow," Sutter's role was not heroic. He was planner and outfitter, not rescuer per se. A number of his men marched with the relief columns, but not Sutter. At forty-three, "old" Sutter was content to let younger and braver men risk their lives in the Sierra snows. But the promises to the people of California made by Sheriff George McKinstry of the Sacramento District (published in the *California Star*) that the refugees would be received by Sutter "with all the hospitality for which he is celebrated," held. Sutter's wholehearted generosity and sympathy toward the distressed immigrants won him many friends and much acclaim, all of which was deserved. Although a few men suspected that self-interest was somehow his motivation, most Californians agreed with the *California Star* which editorialized, "But for the timely succor afforded them by Captain J. A. Sutter, one of the most humane and liberal men in California, they must all have perished in a few days."

Sutter had considerable justification for staying at the fort, besides his age. First, there was the matter of watching over his own property as well as protecting the women, children and civilians gathered there. He was Kern's second in command, and the young lieutenant was often ill. And, although Kern turned the fort over to Sheriff McKinstry rather than to Sutter when he dashed off, first, to participate in Donner relief operations and, second, in a punitive expedition up the Sacramento Valley against Indians, Sutter was really in control during Kern's absence. McKinstry was not only his close friend but Sutter's chief clerk! He deferred to him, and when he wrote Commodore Hull for help in rescuing the Donners he stated that he wrote "with Captain Sutter's permission." Sutter, for his part, described McKinstry fondly as "all time, the same—full of fun and wit."

Although McKinstry let Sutter run his own fortress, he confided, privately, to Reading after trying to unsnarl his employer's business affairs, that he thought that New Helvetia was already too much for Sutter. He hoped that his friend and patron would be successful in selling the fort to the United States government and helped him by suggesting to Commodore Stockton that he secure the establishment. McKinstry wanted Sutter to be able to retire to Hock Farm with a "pretty fortune."

In April 1847, the California Battalion was discharged in Los Angeles, but Kern did not surrender control of the fort to Sutter, although the thrill of playing soldier had waned and his protector, Frémont, was under a cloud for insubordination and disobedience of Gen. Stephen W. Kearny. Kern was apparently relieved of his New Helvetia command on May 24 but not by the patient Sutter. Lt. Charles C. Anderson, with half of Company C of Gen. Jonathan D. Stevenson's regiment of New York Volunteers, camped on the American Fork, then took over the fort itself on June 1. Not until the volunteers were pulled out on September 20, 1847, did Sutter regain control of his own property. After a year of relegation to the role of subordinate, he now reasserted himself as master of New Helvetia, attempting to repress the painful year and more which had just passed. He would later claim that when Lieutenant Misroon came to the fortress to reorganize his garrison, he left Sutter in command. So tangled did his stories become that he would maintain that it was he, not

Kern, who turned the post over to Lieutenant Anderson, forgetting that he had insisted that no one took over from him at any time. Sutter's defensiveness was pathetic. The raw truth was that he had been passed over not only for military commands but also in civilian appointments. The Americanized Sacramento River had a sheriff and an *alcalde,* but they were McKinstry and Sinclair—not Sutter. When Stockton appointed Frémont governor of California and chose seven men to form a legislative council for him, Sutter's name was conspicuous by its absence. He missed nothing in this case, of course, for Kearny thwarted Frémont's gubernatorial ambitions before the council could ever convene. Nevertheless, these rebuffs wounded Sutter, and it was an infinitely bitter experience for him to find himself billeted in his fort instead of commanding it.

But 1847 saw Sutter beginning to recoup his losses, gradually reestablishing his position of preeminence in the Central Valley. Carding, spinning, weaving, wood cutting, brick making and the building of a lime kiln and a new bake oven could not absorb all his energies. He embarked on his ambitious plans for a great expansion of New Helvetia by hiring James Marshall and another man to survey and dig out a race for his flour mill at Natoma, a few miles upriver from the fort. Sutter's flouring mill would consist of four four-foot stones, operated by more waterpower than that provided by the Genesee at Rochester. The stones were capable of grinding 20 *fanegas* of grain every hour. Sutter fully expected them to be in operation by Christmas, easily handling the entire Sacramento Valley production of wheat in the future. He was losing money selling wheat at $2 a bushel, and he intended to supply his Russian and other creditors with flour, not wheat, from 1848 on. He knocked the interior walls out of his "penitentiary" in order to make it into a granary, and he kept his horse-powered mill going at night in order to accommodate his neighbors.

Gen. Stephen W. Kearny dropped by the fort on June 13 and Lt. Charles Anderson and Sutter lined up the garrison for inspection, while the cannon belched a smoky salute. On the four-teenth, Sutter gave a dinner, with the general as his guest of honor. He also buttonholed him about the sale of the fort and was pleased by Kearny's reaction to the idea.

Piopiomoxmox, the Walla Walla chieftain, and his braves threatened to make new trouble around New Helvetia at this time. They demanded their pay for service in the California Battalion's campaign. Frémont had Kern pay them off in "government" or "war" horses—stock captured from the Mexican-Californians. Sutter thought that they looked contented enough when they left for the north, but he soon heard they were raiding again. He did not like the Walla Wallas, writing, "They are a very bad tribe of Indians, and very warlike." Perhaps this was the reason for Lieutenant Anderson's lack of success in recruiting a force to punish them. Sutter himself was much more interested in visiting Kearny's camp, though it might mean meeting Frémont, under something resembling house arrest in the general's entourage. The Pathfinder was on his way east to a court-martial for conduct prejudicial to good order and discipline.

On July 4, 1847, Sutter participated in Independence Day celebrations by firing a national salute from his battery at sunrise, as he hoisted the Stars and Stripes. In mid-July, he visited the camp of Commodore Stockton on the Bear River. Here, in a typical gesture, he presented the naval hero with his own fine riding horse, just as he had once done for Frémont.

Partially restored to his old position of power by summer, Sutter sent his new jack-of-all-trades, James Marshall, out with an Indian to select three Sierra sawmill sites. Toward the end of August, Capt. Jefferson Hunt led a contingent of Mormon Battalion veterans into the fort. They were on their way back to Great Salt Lake. Sutter's keen ear picked up the clink of their pay in their pockets. This made them doubly welcome, and he saw their arrival as a great windfall. His blacksmiths were soon shoeing their horses for $1 a shoe. He sold them unbolted flour at $8 a sack and peas at $1.50 a bushel. Since they had orders for some of the "war" horses, Sutter delivered some of the captured stock to them. With such fair treatment, and an offer of good wages, he won some of them over to his employ as laborers, ready to build the flour and sawmills and to dig the two millraces.

It was on the twenty-seventh day of August that Sutter signed the historic contract with Marshall to build a sawmill at a site on the South Fork of the American, which the Indians called Coloma, far beyond the limits of Sutter's land grant. The next day, Marshall set to work, and Sutter predicted his mill would be sawing timber by December. In September, he hired dependable Heinrich Lienhard as his major-domo, or overseer and storekeeper. Lienhard had earlier worked for Sutter in his melon patches at the Mimal farm above Hock Farm. By October, the thirty-odd-mile road to the mill site from Sutter's Fort was so good that Sheriff McKinstry, the Sacramento correspondent to the *California Star,* was bragging to San Franciscans that it was "superior to the streets of your city." McKinstry optimistically predicted that Sutter would soon float great rafts of cut lumber down the South Fork and American to the Sacramento and from there to Suisun Bay and the proposed metropolis of Montezuma. Sutter intended some of this lumber for his own entry in the town-founding sweepstakes. He was not only confident that Hastings' and Semple's Montezuma would never rival his own Sutterville but also advised Larkin, "I am convinced that she will improve a great deal faster than your own town of Francisca [now Benicia]." Rafting lumber down the shallow, rapid and rock-strewn American River was more Marshall's pipe dream than his employer's, but Bidwell was unable to convince Sutter that it was impracticable.

Sutter needed laborers desperately. At times, when he could use 200 Indians, disease reduced the number of field hands to 20 or 30. He was afraid, in September, that he would lose 3,000 *fanegas* for lack of harvesters. To Larkin, he wrote of sickness sweeping northern California, "I hope it will not be so again for the next eight years." Looking ahead to a time when agriculture would become a true industry in California, Sutter told Larkin, "The time is past when it could be depended on Indians. Now, we need cutting and threshing machines or it is not possible to raise large crops." William Heath Davis had sold his launch to the government, so there were not enough river craft to haul all Sutter's harvest to the Russians, anchored in the bay. He urged Leidesdorff to charter a schooner or small brigantine to come up the Sacramento to his *embarcadero* to load the wheat. He even offered to supply him with a pilot. He also asked the merchant to get someone to send the launch *Londresa* to New Helvetia for wheat. Perhaps Sutter's hopes rose when he greeted the first Sacramento River steamer, Leidesdorff's little *Sitka,* slow and cranky as she was. But, if so, they were dashed when the tiny Russian steamboat sank on its homeward journey to Yerba Buena.

About thirty of the Mormons who had not gone to work for Sutter returned to the fort after meeting an elder near Truckee Lake who told them to remain in California until spring, on Brigham Young's orders, because food was short in Zion. At last, Sutter found himself with a plentiful force of strong, dependable workers. Although Heinrich Lienhard found some of them rude and inhospitable, Sutter liked them very much. He hired a number of them to dig the millraces at twelve and a half cents a yard. He recalled, for Bancroft's benefit, "They were very glad to earn some money in order to buy horses and cattle for their new homes at the Salt Lake, to which they longed to go. They were very good people. . . . I had not a word of difficulty with any of them. (When the gold excitement broke out, they said they were very sorry I was so inconvenienced by it and some of them even remained and finished the jobs they were engaged in.)" He said much the same thing to Larkin: "All the hands on my mills are Mormons and the best people which ever I have had employed. If I would have had Mormons 4 or 5 years past, I would have a fortune. But so long as I am here, I have had only a few good men. The balance was a bad kind of people." In his diary he marveled at an unheard-of situation: "A good many of the Mormons are sick on account of their working too hard."

By October 1847, Sutter had five parties working on the American River, making shingles, barrel hoops, getting out timber for windmills and ferry boats, building the mills and ditching their races. By December, his thirty-four men at Natoma had the flour mill all but finished. His tannery was working again, too, and he began to feel that he was out of his difficulties at last. Except for occasional pleas for files, cranks and six great saws for his mills, Sutter virtually vanished from Larkin's correspondence. He was simply too busy to take the time to write. He explained this period to Bancroft: "After the war, things went on prosperously with me. I found a good market, both in the newcomers and at the Bay. People from below came to me to buy leather, shoes, saddles, hats, spurs, bridle bits and other articles. My manufactures increased. Good mechanics were plenty. I had large fields of grain and large herds of cattle, horses and sheep."

He was still miffed about his treatment by Uncle Sam, after his long display of loyalty to the American cause. He growled to the historian, "For all my services during the Mexican War I did not receive a single cent. Nor were my soldiers ever paid. The muster rolls of the Indians were lost and they complained that the Americans did not pay their soldiers any better than the Mexicans." Sutter's complaint was not entirely justified. While his pay for government service as a lieutenant of dragoons ($50 a month), *if* received, was far from lavish, he certainly took advantage of the perquisites of military service, drawing tobacco, blankets, Navy blue trousers, socks, neckerchiefs, a mattress and a pea jacket. What really annoyed him was that the government of the United States showed no inclination to pay him anything for the use of the fort as a garrison. If only they would come through with the modest sum of $1,000 per month for rent, over a year's time, he was saved! He explained to Larkin, "I hope this year will be a great alteration in my affairs and I will be out of most of my debts. I would be, entirely, if I could get my pay, due to me from the government, about $12,000 or $13,000. I hope we will get it in about a year."

For once, Sutter found himself in the strange role of creditor instead of debtor. When he tried to collect $40 due him for a load of bread which he had supplied the U.S.S. *Portsmouth,* Lieutenant Misroon told him that he was not aware of the debt. He warned Sutter that if he did not have good grounds for dunning him, he would consider it "a very unhandsome, if not dishonest, transaction." Where once these words would have ignited Sutter, in 1847 he merely had his clerk, McKinstry, send the forgetful lieutenant a copy of his 1846 order, which he had filled. Sutter was indeed mellowing. He was also branching out into new activities. For one, he became the Fort Sacramento-New Helvetia sales agent for publisher Sam Brannan's *California Star.* For another thing, Larkin asked him to build, or contract to build, a wooden or adobe home for him on Flügge's old ranch, which the consul had bought.

A more important new assignment for Sutter came on April 7. The sometime slaver of war-orphaned Indian children was appointed Indian Sub-Agent for the tribes of the Sacramento and San Joaquin rivers by Military Governor Kearny, upon Consul Larkin's recommendation. This was just twelve days before David Dutton wrote Larkin to warn him, "Your Indian girl was delivered according to agreement (one week after you left here) at Captain Sutter's. She is a smart girl and is learning no good habits there."

General/Governor Kearny sent Sutter his commission on the seventh, with a covering letter. (A week later he appointed Vallejo to a similar position for the Sonoma area.) In this letter, the general reminded Sutter that the Indians had given recent settlers considerable harassment by attacking small parties and running off horses and cattle. Sternly, he ordered, "This conduct *must* cease." He hoped that Sutter's good advice and counsel and his perfect acquaintance with all the Indians would induce them to end their acts of violence. If not, he guaranteed that they would be punished by an armed force which he would dispatch. Kearny asked Sutter to pass the word on to the chiefs of the Horsethief Indians and to explain to them the change in administration in California. Sutter was to point out to them that they must now look to their Great Father, the President of the United States, and that Americans and Mexican-Californians were united as one people under his protection. The general also promised to send Sutter some presents to give each tribe that would promise to conduct itself honestly and peaceably. In signing off, he ordered Sutter to report to him and future governors, from time to time, on any occurrences which he might deem worthy of attention. He also solicited Sutter's suggestions for appointees in the field of Indian affairs. The general noted that Sutter's salary was $750 a year and that he was not to expend any public money or contract any debts against either the United States or California as an Indian agent.

Sutter was an obvious choice, and a good one. Not only did he have a vast amount of experience with California's Indians and others met in his early travels, but he had a genuine way with them. Sutter was able to transform savages into efficient farmers, trappers, soldiers and sailors. In comparison with most Americans and Mexican-Californians, he was pro-Indian, in a decidedly paternalistic way. Even Bancroft, hardly Sutter's best friend, had a good word for him as an Indian diplomat: "His Indian policy was, undoubtedly, a wise and successful one, its chief features being constant vigilance, prompt punishment of offences and uniform kindness and justice, especially to those tribes near home. He had unusual tact for making friends of all men, irrespective of race."

Sutter was not only familiar with Indian warfare, he had made treaties with them, issued good-conduct passports to chiefs and documented their ownership of horses. He could be ruthless on his punitive expeditions or when he hired scalp hunters, but he could also be a friend. In his account of California travel, the Swede, Waseurtz af Sandels described a treaty pow-wow where

Sutter demonstrated his Indian savvy. Of all the Indians gathered about him, he allowed only the chiefs to bear arms. After some graceful dancing by these warrior chiefs, they made long speeches to which Sutter apparently paid rapt attention. Then each chief, laying his weapons at Sutter's boots, said, "Take these and with them penetrate my heart if I or my tribe betray the trust you now put in us and which we now solemnly swear to keep." Sutter then forced the bows and arrows back upon the chiefs and they departed as friends and allies.

Sutter even managed to work (minor) miracles with the mountain men who, whatever their other qualities, were usually arrogant racists. They despised Indians even more than "greasers" or "Bugs," as John Gantt termed the Mexican-Californians. Waseurtz af Sandels noted that though the Rocky Mountain men who lounged about Sutter's Fort were initially at odds with the Indians, Sutter was able to handle them: "At first, they very much affected Sutter's management of the Indians by inflicting many unnecessary cruelties very contrary to the wishes and will of Sutter. Gradually, he brought about a milder way of treating the aborigines, conciliating their feelings toward the white men and furthering his own views of civilization."

"Growling Sam" Smith, an up-valley settler, brought news to Sutter of his first major Indian problem of 1847. Smith reported an Indian battle which had taken place sixty miles north of New Helvetia. As Sutter questioned him, it emerged that the battle had been, in fact, a brutal slaving raid by Smith himself and two companions, Antonio Armijo and John Egger. Received kindly and furnished with berries and other food at a *ranchería,* the threesome had responded by attacking their hosts, killing thirteen braves and taking thirty-seven Indians as prisoners, or slaves.

Sutter quickly notified the *alcalde* of Sonoma, Lilburn Boggs, and ordered Smith to go before him and to make out an affidavit on the affair. Before he could take much further action, another incident occurred. A chief of the Consumnes River country reported to Sutter that two white men had claimed a horse at his village as theirs, although Lieutenant Revere had left it with the Indians, complete with proper papers of ownership. Before the two men seized the mount, they whipped the chief, cut up his hat, and abused his people. Sutter immediately informed *Alcalde* John Sinclair of this outrage, but it was too late; the raiders escaped.

Next, Sutter wrote to Governor Richard B. Mason for instructions on how to police northern California properly against such unwarranted attacks on the Indians. Mason replied by urging Sutter to use every effort to arrest the guilty parties, advising him to call in not only decent citizens for help but also any military officers in the area. All who valued peace would help him, said Mason. He advised Sutter to arrest the culprits and to organize a tribunal for their trial. Should the death sentence be pronounced, the governor promised to see it carried out. He ordered Sutter to find the enslaved Indians, to release them, and to restore them to their people. He was to make clear to them that the United States government condemned violence and disorder: "The safety of the frontier shall not be put at hazard by a few lawless villains."

Lt. Henry W. Halleck, U.S. Army Engineers, was Secretary of State for the Territory of California in 1847. He responded to Sutter's letters to the governor and requested that he communicate freely with the governor's office about the measures which he felt might best be taken to govern the Indians and to bring them security, quiet and happiness. With his letter, the Secretary of State included a circular of instructions. Sutter was to watch over the Indians, the wild tribes particularly but also the Christianized ones from the missions and *ranchos,* although they were also subject to the *alcalde* (Sinclair) of his district. Halleck made it clear that the governor wanted Sutter to be the "Protector of the Indians." The Secretary advised him to correct any ill treatment of Indian workmen by employers. Should they abuse any Indians, Sutter was to arraign them before the *alcalde* for trial. The governor left a great deal to Sutter's discretion and good sense, flattering him by stating that he expected much of him because of his great experience. He was confident that Sutter would persuade the Indians of his domain to pursue honest and industrious courses of conduct.

The circular stressed the fact that the government wanted peace with the Indians. Sutter was to send messages to hostile tribes or, better, to hold pow-wows with them in which he was to satisfy them that the government's intentions were not only strictly honorable but also peaceable. He was also to tell them that the Great Father would forgive their past offenses. *But,* he was to warn them that the government ruling California would inflict severe punishment on them for any and all disorder. Halleck stressed that in cases of Indian abuse by whites, the injured parties were to appeal to Sutter. As the only authorized agent of the United States government, he would inflict punishment in all offenses perpetrated by whites upon Indians or vice versa. Offenders, Halleck told Sutter, were to be arrested, arraigned by him before the *alcalde,* and jailed by him until he should receive instructions from the government.

A less pressing chore was a census which Halleck, on behalf of Governor Mason, asked Sutter to take in order to collect data on the location, number and character of all Indian tribes in his Sacramento district. Since Sutter knew the chiefs already, Mason expected him to deliver a great deal of valuable information. From Sutter he hoped to learn the tribes' manner of subsistence, their weapons, mode of warfare, their history and their present condition. Further, Sutter was to seize any and all stolen property he might discover in the *rancherías* and to restore it to the proper owners upon evidence of ownership. Halleck was sorry to report that, as yet, there were no territorial funds for the purchase of presents to send to Sutter, for distribution to the Indians, to make his peace-making and census-taking easier. But he reported that the governor had asked Washington for a supply of presents, and that he expected them to be sent before long.

Only a few days after receiving Halleck's communications, Sutter received a letter from Mason himself. The governor granted him (and Vallejo) a commission to hold a special court for the trial of prisoners Armijo, Smith and Egger and charged him with the impaneling of a jury of twelve good men. Sutter was to see that the men decided on the guilt or innocence of the trio and, if they were found guilty, he was to act as judge in pronouncing sentence. Mason insisted that Sutter give Armijo and his cronies a fair and impartial trial and that he furnish them with a copy of the charges against them. He was also to swear all witnesses, jurymen and interpreters properly and to keep a full record of the trial. This transcript he was to send to the governor, together with his views and recommendations. With the letter, Sutter found a copy of a circular which announced his appointment, and Vallejo's, as special commissioners, or judges, to hold court at Sutter's Fort at his convenience in order to try Armijo, Smith and Egger for murder and slaving.

Sub-Agent Sutter received another circular from Halleck which asked him to provide all hired Indians with a certificate of good conduct, to help distinguish them from horse thieves and murderers. Without such a passport, Halleck informed Sutter, an Indian found beyond the limits of a town or ranch where he was working would be liable to arrest. And, he added, as of November 1, 1847, any "wild" Indians visiting the settlements would have to secure a passport from Sutter or Vallejo.

Although he now had Armijo and the others in custody, Sutter did not try them at the fort. He scheduled the trial for August 31, but Armijo was sick and no prosecuting witnesses showed up, so he and Vallejo adjourned the court to October 18. However, Governor Mason decreed a change of venue and moved the trial to Sonoma. He also added *Alcalde* Boggs as a commissioner, in order to break a possible tie between Judges Sutter and Vallejo. On September 10 he set the date for the trial at October 28: he wanted the matter settled fairly but quickly. Meanwhile, Armijo was admitted to bail, with Halleck's approval. The governor then appointed a prosecutor for the case. But, apparently, justice was not done. The prisoners at the bar were acquitted of the charges against them. The whole affair ended in a wrangle between the governor on one side and his commissioners on the other because they wanted $8 a day for their expenses, whereas he would authorize no more than $2.

For all his love of glory, Sutter did not become attached to the bench. Perhaps he preferred his role of census-taker. In any case, during December 1847 he tried to carry out the gigantic roll call. He sent Heinrich Lienhard to the Hock *ranchería,* lending him two Indians as interpreters. From there, Lienhard made his way to the various villages of the Feather River, writing down their names, phonetically—Deitchera, Boga, Honcut, Yuba, Mimal, Hock and Seshun. When he read them back to the natives, they covered their mouths trying not to laugh at his Teutonic mispronunciations. Next, he asked, "How many men live in this village?" The Indians would provide him with a count by breaking off small pieces of reed. They were usually reluctant to answer any questions until he informed them that the chief, *Tscheba* Sutter, had sent him. Then they always complied. Apparently, Sutter took care of the area around New Helvetia, Lienhard the Feather River area, and Bidwell the Sacramento Valley north of Sutter Buttes. In any case, the figures were estimates, and wild enough. Bidwell reported to Sutter that there were 82 whites in his district, 19 tame Indians and 19,500 wild Indians. Sutter's report to Mason was late and incomplete. He apologized but reminded the governor that there was no mail service in California. He confessed his inability to supply any estimate of the number of wild Indians in the Sierra, but he figured that there were 70 small tribes, speaking about 120 different languages, in the area. For the zone between the Sacramento and San Joaquin rivers and the Sierra Nevada, he gave rather exact figures—60 dwellings, 289 whites, 5 Kanakas (4 men and a woman), one Negro, 479 neophytes, or tame Indians, and 21,873 *gentiles,* or wild natives. His survey of the amount of stock in the area resulted in figures of 20,000 cattle, 2,500 horses, 70 mules, 2,000 sheep and 1,000 hogs. As for improvements, he regretfully reported that there were no schools, though he planned one for Sutterville, only one working flour mill and another, under construction and one saw-mill, also being built (all three of them his). At the fort, he reported his three horse-mills and a tannery. His 1847 wheat harvest was 14,000 *fanegas,* but he could supply no figures on his barley, corn, peas and beans.

Sutter should have been more effective as an Indian sub-agent than he was. But his grip over the natives was loosening badly by 1847. It was Lienhard, not the *patrón* himself, who discovered that the Indians in the fort were stealing meat when steers were slaughtered, and it was the young major-domo who punished them by slapping them smartly on their vermin-infested heads. A major reason for Sutter's general loss of control was his growing addiction to alcohol. According to Lienhard, by 1847 Sutter was already an out-and-out drunkard. Even early in the morning, he was often in his cups, and every time Lienhard came to his quarters to get or to return the daybook, his employer forced him to take a drink. In his reminiscences Lienhard recalled, "Sutter liked his liquor. For some time, however, I had no idea he drank as much as he did. . . . [But] during my second week at the fort, I believe, I saw him walking with an unsteady, swaying, motion, which left no doubt as to his condition." Several times, Lienhard had to help Sutter to his room and put him to bed. Once, Lienhard scolded Sutter's Indian servant for setting too few plates at the table for a meal. When ordered to get more, the boy replied that he couldn't because Sutter, in a drunken rage, had smashed all the crockery.

CHAPTER XVI

THE PROSPECTOR

THE cloudburst of January 28, 1848, which turned New Helvetia into a churned-up sea of mud and transformed Sutter's placid pond into a rushing tributary to the American River, also washed into the fort a rain-soaked and mud-spattered James Marshall. While his arrival was completely unexpected, such behavior by his sawmill partner failed to surprise Sutter. His eccentric and surly millwright was a sometimes spiritualist, thought by many to be at least half crazy.

Marshall fidgeted nervously with his broad Mexican sombrero as water dripped from his serape, soiled white linen trousers, and buckskin leggings, and puddled on the floor around his muddy moccasins. The room, Sutter's office next to the guard house, was not private enough: Marshall asked to see him alone in his quarters in the *Casa Grande*. Sutter could not imagine what the moody Marshall wanted with him. The very day before, he had sent him a load of supplies, including pork on the hoof. But he put aside the letter he had been writing and led Marshall into his quarters, furnished with old pepperwood furniture from Fort Ross. There, he shut the door and asked his partner what he wanted. Instead of answering his question, Marshall nervously asked if he had locked the door. Puzzled, Sutter replied, "No, but I shall gladly lock it." He was unarmed but he did not fear Marshall in the least, for all his erratic behavior. Sutter thought that the visit was inspired by one of his wild whims. "Are we alone?" asked Marshall. Hardly had the Swiss answered "Yes" before the millwright demanded two bowls of water. Wondering if Marshall mightn't be mad after all, Sutter rang a bell. (He had six varying signals for a half-dozen different servants and clerks.) When a servant appeared, he sent him for the bowls. "Now I want a stick of redwood and some twine and some sheets of copper," Marshall continued. The dumbfounded Sutter protested, "But, Marshall, why do you need all these things?" His matter-of-fact answer was, "I want to make some scales." Sutter resolved to humor his associate. "Well, I have scales enough in the apothecary shop." And he went to get them himself.

When Sutter returned, he shut the door behind him but neglected to lock it. Marshall, with a mixed air of triumph and expectancy, pulled a white cotton rag from his pants pocket and began to unroll it. Just then, the door opened and a clerk entered, unaware that the room was occupied. "There!" exclaimed Marshall, jamming the bundle back into his trousers pocket. "Didn't I tell you that we had listeners?" Sutter hustled the clerk out, relocked the door, and managed to calm his visitor. Once more, Marshall drew the rag from his pocket. Opening it up, he took out a one-ounce vial of greenish glass. Inside were metallic pebbles and grains. One looked like a melon seed; none of them was even the size of a pea; many were no larger than pin heads. "I believe this is gold," he said.

Sutter got the full story from him. Marshall had found the dull yellow grains while inspecting the brush dam and the tailrace of the Coloma mill. On January 24, he had examined the raceway, being deepened down to its rotten granite bedrock by daytime digging and by flushing (scouring) by leaving the gate, between forebay and channel, open all night. Picking up some of the grains, he had compared them with a half-eagle ($5 gold piece) which one of his Mormon Battalion veterans had kept from his mustering-out pay. Still uncertain, he had bitten the metal flakes and tested their malleability better by hammering them flat on an anvil. Finally, he had subjected them to fire and to the soap-making lye pot of Mrs. Wimmer, the camp cook. The flakes of metal showed no ill effects and he had exclaimed, "Boys, by God, I have found a gold mine!" But, still, some of the mill hands laughed at him and called him crazy. Others gently tried to dissuade him, with "I reckon not," and "No such luck." So he had decided to ask Sutter to determine if what he had found was really gold.

Sutter examined the material closely, saying only, "Well, it looks like gold. Let us test it." Going back to his apothecary shop, he got some *aqua fortis* and applied it to the metal. The nitric acid failed to disturb it. Then Marshall asked Sutter if he had any silver. The Swiss produced some coins and they put an equal amount of each metal in the scales, so that they balanced. Submersing the scales into the two bowls of water, they saw that the silver was outweighed by the other metal. Finally, Sutter turned to the *Encyclopedia Americana* on his shelves and read the article on gold until he was convinced that the metal was, indeed, auriferous. When he was done, he pronounced the specimens to be of twenty-three-carat purity, at least. Snapping the volume shut in a gesture of finality, Sutter told his associate, "I believe that this is the finest kind of gold."

Marshall now insisted that his partner leave with him, immediately, for the mill site. But Sutter was not about to make a fifty-mile ride in the rain without dinner. He tried to persuade Marshall, "You had better take supper now. I will go up early in the morning, as soon as I have given my new orders and arranged the affairs of the day." According to Sutter's highly colored reminiscences, Marshall would have none of it. Without waiting for supper or anything else except Sutter's oath of secrecy, he strode out into the night. Actually, he *did* have dinner and stay the night, as Sutter urged, and the latter could not tear himself away from the fort's pressing duties until Tuesday evening, February 1, 1848.

On the night of January 28, Sutter tossed restlessly in his bed, rolling over in his mind all that he knew about gold in California. He was aware that Francisco López had found modest quantities of the metal in southern California and that his own men, John Bidwell and Pablo Gutiérrez, had found traces in both the Bear and American rivers. But he also remembered that the Swedish traveler and scientist, Waseurtz af Sandels, had told him that California's gold deposits were not rich enough to be worked profitably. He recalled his joshing Sandels in 1843—"Doctor, can't you find me a gold mine?" His reply had been serious advice, "Captain Sutter, I'd never think of gold mining. Your best mine is the soil." Sutter was inclined to agree, largely because the Indians possessed no gold. Nor did they even seem to be aware of its existence. As he told Bancroft later, "Strange it was, to be sure, that the Indians had never brought a piece of gold to me although they very often delivered other things which they found in the ravines. I always requested them to bring curiosities from the mountains to the fort and I recompensed them for their efforts. I received all kinds of animals, birds, plants, young trees, wild fowl, pipe clay, stones, red ochre, etc., but never a particle of gold." But deep in his bones, Sutter sensed something great, yet ominous, in Marshall's discovery. He wrote nothing in the New Helvetia diary but the laconic phrase "Mr. Marshall arrived from the mountains on very important business." But, in later life, he always claimed that he had fearful premonitions of what gold would mean for his plans. "At once, and during the night, the curse of the thing burst upon my mind. I saw from the beginning how the end would be. . . . Of course, I knew nothing of the extent of the discovery but I was satisfied, whether it amounted to much or little, that it would greatly interfere with my plans."

Because three boats arrived at New Helvetia right after Marshall, Sutter was too busy to set out for Coloma on what he, ever after, called his "melancholy ride" until late in the evening of the first of February. He camped that night on the dam at the Natoma flouring-mill site, filled with apprehension over the future of his garden empire. Continuing on next day, he was about half-way to his goal when he saw someone or something stirring in the blooming manzanita brush alongside the road which his Indians had cut from the fort to the mill. Twisting around in his saddle, he asked his Indian companion, "What can that be?" The Indian peered through the drizzle. "The same man who was with you," he said. Riding on, Sutter saw that it was Marshall, soaked to the skin. He asked him, "Have you been here all night?" "No," Marshall answered, "I spent the night at the mill and came back this far to meet you." (Marshall, not sure when Sutter would arrive, might have gone down the road to intercept him on four different days.)

The restless Marshall then poured out his ideas to Sutter. He believed that the entire countryside was rich with gold. He took his partner directly to the mill race. Marshall told the ditchers who were widening and deepening the race to knock off work and to open the headgate to let the water through. When the rush of white water had cleared away the rubbly evidence of their labors, he had the men shut the race's gate again. Then he and Sutter explored the cut for traces of gold. They soon found some, but in the hands of one of the workmen's little boys. What they did not know was that Marshall's workmen had "salted" the ditch to get Sutter into a good enough frame of mind so that he would give them a bottle of liquor. But, just as he had arrived, one of the youngsters spied the planted flakes and collected most of them. He ran to his papa and exclaimed, "Father, see what I have found!" Sutter was almost as excited as the boy. He stabbed his cane into the sandy soil and exulted, "By Joe, it is rich!" The salters had to swallow their joke. ("We dared not to say a word but let the boy claim and keep the gold, least we lose our expected drink.") Sutter examined the mill race himself, and picked up enough pieces, together with those given him by the Mormon workmen, to fashion a trinket. Treating the men to *aguardiente* and giving them pocket knives as gifts, their employer told them, "By Joe, I shall have a finger ring made of this gold as soon as I can get hold of a goldsmith." (He did just that and was wearing it, with its engraved inscription—"The First Gold Discovered in January 1848"—and a Sutter coat of arms to which he was doubtless not entitled, when Bancroft visited him in Pennsylvania, twenty-eight years later, shortly before his death.)

The next day, Sutter and Marshall went upstream from the mill and found gold all along its course. There was even better "color" in the dried-up creeks and ravines tributary to the American's South Fork. Reported Sutter, "I, myself, with nothing more than a small knife, picked out gold from a dry gorge, a little way up the mountain, a solid lump of gold which weighed nearly an ounce and a half." Sutter was now convinced that Marshall had found the legendary land of El Dorado. He gathered the workmen around him and got them to promise to keep the discovery a secret for six weeks, until his grist mill as well as his sawmill should be in operation. Some of the hands were eager to abandon the mill work for mining. One wrote in his diary, "The fever set in and gold was on the brain." But the natural conservatism of the Mormons prevailed over their gambling instincts. Since the mill was nearly completed, they agreed to stick with Sutter, prospecting only on their own free time.

For the moment, Sutter was safe. The gold discovery was a secret. "But this was not to be," he grumbled, in recall. "Women and whisky let the secret out." Actually, Sutter himself spilled the beans first. On February 10 he wrote to Vallejo, "My sawmill is now finished and promises well. All my other works are progressing rapidly and I have made a discovery of a gold mine which, so far as we have examined it, is extremely rich." Even earlier, he had hinted at important goings-on at the mill to Heinrich Lienhard, but he had shrugged it off as more Sutterian bombast. Nor could Sutter keep the news from Bidwell, who passed it on to Vallejo again. Now the most reformed of enemies, Vallejo generously said to Bidwell, "As the water flows through Sutter's mill race, may the gold flow into Sutter's purse."

The Mormons kept the secret well until Sutter sent Jacob Wittmer to Coloma with supplies. They did not break faith; Sutter simply forgot to swear the children to secrecy—as if it would have done him any good. One of the boys told Wittmer that he had gold. The teamster laughed at the lad and so angered his mother that she showed him specimens and told him the whole story. Word leaked out on St. Valentine's Day, 1848. Sutter, who groaned, "I should have sent my Indians," sadly registered Wittmer's return in his logbook: "Wittmer returned with the two wagons from the mountains and told everybody of the gold mines there, and brought a few samples with him."

Actually, the teamster at first had a hard time peddling the secret of Sutter's gold. A hard drinker, like his employer, he rushed over to the shirt-tail store of Sam Brannan and C. C. Smith, which doubled as a *cantina*. (Since Columbus Day 1847, the partners had rented one of Sutter's outbuildings.) There Wittmer produced his gold dust and demanded a drink. Smith, tending bar, fixed a fishy eye on the teamster and bellowed, "What's that? You know very well that liquor means cash money!" But Wittmer held his ground. "This *is* money," he insisted. His stubbornness did not convince the suspicious Smith. "Damn you, do you mean to insult me?" growled Smith, menacingly. An exasperated Wittmer threw up his hands in apparent capitulation: "Go to the fort and ask the captain, if you don't believe me." Greed began to shoulder suspicion from Smith's mind and by the time he reached Sutter's headquarters he was running. Craftily, he backed into his question: "Your man came to me and said that this is gold. Of course, I know that he is lying. . . . I told him so—" Before he could finish, Sutter blurted, "Nevertheless, it is true." He simply could not keep a secret, and years later he put the rhetorical question to Bancroft which, in his own mind, excused him. "What else could I do? The secret was out."

Smith passed the word to his partner, slick Sam Brannan. On

May 5, the two took a personal look at Coloma. When Brannan sailed on the launch on May 8 he had a vial of gold dust with him. When he arrived in San Francisco, he ran down Montgomery Street, hat in one hand and dust in the other, shouting "Gold! Gold! Gold from the American River!" He intended to stir up a little trade for his firm at the fort. But he got more than he bargained for. His was the shout heard 'round the world. Before its echoes would die away, the world would be turned upside down by the greatest gold rush in history. Earlier, Sutter had sent specimens to San Francisco for assay but Capt. Joseph Folsom's judgment—"mica"—had been accepted by the citizens rather than Dr. Victor Forgeaud's diagnosis—"pure gold."

At the fort itself, Wittmer continued to spread the word. He showed Lienhard some eighteen to twenty *chispas,* or flakes. Lienhard, a doubting Thomas if ever one lived, thought Sutter's smith ought to test it. The blacksmith heated the flakes and pounded them with massive blows of his hammer. As the flakes expanded, pandemonium broke out in the smithy. John Montgomery jumped about, chanting, "Gold! Gold! It's gold, boys, it's gold. All of us will be rich! Three cheers for the gold!" Sutter, hearing the noise, came out of the Big House. "My secret, I see, has been discovered. Since we expect to be rich, let's celebrate with a bottle of wine." Sutter got a bottle of red from his wine closet and he and Lienhard finished it then and there.

Strangely, no rush for gold followed Wittmer's announcements. For a variety of reasons, the news caused very little excitement until May. It was thought to be a localized strike, at the Coloma mill, and on Sutter's property. Then, too, the spring rains were not over and heavy downpours—which meant snow in the mountains—discouraged would-be gold seekers. The men went about their work at the fort, when the filthy weather permitted it. Sutter, too, tried to return to normal. Whenever he was beset with a new problem, he preferred to throw himself into frenetic work rather than brood. He had been busy all fall, harvesting and cleaning wheat. Now he rushed it aboard his boats for shipment and dispatched wagons, launches and canoes on a thousand errands to the far-flung satellites of Sutter's Fort—the hog ranch, the fishing *ranchería,* still-dormant Sutterville, the sawpits, the riverside tannery, the Natoma flour mill, the Coloma sawmill, John Sinclair's Rancho del Paso and his own Hock Farm. So involved was he in his various projects that he could not build Larkin's log ranchhouse for him and had to turn the job over to Bidwell. Larkin wrote Bidwell of their common friend, "Say to Captain Sutter I rejoice at his prospects." But Sutter still had greater faith in agriculture than in a mining fortune. He feared the gold would prove a curse, rather than a blessing, because it would bring hordes of men who would not respect his hegemony over the valley and it would, doubtless, tempt away his best workers. And he was absolutely correct.

Sutter was no fool. While he sowed wheat and peas and worried over his prize merino ram, and while his Coloma workmen were the only argonauts, picking at crevices during their free Sundays with the jackknives he had given them, he worked out a plan to monopolize the metal. As Indian sub-agent, he drew up a treaty between the chiefs of the Coloma and Yalesumne tribes and the partnership of Marshall and himself. For some $150 or $200 worth of trade goods—shirts, hats, handkerchiefs, flour and peas—at San Francisco prices, he secured from the Indians a three-year lease on an area ten to twelve miles square, centering on the sawmill. Since he knew that the mill site was far beyond the boundaries of his Mexican land grant, this was the best plan he could devise. He sent the document, properly signed and x'd by the parties of the first and second parts, to Governor Richard B. Mason on Washington's Birthday. He asked the general for his approval of the preemption contract, or treaty, on the grounds of the many benefits it would offer Sutter's wards—food, clothing, and the habits of industry. Since he knew General Mason was very busy with gubernatorial duties, Sutter kept his letter short, and the treaty document likewise, not bothering to cite the benefits which would accrue to him and Marshall. He mentioned the possibility of lead and silver deposits in the area but forgot to mention that gold, as well as mill-ripe timber, was there for his harvesting on Indian lands.

Governor Mason replied in a communiqué dated March 5. He regretted that he could not sanction any such lease as Sutter's, since the United States government did not recognize the right of Indians to sell or lease the lands they occupied. Should the government extinguish the Indian titles, it would find them encumbered with private claims, like Sutter's. Thus, Washington would never recognize such claims, since lands upon which Indian titles were extinguished reverted to the public domain.

Charles Bennett, Sutter's messenger to the governor, proved to be a poor choice. En route to the capital, he stopped off in Benicia. In the local store *cum* saloon, he eavesdropped on some men discussing newly found coal deposits on the slopes of Mount Diablo. Unable to contain himself, Bennett snorted, "Coal! I've got something here which will beat coal and make this the greatest country in the world!" With a flourish, he poured the gold dust out on the counter. In San Francisco, he showed the gold to an old miner, who pronounced it the real McCoy. Some skeptics thought Bennett's tale a hoax of Sutter's, to lure settlers to New Helvetia. Robert Semple, for example, ventured that he would give more for one solid, single, coal mine than for all the gold mines in the universe. But most of the men who heard Bennett were curious, if not completely convinced, and many were soon mining at Coloma.

Unfortunately for Sutter, California enjoys, every February, a delightful interlude of a week or two of sunny, warm weather, between rainstorms. This inside-out Indian summer, actually a false spring, induced Levi Fifield and Wilford Hudson to go prospecting around Coloma on February 25. Their expedition is a likely enough starting point for the California Gold *Rush,* as distinguished from the *discovery,* itself. The recurrence of rains halted further prospecting until March 7, when Hudson made a second trip to Coloma. On the eleventh, the sawmill was finished.

The next day, the first plank was produced and the Coloma Mormons no longer had any qualms about full-time mining. Late in the month, Bidwell went to Coloma for a look at the gold mines. He was followed in early April by John Sinclair, Sheriff McKinstry and Baptiste Rouelle. More and more "dust" made its appearance at the fort and the trickle of men up into the mountains began to increase.

On April 17, Sutter was ready for another look himself. With two of his Indians, he acted as a guide for his old friend Reading and Edward Kemble, the young editor of Sam Brannan's *California Star*. After welcoming them warmly, and feeding them hearty meals of beef and frijoles, he led them out on the nineteenth. The now graying, distinguished-looking Sutter was never a good rider, and he demonstrated his equestrian timidity on the rough road to Coloma. Once his mule, normally as solid and secure as a Morris chair, stumbled in a stony bog and Kemble heard the blue-eyed, ruddy-faced captain soothing the animal: "God bless me, Katy! Now, den, child. De oder foot. So!" But Kemble and the others could never really poke fun at the well-dressed gentleman in the broad-brimmed planter's hat who carried a gold-headed cane. Instead, Kemble would write of Sutter's "overflowing kindliness of heart and the unselfish generosity that characterized his whole life."

The travelers saw not a soul on the road; proof enough that there was no real rush as yet. When Sutter led the men into Coloma, it was a silent and vexed partner who greeted him. Sutter, polite as ever, ignored Marshall's rudeness and introduced his friends, explaining that he had no secrets from them. When they asked where they might look for gold, Marshall just waved at the river. Only Reading found a few samples, by panning with an Indian basket, and, in his own words, there was not enough to buy a drink.

At the campfire supper that night, the chiefs of the area came in to pay their respects to their *alcalde grande*. Several of them were a little independent, and one was bold enough to harangue

Sutter against looking for gold, which was bad medicine. He told the whites that it lay all over the mountains and that one Sierra lakeshore was crusted with it. Kemble guessed that the *padres* had persuaded the Indians to keep it a secret for so many years in order to prevent the ruination of quiet, mission-period California.

On their way back to the fort, Sutter demonstrated his impulsive generosity. Although he was hungry for wealth and certainly did not despise gold any more than he did land, when one of his companions expressed admiration for the Weber Creek Valley, Sutter immediately offered to give him a deed to the land. He never even stopped to consider whether it was really his to give; such gestures were a part of him. Not too long afterward, Charles Weber and Bill Daylor with a crew of Indian diggers, would take $50,000 in gold out of the creek before any other miners arrived to compete with them.

The skeptical Kemble had mentioned California gold in his paper with hardly any comment, but upon his return from the expedition to Coloma he said not a word more about it. For some reason, he thought the gold discovery was a hoax, got up to "guzzle" the public. The rival paper, the *Californian,* broke the news of gold in print, but hardly in exciting fashion. The story, in its entirety, read: "Gold Mine Found. In the newly made raceway of the saw-mill recently erected by Captain Sutter on the American Fork, gold has been found in considerable quantities. One person brought thirty dollars worth to New Helvetia, gathered there in a short time. California, no doubt, is rich in mineral wealth; great chances here for scientific capitalists. Gold has been found in every part of the country."

By May, however, the combination of rumor, modest newspaper reports and the word-of-mouth reporting of returned prospectors, began to take effect. Sutter first noticed the difference on May 11 when he found that his entire grist-mill crew had deserted to the mines. By the middle of the month, a real rush was on from Sonoma, Benicia, Monterey and San Francisco. Henry Bigler was bragging of making $16 a day digging. A neighbor pre-

When John C. Frémont met John Sutter, two powerful egos clashed. Frémont became an enemy of Sutter's, and his machinations with the Bear Flag rebels were instrumental in toppling Captain Sutter from a position of power in California in 1846.

Union Title Insurance and Trust Company Historical Collection

California Beaches & Parks

The well-laid plans of such California pioneers as John Sutter and Thomas O. Larkin, for a peaceful and gradual Americanization of the territory, were ruined by the violent outbreak of the Bear Flag Revolt in 1846. Briefly, Sutter was forced to fly the Bear Flag of the filibustering mountain men and drifters before hoisting the Stars and Stripes over New Helvetia.

VIEW OF SUTTER'S FORT—RAISING THE AMERICAN FLAG, 1846.

California Beaches & Parks

Largely because of the bastion—Sutter's Fort—which was the heart of New Helvetia and which dominated all of northern California, John Sutter was able to make himself into the most powerful man in California in a mere five years, after arriving with a few letters of introduction, a handful of Hawaiian followers, and a bulldog from Oahu.

VIEW OF CAPTAIN SUTTER'S FORT, NEAR SACRAMENTO CITY, CALIFORNIA, NOW MANNED BY U. S. TROOPS.

California Beaches & Parks

Although Sutter lost control of New Helvetia and his fortress during the Mexican War, the bastion—renamed Fort Sacramento—became one of the major centers of Yankee power during the Mexican War and its aftermath, with Sutter serving as second-in-command to U.S. Army officers.

At this site in the cold waters of the South Fork of the American River at Coloma, California, a New Jersey carpenter and spiritualist, James W. Marshall, turned the world upside down by finding a few nuggets of gold on January 24, 1848. Ironically, what should have made his employer, Capt. John Sutter, a millionaire instead very nearly transformed him into a pauper as he was swept aside by hordes of '49ers.

The on-the-spot report of Governor Richard B. Mason of California and the detailed map of Lt. William Tecumseh Sherman, drawn in July 1849, changed the gold discovery of 1848 from a local affair into a world-wide rush for riches.

Captain Sutter's ruin was assured when James Marshall picked golden nuggets out of the Sutter's Mill tailrace in January 1848, thereby setting off one of the major mass migrations of mankind in all recorded history.

John Sutter was never a good miner. He gave up prospecting and mining as a bad investment after only a short trial because he was so unsuccessful in finding rich placers anywhere in the Sierra foothills, even when he prospected immediately upstream and downstream from Mormon Island (above), which yielded thousands to its South Fork (American River) diggers.

Sutter's dream metropolis of Sutterville, three miles downriver from his *embarcadero*, never really got off the drawing boards, although fine plates of the paper city were drawn to attract European immigrants. Sutter's son threw his support to the infant city of Sacramento, which soon overwhelmed its rival neighbor. Sutterville became a ghost town.

Between the discovery of gold in 1848 and the silting up of the Sacramento River, largely from hydraulic mining, the city of Sacramento became a deep-water port. To Sutter's old *embarcadero*, there came sailing ships and steamers from all over the world. But Sutter, ironically, banked not on the future of the land between his landing and his fort—that is, Sacramento City—but on his rival town of Sutterville, three miles downriver.

Most of Captain Sutter's friends drifted away from him in the difficult days after his establishment was swamped by the '49ers. But a few like Thomas Oliver Larkin (above) and John Bidwell remained loyal to him. Larkin, U.S. Consul at Monterey, was second only to Sutter in importance in the transformation of Alta California into an American state.

California Historical Society

California State Library

By the early 1850's, Sutter's lonely sawmill site, Coloma, was a boom town of gold miners and the seat of government for El Dorado County. Many of its citizens became rich, but Sutter was unable to find wealth either in mining there or in the trading post he set up with Lansford Hastings.

Sutter abandoned his New Helvetia to the hordes of gold miners and land speculators that overran California in 1849 and literally fled to his country estate, lovely Hock Farm on the Feather River to the north of Sacramento. But bad luck followed the pioneer even here; an arsonist burned the rustic manor down and drove Sutter from California, forever, in 1865.

William S. Jewett, 1812–73, California's finest nineteenth-century portrait artist, painted John Sutter a number of times. One portrait hangs in the Capitol; two are held by the Society of California Pioneers in San Francisco; and one (above) by the Oakland Art Museum as part of the Kahn Foundation collection.

dicted to Bidwell that the Sacramento Valley would shortly be full of gold-seekers. But Sutter, intent on maintaining his normal routine, was busy whitewashing one of his powder magazine-granary-jail cells for a store for C. C. Smith, since his old shop was to be made into a boarding house. On the nineteenth, so many argonauts arrived that Sutter wrote: "The great rush from San Francisco arrived at the fort. All my friends and acquaintances filled up the houses and the whole fort. I had only a little Indian boy [to help me]. . . . My cooks left me, like everybody else. The merchants, doctors, lawyers, sea captains, merchants, etc., all came up and did not know what to do. All was in a confusion; all left their wives and families in San Francisco and those which had none locked the doors, abandoned their houses [or] offered them for sale, cheap. . . . Soldiers deserted their flag and sailors left their ships to rot in the harbor. The recently opened school had to be closed; teacher and pupils had gone off to the mines."

On March 25, Sutter wrote Leidesdorff: "We intend to form a company for working the gold mines, which prove to be very rich. Would you not take a share in it? So soon as if it would not pay, we could stop it, at any time." On April 2, he had formed his gold-mining company in partnership with Marshall, one of the workmen, named Wimmer, and a veteran Georgia miner, Isaac Humphrey. But he continued to reside at the fort, letting his partners dig while he supplied them with Indians, food and supplies. He was more ambivalent than ever, torn between mining and agriculture. He still had his days of gloom. When he showed Cordua three ounces of fine gold he also told him that the securing of it had cost him three times its worth of $50. Yet he predicted the development of quartz mining, writing a friend: "Not only *plazeros* but also rich gold veins have been discovered on our property, which we shall explore more thoroughly before it pleases Uncle Sam to lay his fatherly hand on it." And when he ordered new clothes with which to greet his family, expected from Europe, he was superbly confident in a newsy letter to his tailor: "Possibly you hesitate on account of the payment. You need not hesitate on account of this because we now have plenty of gold in Sacramento and as soon as you send the clothes, we will send you the amount, which will be in the purest gold that exists." Sutter told the tailor that the mines extended for 100 miles north and south and 80 miles east and west, adding that he and Reading had discovered not only gold but quicksilver and iron ore— eighty-five-percent iron, he bragged—in inexhaustible quantities. Finally, he boasted that the miners who had been making $5 a day were now clearing from $10 to 16; that some Mormons cleared between $600 and $1,000 a week; that a fifteen-year-old had found $70 worth in one day and that another lad had washed a pound of pure gold in a few weeks.

Although Sutter was not ready to leave New Helvetia and join the rush to the mountains, he could no longer maintain his business-as-usual attitude to the California Gold Rush. Customers at the fort's store so overwhelmed him that he had to abandon his diary on May 25, 1848. The Gold Rush was in flood.

CHAPTER XVII

THE '49ER

THE first gold in the Sierra was picked up, by hand, by Jim Marshall and his men. Sutter first "mechanized" the process by giving his workers knives with which they explored the crevices in and under boulders in the stream beds, recovering trapped gold dust and flakes. The next step was to imitate the *batea*, the wooden gold-washing bowl of the Latin American miners. All manner of bowls, metal pans, and even Indian baskets were pressed into service. Placers—sand bars—were excavated with pick and shovel and the sand and gravel washed, a pan at a time, just under the surface of the swiftly flowing streams. The action of the rushing water carried off the dirt, sand, pebbles and other debris, leaving the heavier gold in the bottom of the container.

Then Isaac Humphrey introduced the gold-washing machines he knew from the North Carolina and Georgia mines. These were called cradles or rockers. They were cradle- or coffin-shaped boxes, mounted on rockers. The bottom end was left open for the escape of water and rubble, while the head bore a sieve or hopper to screen out large rocks. Buckets or shovels were used to dump dirt into the hopper. The lighter material was swept

away by the miners' bailing great quantities of water into the
head of the box, via the hopper, while the weightier gold lodged
behind cleats nailed to the bottom of the box. Mining was no
longer a one-man operation now. It took a team of men to dig
the gravel, haul it to the cradle, keep the water flowing and the
cradle rocking so that the paydirt would more easily become
separated from the worthless soil and sand.

Quartz-mining or hard-rock mining, as distinguished from the
washing of placer gold, was still far in the future as Sutter gave
some thought to doing some prospecting on his own. The industry was still tied to the deposits in riverbanks and sand bars. But
the machines grew steadily more sophisticated. First, there was
the introduction of the more complicated long-tom, a kind of
super-cradle or outsized rocker. Later, pumps and steam engines
were applied to the task of securing gold flakes, and eventually
an engineer named Lerwheel advertised his services in the *Placer
Times*. He would explore the very bottom of the streams with his
diving bell and he promised fourteen years of experience, gained
while a diver for pearl shell with the Sub-Marine Society of
Tahiti. But this cumbersome device had no real future in the
shallow streams of the mother lode. The miners found it simpler
to divert the water courses with cofferdams, in order to reveal the
treasure lurking in the very stream beds themselves.

A *Placer Times* correspondent described the teamwork of a
group of miners:

> Here a dozen picks were tumbling down masses of dirt and as
> many shovels turning it into baskets; there a line of laborers,
> bearing baskets on their heads, extended to the water's edge,
> passing and repassing with loads of earth, which was deposited
> by the sides of the machines. Half-leg deep in the water stood
> some, hard at work dashing water on the dirt as it was thrown
> into the sieve, while others jerked up and down at the levers and
> rattled the dirt and gravel down the inclined plain into the river,
> to be swept away by its swift, boiling, current.

By June 1848, the Gold Rush had picked up so much momentum that it was threatening to swamp Sutter. He still tried to be in two places at once, but the miner-agriculturalist found it increasingly difficult to survive. As usual, Larkin was more prescient than most of his contemporaries. Although he declined to predict what the good or bad consequences of the Gold Rush might be when he reported on the discovery at Coloma to Secretary of State James Buchanan on June 1, he was considerably more candid when he wrote a personal letter to Stephen Reynolds in Honolulu, only two days later: "You have often requested to know in what manner you could obtain dollars in California. . . . Come to California, bring 100 Kanakas, 1,000 spades, shovels, picks, with 100 dishes or bowls. Go up the Sacramento (I have 20 leagues there; take a league), dig, delve and wash, turn up the bottom of the American Fork, dig down the banks of the Feather River, fill your barrels, take into your constitution the ague and fever, bury half of your Kanakas, and go back."

Although Governor Mason had at first underestimated the importance of what he called the Golden Yellow Fever, he finally decided to see the placers for himself. On July 2, he arrived at Sutter's Fort with Lt. William T. Sherman and Capt. Joseph Folsom in tow, along with the remains of an escort rapidly deserting to the mines. Sutter always loved celebrations so he dragged out an old iron cannon and loaded it to fire salutes. Lienhard was afraid that it would blow up, but the old piece survived Independence Day. Sutter began the Fourth of July festivities by firing the gun, then raising the Stars and Stripes at sunrise. His mind was, for the moment, taken off the flood of mankind swirling and eddying around New Helvetia, threatening to wash it away. He recalled, "It was a universal holiday and, being the first [sic] national holiday to be celebrated under the American flag, everybody was in high spirits. All rejoiced in being under a good and strong government, now." Sutter invited all the prominent men of the valley who had not gone to the mines to a great banquet in honor of Governor Mason. Sinclair presided. Charles

"Philosopher" Pickett was chosen by Sutter to be Orator of the Day. Sutter served his guests beef, wild fowl and venison, and, in his own words, "all the luxuries which a frontier life could offer." Luckily, a launch had just delivered a new supply of sauterne, brandy and other liquor, so there was no shortage of toasts proposed and drunk.

Under great pressure from the prospectors, Sutter was drinking more heavily than ever by the summer of 1848. At his Fourth of July party, he overindulged. Sherman wrote in his *Memoirs,* "Before the celebration was over, Sutter was very tight, and many others showed the effect of the *aguardiente.*" In his own reminiscences, twenty-eight years after the fact, Sutter denied it. "General Sherman says in his memoirs that I was 'tight' that day, but I was no more intoxicated than he. Men cannot drink liquor without feeling the effects of it. I believe it was in bad taste for an officer of the Army to partake of my hospitality and then make flippant remarks about it, accusing the host of drunkenness. I think that Sherman was later ashamed of his words; in a letter which he wrote to me he took back everything and begged my pardon." Perhaps Sutter's inebriation on July 4, 1848, suggested to John A. Stone, alias "Putt," the bit of doggerel which he put into his popular *Putt's Original California Songster:*

> I went to eat some oysters, along with Captain Sutter;
> And he reared up on the table, and sat down in the butter.

Sherman actually enjoyed the banquet, as well he might. It set Sutter back some $2,000. He paid Sutter an honest compliment shortly after the celebration: "This man, Sutter, has played a conspicuous part in the history of the country and is likely to continue his onward career."

Unfortunately for Sherman's prediction, Sutter's career was in decline. Although his establishment impressed the governor greatly, standing out as it did in an area of abandoned homes, farms and fields, Sutter was finding it difficult even to harvest his wheat, claiming that he had to leave two-thirds of his harvest in the fields. There was no denying that rent was pouring into his coffers. He was getting $1,800 a month and expected $2,000 to $3,000 before long. One visitor to the fort in July found it bedlam, jammed with men and horses, piled high with casks, boxes and bales, and resembling nothing so much as a European market square or a Turkish bazaar. But the Mormons had left Sutter; also the *gentiles* and now the Indians were clamoring to go and mine for gold. The shoe, saddle, hat and blacksmith shops and the distillery had to be abandoned for want of help.

In July, he appointed a caretaker for the fort and led some 100 Indians and about 50 Kanakas, just arrived, with wagonloads of provisions, to a bar about ten miles above Mormon Island on the American's South Fork. He also formed a partnership with Lienhard, who gave up the New Helvetia nursery and garden to lead eleven Indians to diggings downstream from Mormon Bar. Sutter supplied Lienhard his diggers, food and equipment for one-half of the take. Before long, Lienhard regretted his arrangement because he found Sutter could not keep his word in money arrangements. Several times, Sutter moved Lienhard and his party to placers which he promised would yield $50—or $150—a day per man, but none of them really panned out. Sutter kept up a steady flow of optimism and promises, but he and Marshall finally split up. Sutter had twice staked the eccentric Marshall to prospecting outfits, but he always failed.

When, in July, Sutter found himself hemmed in by other miners about ten miles above Mormon Bar, many of them lawless men who openly resented his Indians, beating them up and kidnapping them for servants, he moved from the South Fork to Sutter's Creek. But even here mobile saloons followed him and persuaded his diggers to squander their dust in drinking and gambling. His men were often unfit for work, and they fell deeper and deeper in debt to him, especially the Hawaiians. Although men like Suñol, Daylor, McCoon, Job Dye and Jim Savage, by imitating Sutter and using Indians, secured tens of thousands of dollars in gold, there was no success for his own mining company.

Lienhard thought that the reason Sutter could not control his drunken miners was that he was himself the traveling saloons' greatest customer. Be that as it may, he found himself unable to find good placers and uncertain of how to cope with the wild element of society, to the fringe of which he had once belonged. He never spelled out the reasons for his mining debacle, but Lienhard's description of the society around him may be part of the answer: "Most miners were so greedy, treacherous and unreliable that no man's life was safe. Law and order were unknown, fights occurred daily and anyone who could not protect himself with his fists was unfortunate. Every man carried a gun. . . . Robbery and murder were a commonplace because many men still preferred to steal gold dust rather than work for it." Even seasoned frontiersman George Yount was appalled: "There is nothing in all the history of the natives of America to equal the deeds of cruelty perpetrated by individuals who early immigrated to this Land of Gold. In the states east of the mountains, villainy is held in check by law and the restraints of public sentiment. But, allured by the discovery of gold, the dregs and scum of the cities rushed into California and murder and rapine marked their every footstep." Conditions at the fort were no better. A visitor described its moral climate to Larkin: "Self-interest is so great here that they cannot take time to bury people when they die."

Sutter said very little about his failure. "It was high time to quit this sort of business, in which I only lost time and money. I therefore broke this camp, too, and returned to the fort where I disbanded nearly all of the people who had worked for me in the mountains digging gold. The whole expedition proved to be a heavy loss to me." With a small army of diggers, paid largely in clothing, liquor and food, he could not make a go of mining in a region where a lone soldier, on furlough, made $1,500 in a single week's washing. Most of the dust which Sutter did get he managed to scatter to the winds. Observed Lienhard, "He was so careless with his gold that I was amazed that all of it was not stolen, when he had so many men of questionable character among his associates."

Sutter turned his back on the mines, resolved to make his fortune on the Sacramento plain. He had good reason for optimism. As late as September 1848, one of Larkin's subordinates would write him that he believed the government would move from Monterey to New Helvetia. It was as much his preference for agriculture over mining as it was indecision which led Sutter to quit the placers. He found his fort in chaos. Whoever wanted meat killed one of his sheep, hogs or steers. Dismayed, he observed the near ruin of his fort: "Stealing began. Land, cattle, horses, everything began to disappear." His 200 salmon barrels vanished, along with the fort's bells, cannon and gate-weights. Said Sutter, "There is a saying that men will steal everything but a milestone and a millstone. They stole my millstones." His fences were torn down piecemeal for firewood or to allow hungry horses into his grain fields to graze. His crops were trampled into the soil. Sutter's fame as "the man of gold" brought the ruthless plunderers of the Rush down upon him. He sadly acknowledged, "The miners would not buy flour from me when they could more easily steal it." Jim Marshall was far more bitter than Sutter about their joint eclipse. Of the California prospectors he wrote: "They left honesty and honor at home. . . . They commenced a course of rascality of which Sutter and myself were the principal subjects . . . [and] plundered the persons who had given them wealth by their enterprise."

The suspicious Lienhard tried to warn him away from the flatterers and schemers who surrounded him when he had dust in his pouches, but Sutter's vanity could never resist admiration. When he finally realized that he had been fleeced by a friend—again— he would only pace back and forth, frowning, and say, simply, "That's too bad." As the worst judge of men ever to handle wealth in California, Sutter's end was readily predictable to Lienhard and others by 1848. Late in life, afflicted with self-pity, Sutter looked back to this period as the onset of his ruin. Actually, the blackest days still lay ahead of him, but he complained, "The damage which I suffered in 1848 is inestimable. What a great misfortune was this sudden gold discovery for me. It has just broken up and ruined my hard, restless, and industrious life. . . . My property was all left exposed and at the mercy of the rabble. . . . The country swarmed with lawless men. I was alone; there was no law." He was right, of course. A few other men, as foresighted as himself, saw the Gold Rush as the end, not the beginning, of an almost fabulous California paradise. Larkin was one. John Coffin Jones, writing "what a curse it will prove to the country," was another. Sutter told Bancroft twenty-eight years later, "I regret that I did not abandon Fort Sacramento, at once, in order to settle at Fort Ross. The location was beautiful and healthy, there was good soil and plenty of timber and, by far, more improvements than at New Helvetia. There would have been no gold hunters to rob me. Indeed, gold might never have been discovered."

In 1848, Sutter was not as badly off as he suggested to Congress when he later begged compensation for his losses. He claimed that he lost $10,000 at Coloma and $25,000 at Natoma, but he was getting at least $2,000 a month rent from the fort and Alden S. Bayly and John Winters paid him at least $1,000 (some sources say as high as $6,000) for his interest in the Coloma mill.

The direct catalyst to Sutter's return from the mines in the fall of 1848 was news of the arrival of the ship *Huntress* in San Francisco on September 14. On board was his oldest son, John August Sutter, Jr. Captain Sutter was now ready to clutch at *any* straw, no matter how slender. So he banked on his green, twenty-one-year-old son, a stranger to him after fourteen years of separation. He needed someone, desperately, in whom he could place his trust. With several of his impressive, lance-bearing Indian bodyguards he rode up to Lienhard's camp to tell his partner of his son's arrival and to brag about the youth's scientific education and knowledge—*and* to borrow what gold Lienhard had ($1,000) in order to make a better impression. It was well that Sutter worked to improve his image. Young August's eyes were being opened wide in San Francisco and New Helvetia by tales of his father's drinking and his profligacy. He was also warned that his father was surrounded by conniving rogues intent upon his utter ruin, financial, moral and physical. Whatever doubts the young man may have had on the boat trip up the Sacramento about the truth of these rumors disappeared when he reached the fort. He found that all his father's property was at everyone's disposal, his books in chaos, and his important legal documents and maps lying about as if they were waste paper. Worse, he found that his father was in debt by at least $80,000. The captain had been drawing on the fort's rents, in advance, up to $3,000 a month, and was using for his own purposes (just like a banker, but without any books!) the gold dust entrusted to him by miners for safekeeping.

To August, it seemed that there was no one man in San Francisco or New Helvetia who did not maintain that he had claims against his father. But the young man buckled down to the task of unsnarling the tangled skeins of Sutter's accounts, hiring Henry A. Schoolcraft to help him as bookkeeper. Before Sutter arrived from the mountains, August conferred with McKinstry and Reading. Both friends of his father urged him to take over his parent's property in order to stay the execution of the attachment on New Helvetia which Leidesdorff had originally levied in 1846. In 1848, the Russian American Company, completely out of patience, had passed the matter on to Washington, and the United States government was applying pressure on Sutter to pay up or forfeit his private empire.

Sutter at last arrived. Father and son had a tear-stained, joyful, reunion. The young man, finding his father so kind and affectionate, regained his confidence in him and dismissed all the tales of his loose living. When McKinstry proposed the unethical—illegal, in fact—idea of signing over all his property to his son, to avoid foreclosure, Sutter readily consented.

Two of August's new friends, both lawyers, drew up the papers, although they were well aware of their illegality, since Sutter could not convey property after its attachment. But desperate measures were necessary. Neither father nor son wished to cheat the Russians. But both were determined to fight for time with any weapon at hand, time in which to work hard to pay off the Russian debt, along with all others. On October 14, August paid (on paper, at least) $50,000 to his father, who conveyed to him all his Sacramento Valley properties and a lot in San Francisco, plus six leagues of land at Fort Ross, which he did not own, and a square mile at Coloma which he likewise did not own. In a second legal instrument, Sutter turned over all his personal property to his son, for $15,000. This included 1,500 horses, 50 mules, 600 cattle, 20 saddles and bridles, and the schooner *Sacramento*. The number of head was far below his usual estimate of his stock but probably referred to his tame cattle, whereas most of his beasts roamed the Sacramento Plain free and could only be counted, much less transferred, after a rodeo. Sutter's excuse for this bald fraud was not a bad one—the unsettled state of California law. It was this very lawlessness which threatened him; he would make use of it in his own way.

On the following day, Sutter took the next step in his little plot against bankruptcy. He had his son enter into the firm of Hensley, Reading and Company, with Samuel J. Hensley, Pierson B. Reading, and Jacob Rink Snyder, three men of excellent character—a rare commodity in California of 1848. The three each put up $3,000 in gold; Sutter, Jr., fronting for his father, bound himself to supply the firm with suitable buildings at the fort for its operation; to secure to the company the exclusive use of the schooner *Sacramento;* and to obtain a 300-yard strip of land on the Sacramento River's east shore for 1,000 yards downstream from the mouth of the American. Here the firm was to have the exclusive privilege of building houses and cutting timber. Hensley, Reading and Company was also to secure control of the ferry as soon as the lease granted by Sutter to George McDougal in August should expire. On November 1, the partners had to add a codicil to their agreement, releasing the land and ferry clauses, because the newborn city of Sacramento was appropriating the riverside land for its own municipal use.

Sutter was delighted with his son's intelligence and diligence. Since he had made such a good beginning and because Hensley and Reading were his most trustworthy friends, along with Bidwell, he was sure that he had been right in turning over his properties and debts to the boy. He gave him free rein, feeling no qualms about leaving the fort, and rushed off to the mines although it was October and, with winter closing in, most of the traffic was going in the other direction. One reason for his trip was his desire to check on his trading post in the double log cabin of the mill hands at Coloma. There, he, Lansford Hastings, and two others ran a store handling miners' supplies. He took with him whole wagonloads of goods, of which he was shortly either cheated or robbed and, according to his son, by none other than his partners, whom August denounced as insatiable parasites.

Young August quickly proved himself committed to Sutter's financial rescue, and far more ethical than his father. But he was even more naïve, completely inexperienced in rough-and-tumble frontier living, and only twenty-one years old. Despite his part in the property conveyance (actually McKinstry's idea), August was virtually guileless. Sutter had, in fact, left his fate in the hands of a novice. Although young Sutter struggled valiantly to stem the outward flow of money and to pay off old bills faster than new ones accumulated, he soon revealed his weaknesses. August's judgment in dealing with his father's friends was bad. He annoyed John Sinclair by pressing him for money due his father. Whatever his other faults, Sutter, Sr., had never been a dunning creditor. (August annoyed his father, too, by selling Vallejo the fort's still, against Sutter's wishes, and by moralizing with him about his zest for the bottle and for handsome Indian girls.) He angered Lienhard by being unable to pay that patient man after his father had told him to do so, finally mollifying him by giving him 1,100 sheep and a silo. But the young man also made enemies of those who *deserved* to be his father's enemies. Catching on to the way Lansford Hastings was using his father earned him Hastings' hatred. Hastings even blustered, in Captain Sutter's presence, that he intended to kill his son.

But August Sutter's incompetence was most brilliantly displayed in his handling of the parasites who loafed about the fort. When some of them threw firecrackers on the dry shakes of one of the buildings, he shouted, "Stop it, you fools!" before he remembered that he was not in orderly Switzerland but on a lawless frontier. Some of the roughnecks, just itching for a fight to vary their daily round of loafing, wenching and drinking, gathered around the slim young man. Two spoiled sons of respectable Eastern families marched belligerently up to him. The former, ironically, one of Captain Sutter's bodyguards, hired to protect him from robbery (on the principle of "set a thief to catch a thief"), demanded roughly that August repeat his words. Young Sutter was frightened. He swallowed his pride—and his heart, which seemed to be working its way up into his throat—and abruptly backed down, stammering, "I did not mean anything by it, but was merely afraid that the fort would be set on fire."

Shortly afterward, August was involved in another set-to. Filling in for his father as Indian sub-agent as well as master of New Helvetia, August heard the complaints of several Indians that one of their horses had been stolen by a white loafer. When August accused the suspect, a hoodlum who doubled as bartender and constable in the fort, he answered that the Indians had stolen the animal first. When August continued to take the Indians' part, the barman attacked him. Lienhard tried to separate them but was discouraged by the *alcalde*, a friend of the barman, who waved Lienhard away with a club. August was no match for his young antagonist. The young Swiss was soon flat on his back in the dirt, being pummeled unmercifully. Lienhard persuaded him to give up, and he escaped from the scuffle with no broken bones, only a battered and scratched face. But his pride, too, was battered, causing him to shut himself in his father's room to lick his wounds and sulk.

August did not have long to worry, however. The barman made the fatal error of hazing eccentric, but tough, Charles "Philosopher" Pickett, by claiming and trespassing upon the space adjoining Pickett's in the fort's northeast quarter, space Sutter had rented the Philosopher for a store. Pickett warned him off in no uncertain terms, and when he ignored him, Pickett either nailed the connecting door shut or fenced him off from the space. Soon, the barman returned with an axe and Pickett felt obliged to shoot him. Sutter's sheriff disarmed the Philosopher, but since *Alcalde* Bates was the barman's business partner, and hostile to Pickett, he wisely delegated authority in the case to the second *alcalde,* John Fowler. But Fowler, aware of the Philosopher's hot temper and superb aim, immediately resigned his office, for reasons of health. Bully-boy Sam Brannan then volunteered to try the case and, helped along by plentiful nips from the brandy bottle which he installed in the courtroom, did a fair job as judge. However, his arrogance got the best of him and he leaped up to make a plea for the prosecution. Pickett protested, "Hold on, Brannan, you are the judge!" The apostate Mormon overruled him. "I know it, and I am prosecuting attorney, too!" Captain Sutter, back from the mountains, had been impaneled as a juror. Now he provided the spectators with some entertainment after overdrawing from his account in the brandy bottle. He awoke in the makeshift jury box while testimony was being heard as to the bad conduct of the deceased. Sutter listened a moment, lurched to his feet and cried in outrage, "Gentlemen, the man is dead and has atoned for his faults, and I will not sit here and hear his character traduced." With that, he started to stalk—or, better, weave—his way out of the courtroom, but Justice Brannan persuaded him to stay. Since Sutter no longer had a jail, the accused murderer had to be let free on bail. The next day, the jury disagreed, and in a new trial Pickett was acquitted of homicide.

This farce-trial featured two men who, like Frémont, became

Sutter's enemies. Brannan ultimately became a virtual nemesis for both Sutter and his son. Surprisingly, the other was Pickett. August rented his quarters in the fort out from under him, for some reason, and turned the eccentric from one of his father's friends into a vindictive foe. Ironically, Pickett not only nursed his grudge but he harassed the elder Sutter more than the guilty party, August, over the years.

Up in the diggings, before his return to the fort, Sutter had had a little better luck than before, though his Coloma store turned into another disaster for him. In a boom town, where butter sold for $6 a pound, sardines for $16 a box, and miserable New England rum for $8 a bottle, he expected to share $100,000 quickly with Hastings; instead, he only sank deeper into debt. "The store made money," he said, "but I lost. Hastings was a bad man." But his loyal Kanakas and Indians continued to work hard, and he amassed about $4,000 in gold, according to Lienhard, though he squandered costly presents on Perry McCoon's ex-mistress, the squaw Mary. Finally, he had given the order to return to the fort and some of his party were mounted to accompany the gold-laden pack mules. But Sutter, thanks to too many stirrup cups, had been unable to leave. Lienhard recalled that he was too drunk to ride. In any case, nobody left camp. Instead, they sat around and listened to Sutter's tales of military glory in the never-never land of Charles X's France. "Yes, gentlemen", slurred Sutter in his Germanic accent, which thickened with excitement or intoxication, "during the fight at Grenoble in which I was exposed, I received a bayonet wound in one of my legs. Our major, who happened to be standing hearby, noticed how the blood ran down over my white trousers and called, 'Captain Sutter is wounded! Take him back where he can be treated!' But I told them to go on, and went on fighting with my sword." As the liquor took full effect, Sutter began to brag in a more and more incomprehensible Swiss-German accent that he could converse in four languages—English, Spanish, German and French. "Yes, sir, I can. I am no ordinary gentleman, no, sir. I am an extraordinary gentleman. Yes, sir, I am. I strive to be honored. I will do anything for honor."

Sutter's return to the trials of New Helvetia was thus delayed by a three-day drinking bout. Although Lienhard claimed that it was in no way extraordinary, since the captain was never entirely sober any longer, he was not strictly correct. For on no other drunk had the captain ever caused a near riot by threatening to shoot the lovely squaw, Mary, and McCoon to boot, because she rejected his affections. An old friend of Sutter's, from Cahuenga soldiering days, snatched the pistol from his hand. Nor was it normal for Sutter to form up as a one-man expedition against McCoon, shouldering his double-barreled shotgun and marching and wheeling off to war in a ludicrous parody of military maneuvering. According to Lienhard, one of his companions led him back to his tent, Sutter "daroom-darooming" all the while, in lieu of a drummer, then shoved him in to sleep it off.

After Sutter returned to the mountains for the last time in 1848, he and August began to drift apart. Sam Brannan and others took advantage of their separation to convince the youth that Sutterville, the apple of the captain's eye, was a poor site for a settlement. Instead, they urged him to locate the city between the fort and the *embarcadero*. Brannan persuaded August to take immediate action, even though his father was beyond communication, for winter had closed the road to Coloma. Brannan argued that squatters were moving into the area, threatening to preempt portions of it, and he added that a skilled U.S. Army topographical engineer was available to survey the new city. So, in December 1848, August hired Lt. William H. Warner to lay out Sacramento City during his leave of absence. Lienhard always blamed himself for the choice of name, but Brannan as well as Warner also urged August to consider Sacramento City as a substitute for New Helvetia. He went along, not realizing how badly it would hurt his father's pride not to have the new settlement named Sutter's City. Warner finished his surveying and mapping by January 1849, while Sutter was pulling out of his Coloma partnership with Hastings.

When Sutter heard of the new town and his son's role in founding it, he was furious. He considered himself betrayed by August, a partner of the very men who opposed his plans for his high-ground city at Sutterville. He blamed Brannan, as he should have, and his associates, but he also spoke disparagingly of his son in anger, and gossips gleefully picked up his criticism, exaggerated it and passed it on to August. Speculators gladly exploited the widening breach between the Sutters, and confidence men moved in for the kill. Sutter raged later, "Brannan moved his store from the fort to the river, where Sacramento now is; that was the reason he wanted the town there. The merchants of Sutterville were his rivals, and jealousy built Sacramento. Had I not been snowbound at Coloma that winter, Sacramento would never have been built!" But built it was and it boomed before his eyes.

The fort was another touchy issue. Sutter clung to it, dilapidated as it was, but August considered it a white elephant. He was happy to realize $40,000 from it in rentals but not sorry to see it finally sold, in the fall of 1849, to Bayly for $7,000. It was in February and March of 1849 that August moved everything he could from the fort to Hock Farm, believing it a safer place from thieves and squatters. He asked Sutter's major-domo there, John Ritschard, to fix up the house as the future residence of the entire Sutter family. Eventually, of course, Sutter himself came around to August's way of thinking. He wanted no more to do with the gold mines; the fort was bedlam itself, surrounded by heaps of empty whisky bottles. He saw his one-time citadel transformed by the prospectors into a sink of gambling, whoring and drinking. The only trace of law and order, aside from farcical *alcaldes* and constable-sheriffs, often outlaws themselves, was a squad of men under Corp. Edmund Bray, stationed there to apprehend the worst of the Army's deserters-turned-miners. Talking to a friend, Sutter said, "Sacramento City, my old fort, is becoming too populous for me. I must retire to my Hock Farm on Feather River. I suppose that I shall soon be surrounded there. But, [Fort] Ross is left to me. I can fly there and live on in a good old times." He remarked about this turning point, this retreat, to Bancroft: "I had no pleasure to remain there [in the fort], and moved to Hock Farm with all my Indians who had been with me from the time they were children."

Among those carrion birds attracted by the familial quarrel were George McDougal and his brother John, H. H. Bancroft's "gentleman drunkard," who became governor of California in 1851. Most prominent among the speculators was George McDougal, the ferryman, although he would soon enough be overwhelmed by Brannan. He had tried to pressure August into giving him much of the Sacramento waterfront, because of Captain Sutter's lease to him of a ferry landing. When this maneuver did not work, he—according to August—threatened to establish a preemption claim on the *embarcadero* land. Perhaps, by now, wind of errors in Sutter's original 1841 survey had reached his ears; Jean J. Vioget's faulty skill and equipment ran a line at 38° 49′ 32″ to mark the southern boundary of New Helvetia. With accurate measurements, this line was discovered to run north of the city, not below it.

McDougal's partner was George McKinstry, Jr., Sutter's old friend, who made his associate's work easier at Coloma, to which they hurried. Greasing Sutter's resentment against his son with liberal internal applications of *aguardiente,* they hurried him in late January to San Francisco. The captain had not even stopped to see his son en route. McKinstry and McDougal kept him in liquor there and conned him into signing a bond for $20,000, on March 6, 1849, which obligated him to compensate McDougal for the alleged injury to his exclusive *embarcadero* privileges. The document granted McDougal title in fee simple to a half-mile plot along the river, one mile deep, at Sutterville's south edge. Sutter asked no consideration or compensation whatsoever! Thus, willy-nilly, McDougal became Sutter's ally, for both wanted success for Sutterville, while August became his father's rival.

As McDougal enticed investors and speculators away from Sacramento to Sutterville, young Sutter panicked and fell neatly into a trap of Sam Brannan's. Brannan arranged a meeting with his father in Captain Sutter's room at the fort and there showed August a letter from McDougal, offering him 200 town lots if he would remove his house, store ship—and his influence—from Sacramento City to Sutterville. Brannan told August that similar letters had been sent to both Hensley, Reading and Company, and Priest, Lee and Company. He flatly stated that it was up to August now to either ruin or save Sacramento City. Brannan and the others approached by McDougal (if they were, indeed, really thus seduced) expected August to grant them the same amount of property in his townsite, to protect his own investment as well as theirs. Otherwise, he warned, they would abandon August's town for old Sutterville. A witless Sutter, not at all sure upon whose side he was, said to his bewildered son, "Well, if it is so, you cannot do anything else. You must let Mr. Brannan have the same advantages to induce him to stay." By waving a piece of paper at the Sutters, Sam Brannan and his cronies walked out of Sutter's room owning 200 city lots worth, even then, from $250 to $500 apiece, and without paying so much as a dime for them. It was one of the most flagrant, and one of the most brilliant, examples of confidencemanship in the history of the state.

August did not know it, but there was trouble in the other camp, although McDougal had won new allies in Cordua and William Blackburn. The ferryman took into partnership the slippery Lansford Hastings. Soon they quarreled, and from that time on, Sutterville fell further and further behind Sacramento until it was nothing more than a riverside ghost town.

While Cordua was laying the victory of Sacramento over Sutterville to August Sutter's "intrigues," the supposed victor was sick at heart. His father alienated, he found himself surrounded by confidence men, speculators and enemies of one stamp or another. He was sick with fever and ague and nearly blind from eye inflammation. August pulled out of Hensley, Reading and Company on May 6, 1849. Perhaps his illness helped heal familial wounds; Sutter took him to Hock Farm to care for him. Drawing closer again, they agreed that the moment was at hand to bring the whole family to California. Bidwell was building a fine, comfortable country home for Sutter at Hock Farm. Sutter hoped that August would go to get them, turning back to him control of his fortunes. This was exactly why his son was determined not to go. He narrowed down the list of possible proxies to two men, John Ritschard, Sutter's Hock Farm overseer, and Lienhard. August decided in favor of the latter in April, but Lienhard declined the proposition when young Sutter offered him only $2,000 for his services. Because he had lost so much to the elder Sutter's promises, he held out for $4,000 in salary plus first-class expenses. Finally, August gave in and a contract was drawn, allowing for $8,000 in expenses. Lienhard agreed to escort to Hock Farm from Switzerland Mrs. Sutter, Anna Eliza, twenty years old, Emil Viktor, eighteen years old, Wilhelm Alphonse, sixteen, and Mrs. Sutter's nephew, Gustave Schlafi. (Sutter's youngest son, Carl Albert, born in 1833, had died at the age of six.) Ironically, half of the $12,000 was borrowed by August from the newly wealthy Bill Daylor, the ex-cook, whom his father had once thrown in jail for alienation of Manuiki's affections. Daylor demanded heavy interest so, to make it easier on August, Lienhard took a corner lot at O and Front streets, in Sacramento, in lieu of the first $1,000 of his salary.

Although Sutter and son were thrown together again at Hock Farm, Lienhard found that the wounds had not entirely healed. He accompanied the captain on a ride and found him still very bitter about his son. Although Lienhard tried to tell him that flatterers and deceivers were to blame for the strained relations between them, Sutter was deaf to all explanation. He told his associate that he had heard that his own son had called him vile names. By way of reply, Lienhard reminded him of the widespread story that Sutter intended to ship his son home to Switzerland in chains. Sutter swore that he had never said such a thing. Lienhard acknowledged that he knew it, but he was unable to stop the captain from believing the wildest tales invented to estrange him from his son and business manager. Shortly, Sutter fell into one of his black periods. In this mood, he grabbed up two double-barreled pistols, saying, "I would like to kill him." This threat suggested suicide to him as an alternative to homicide, and he raised the pistols to his head. Lienhard wrestled them away from the embittered pioneer and managed to get him to bed. He found the pistols unloaded—typical of Sutter's carelessness— but the incident troubled Lienhard, since he found Sutter's intoxicated frolics hard enough to bear, much less suicidal depression.

Finally, all was ready. Lienhard offered August a receipt for his pay and expense allowance, whereupon the young man demonstrated his guilelessness by answering, "Why a receipt? If you are honest, everything will be all right. If you are not, a receipt is of no value." Beginning to have belated doubts about the wisdom of his mission, August then asked for Sutter's blessing before he left, half hoping the captain would veto the expedition. But Sutter gave the project his warm approval. Probably because of the coolness between them, Sutter did not accompany August and Lienhard to the *embarcadero* to say his goodbye and bon voyage.

By the time Lienhard sailed in the summer of 1849, August had accomplished the truly herculean task of hauling his father out of his abyss of debt. This he accomplished largely by hiring Peter Burnett as his business agent, giving him his power of attorney, and instructing him to sell as many Sacramento lots as possible, keeping one-fourth of the proceeds as his commission. He paid off the Russian American Company agent on April 13 and settled the ancient Hudson's Bay Company account even earlier. The company's Peter Skene Ogden had intended to go to San Francisco to try to collect from Sutter and other debtors left undunned since company agent William Rae's 1845 suicide. Forbes, the British Vice Consul, had taken over Honourable

Company affairs in San Francisco but had not pressured Sutter
for payment. But Ogden never sailed to California. Because the
British company did not seriously hope to recover even half the
debts outstanding, they gave the chore to George T. Allen and
allowed him a handsome eighteen percent commission. The company had already tried to sell the debts at a discount, but failed.
By January 1849, Allen was in California, on John Sutter's trail.
He hurriedly contacted Burnett when he learned that the Russian
American Company had transferred its claim to the United States
government and that Commodore Jones' secretary was on his way
to Sutter. Allen guessed at interest charges (for Leidesdorff's
books were as unreadable as Sutter's), and Burnett instructed
Reading, in San Francisco, to offer him notes. Allen said, "The
fact is, I don't like notes on every house here." But he accepted
a note for $2,000, due March 12 for one-half of full payment,
having rounded off the principal and interest to a neat $4,000
and having held out a carrot to Sutter in the form of an interest
waiver for the January-to-March period. On February 19, Allen
wrote the company's secretary at the London home office, Beaver
House, "I am happy to observe from a letter just received from
Messrs. Ogden and Douglas that they are perfectly satisfied with
my settlement, so far, of Sutter's account. . . . It may be considered as so much snatched from the fire and should I succeed in
recovering the balance, two thousand dollars more, it will reduce
greatly the outstanding debts here." Late in February, August
wrote to promise that he would pay in full, shortly. August's word
proved far better than his father's. On March 5, Allen wrote
London, "I have succeeded in recovering the whole of the company's claim against Captain Sutter."

By the time Lienhard sailed, June 20, Sutter was all but free
of debt for the first time in his adult life. Burnett paid off William
French in Honolulu, with city lots worth $10,000, and took
care of some long-memoried Missourians who used Sutter's fame
to reestablish contact and to ask for settlements. The last debt to
be paid was Suñol's. Burnett had insisted that August pay every-

one off before sending a dollar to Switzerland, although his mother was clamoring for some of the wealth which—to Europeans—had apparently made Sutter a Croesus. A sick and prematurely aged August now went into virtual seclusion at Hock Farm. Sutter persuaded him to reconvey his property on June 15, and five days later he and Burnett witnessed the boy's last legal action, a surrender to McDougal. He deeded over to the pertinacious speculator the half mile of Sutterville land which his befuddled father had given him in the spring.

With August sick in bed and Lienhard aboard the steamer *Panama,* Sutter took full and typically foolhardy control of his affairs by firing Burnett. August's agent reminded him too much of the painful period in which he had been virtually a ward of his own son. Sutter replaced him with Henry Schoolcraft and a clever attorney, Archibald Peachy. Incredibly, neither Sutter nor his sick son remembered to tell Burnett of the return of all properties to the elder Sutter. Burnett continued to sell lots until the captain finally roused himself from his negligence enough to inform him to close all sales on July 24, 1849. Perhaps understandably, Burnett was not about to just fade away. Instead, he held Captain Sutter to the letter of his contract with August, demanding one-fourth of the value of the lots handed over by August to Brannan and his cohorts. To pay him off, a once again nearly bankrupt Sutter had to give the future first governor of California 82 city blocks in Sacramento, plus 109 scattered lots. With lots in the canvas town of 4,000 people worth from $600 to forty times that figure, it is no wonder that Burnett released Sutter from all further payment and gave him the $10,000 he needed to wipe out his last American debt, to Suñol. August once said, "I have the firm belief that if Judge Burnett could have been retained for the management of our affairs up to the present date [1855], my father would be, now, one of the richest men in California." This is quite likely. But Sutter alienated Burnett and complained, "Burnett made a fortune much too quickly for me."

With Burnett's departure, the brake on Sutter's downward

spiral of business mismanagement was released. Schoolcraft took to drink. Peachy's taste ran more to dollars. According to Sutter, "Peachy made a fortune out of me in a short time—$80,000, which formed the cornerstone of the Montgomery Block. And then, when my land troubles came in, later, and I asked his firm to defend me, they excused themselves, saying, they had more business than they could attend to." Sutter also had unkind words for James King of William, the future vigilance committee martyr, for giving up notes of lot purchasers and releasing them without his permission. In June of 1850, Sutter hired Gen. Albert Winn to handle his affairs. "He sold lots, a great many of them, and never accounted for them." Sutter also claimed that Winn borrowed $5,000 on his account, with interest at ten percent *per month,* and did not say a word about it until Sutter owed $35,000 and the sheriff slapped an attachment on his last stand, Hock Farm. "I was so foolish," admitted Sutter. "I understood so little about business. I gave men powers of attorney to sign deeds and they swindled me on every side." Even his trusted Sam Hensley seemed to acquire a little tarnish at this moment, for it was he, and Hastings, who held Winn's note. (But Sutter did not bear him a grudge.) "I was resting tranquilly at Hock Farm with my family, not knowing that I owed a dollar in the world when the sheriff put on this attachment." Sutter had to hurry to the Sutter County seat, where Hastings and Hensley were waiting to see what luck the sheriff might have. Sutter, alarmed, gave them a $30,000 note which he held against Capt. Bezer Simmons, brother-in-law of Frederick Billings, who was Peachy's law partner.

Next, Sutter found that Winn had had portraits painted of every member of his family, paying for them with Sutter's Sacramento lots. Sutter, finally exasperated, fired him, but his next two business agents never gave him an account of anything. So the captain hired Louis Sanders as his agent and attorney, only to accuse: "As my lawyer, he took fees from both sides and made me lose my cases. He took every advantage to rob me of my property. [William] Mesick was another. He swindled me and

313

robbed me. Very different were these men from Bidwell, Hensley, and Reading, and those I had about me before the gold discovery. These latter so inspired me with confidence in human nature that I seemed ready to trust every sharper who came with the gold excitement. . . ." Sutter always contended that Brannan owed him $50,000 for the Sacramento lots which he had bullied out of August. It was Sutter who gave currency to the incident that faithfully illuminated Brannan's character. With so many of the faithful digging at Mormon Island, Sam had begun to tithe them, as an elder of the church, in order to erect a temple. But the money went into his pockets. When Brigham Young sent a messenger from Salt Lake to collect, Brannan, according to Sutter, replied: "You go back and tell Brigham Young that I'll give up the Lord's money when he sends me a receipt signed by the Lord, and no sooner." Sutter also threw into his bag of villains Eugene Gillespie, Winn's son-in-law, a member of the company formed to get land grants approved by the Land Commission. Instead, according to Captain Sutter, "They bled me freely, got from me a good deal of land which they divided among themselves. . . . Judge [Stephen] Field helped them. He was no better than they."

In 1876, Sutter listed his cast of scoundrels for an attentive H. H. Bancroft, then summed up: "I was the victim of every swindler that came along. These swindlers made the cornerstone of my ruin."

CHAPTER XVIII

THE FAMILY MAN

S NUG as he was in his Feather River retreat of Hock Farm, Sutter was nevertheless distressed by the destruction of New Helvetia. As early as April 1849, editor Edward C. Kemble of the *Placer Times* was describing it gloomily: "the once-frowning but, alas, now time-worn and dilapidated walls of Fort Sacramento." In May of that year, a prospector dug up the yard of Sutter's Fort and took $1.50 in gold from a thirty-foot square of Sutter's old parade ground. *Alcalde* Franklin Bates, in June, sold the Swiss's old horse-drawn grist mill for $3,950 to settle a claim against its new owner. The outbuildings disappeared first, razed for their lumber; then the walls of the fortress began to crumble away. (But Sutter had built well. Despite all the vandals could do, the destruction of his fortress-settlement was so slow that the state was able to rescue his main building in the 1890's, as a historical monument, and to rebuild, over the years, the eighteen-foot-high adobe walls and the satellite structures around Sutter's *Casa Grande.*)

For a time all went reasonably well for Sutter at Hock Farm. August's health improved, as did, somewhat, the health of the

315

relationship between father and son. When the younger Sutter wrote to Vallejo in September, he forwarded his father's regards just as if they had never been at bowie point. The swindling and general mismanaging which followed Sutter's firing of Burnett continued, but it took time to gather momentum, and the captain was still a long way from utter ruin, although he was drinking heavily and squandering his money to the tune of $200 and $300 a day.

On June 3, 1849, Gen. Bennett Riley, as civil governor of California, had called a special election of *alcaldes* and other local officers that was also to elect delegates to a constitutional convention. He scheduled this meeting for September in Monterey because Congress had taken no action on California's desire for statehood. He called for four delegates from the Sacramento district. Because this was such a large area, stretching from the Sacramento River on the north and west to the Consumnes River on the south and the far-off Sierra Nevada on the east, and was— for California—so populous a district, with its mining camps, the convention later raised the number of Sacramento delegates to first eight and then fifteen men. Eight men ultimately took part in the constitutional deliberations—Sutter, Lansford Hastings, John McDougal, Jacob Rink Snyder, Winfield S. Sherwood, Elisha O. Crosby, Morton M. McCarver, and William E. Shannon.

Sutter journeyed to Monterey and stayed at David Spence's house, where he was apparently ill for a time. But he was able to attend most of the sessions of the convention. Delegate Kimball Dimmick was appointed chairman pro tempore on September 1, but there was no quorum so he adjourned the meeting until the fourth. Then, with Dimmick still in the chair, Robert Semple, the publisher, was elected president of the convention. Sutter, who gave his occupation to Recording Secretary J. Ross Browne as "farmer," rather than "capitalist" or "elegant leisure," as he might have, was appointed (with Vallejo) to escort Semple to the seat of honor.

Sutter dutifully cast his *yeas* and *nays* on most motions before the house but played little part in the proceedings other than in ceremonial matters. He was appointed, September 10, to a committee to study and plan an enumerative census of the state-to-be but seems to have exercised little if any leadership even there. He took no real part in the long-winded wrangling over the number of delegates proper for each district. But when the subject was changed and Charles T. Botts took the floor to propose an amendment to the suffrage section of the growing constitution, which would have denied the status of "residents" to Californians who had left their families elsewhere, Sutter threw off his lethargy or insecurity and got to his feet, protesting, "It would be very hard if I should, after my long residence here, be deprived of my right to vote because my family is elsewhere." Botts' amendment was rejected.

Although Sutter had little to say in the debates, his name came up fairly frequently. Thus, Jacob Snyder, in a diatribe against the United States's treatment of California, praised Sutter for the benevolence, generosity, protection and assistance which he had afforded American immigrants. And Sutter's reward? Snyder answered himself; it had been "neglect, gross neglect." When McDougal proposed an amendment to the qualifications for governor that would limit the office to citizens of the United States or California of ten years' standing, William Shannon rose to protest, saying that if he or McDougal should nominate their mutual friend, Sutter, for the highest office, he would be declared ineligible. McDougal countered that Sutter would not be cut off by the amendment since he was a citizen of California for ten years and of the United States for six years prior to that. But his amendment was rejected. When Sherwood opposed the granting of suffrage to Indians, Kanakas and Negroes, one of his arguments was that if his good friend Sutter wished to become a politician, he could simply give a bit of land to each Indian and control 10,000 votes.

On September 24, in the important discussion of the report of

the Committee on Boundaries, Sutter threw off his embarrassment
of his thickly accented and excessively colloquial English. Lansford Hastings got the president's attention after a long diatribe by
Myron Norton about the giving away of great territories east of
the Sierra. Said Hastings, "I understand that my friend, Captain
Sutter, desires to speak on this question. The House, I have no
doubt, will be much pleased to hear him." Sutter took the floor,
thanked Hastings, and immediately apologized for his faulty command of the language of the convention. "I speak English so imperfectly that I shall make only a single remark. Gentlemen who
have passed through the deserts and traveled over these mountains may know something about it; but it is impossible for gentlemen who have come by way of Cape Horn to imagine what a
great desert it is and know how impolitic it would be to the state
of California to embrace within its limits such a country. Except
a small slip of the Great Salt Lake, which is worth something to
the people who are living there, there is such an immense space
between us and that part of the country that I consider it of no
value whatever to the state of California, and believe our limits
ought to be just as much as agreed upon by the committee with
the exception of an amendment which, I think, it requires to
facilitate the trade of the people of San Diego with Sonora and
New Mexico; to include that portion to the confluence of the Gila
and Colorado rivers, which it omits." He concluded, "This is all
I have to say," and sat down.

Sutter was the grand old figurehead of the group, although four
of the forty-eight delegates were older than he was and Larkin
was the same age. His contribution, like that of chaplains Rev.
Samuel Willey and Padre Antonio Ramirez, was largely decora-
tive—and possibly "spiritual." Yet, by and large, the points he
favored were those that prevailed. And he was much in demand as a ceremonial figure because of his record and his still-
prepossessing appearance. Besides escorting Semple to the presidential chair, he was chosen to preside on the closing morning
of the convention, when Semple was ill. The latter, though not

fully recovered, returned in the afternoon to adjourn the convention, sine die, on Saturday, October 13, 1849. With the work all done except for formalities, Riley saluted the delegates with a blank cannonading of thirty-one *presidio* guns, one round for each state—including California. The roar of cannon was always music to Sutter's ears, and as he later told the historian Bancroft repeatedly, "This was the proudest day of my life."

William Gwin having moved that Sutter address General Riley on behalf of the convention (Swiss accent or not), the constitution was signed and ex-president pro tempore Sutter, with Gwin on one arm and Morton McCarver on the other, led the entire body of delegates, secretaries and clerks on a march to Riley's house. There, in a short but flowery speech, Sutter thanked the governor for his cooperation in behalf of all delegates. He ended, "The convention, as you will perceive from the official records, duly appreciates the great and important services you have rendered to our common country and, especially, to the people of California, and entertains the confident belief that you will receive from the whole people of the United States, when you return from your official duties here, that verdict so grateful to the heart of the patriot, 'Well done, thou good and faithful servant.' "

Riley's response was not as flowery as Sutter's tribute, but it was sincere and more graceful. "I never made a speech in my life. I am a soldier—but I can *feel;* and I do feel, deeply, the honor you have this day conferred upon me. Gentlemen, this is a prouder day to me than that on which my soldiers cheered me on the field at Contreras. . . ." The general then brought out wine, and toasts were drunk before wagons and ambulances commanded by Maj. E. R. S. Canby took the delegates to San José, and Sutter returned to Hock Farm.

During the convention, friends approached Sutter to run for governor. Earlier, at Hock Farm, Lienhard had heard others pressuring Sutter and he had also heard his answer: "No, no, gentlemen; please don't try to force that office on me. I don't want it." Sutter declined in Monterey but finally reconsidered and accepted. "Sutter's luck" held. It was late to make much of a race of it. If he did not really want the office, he got his wish. The electorate did not want him. Sutter, with only 2,223 votes, ran a poor third on election day, November 13, 1849. Peter Burnett won with 6,946 and even little-known William Sherwood beat Sutter in popularity. Why did Sutter fare so poorly in this election at which a bare 10 percent of the enfranchised white male population voted? He was well known; he even made campaign appearances in mining towns, Sacramento and San Francisco. The comment of a contemporary, George F. Kent, is illuminating. "Although a very enterprising man, he cannot be said to be very popular. The report is that he has been rather dissipated of late years. How true, I know not." Francis Hoen was not about to beat about the bush, as Kent did. He asked Lienhard, rhetorically, "How can a man in his senses think that responsible men would ever vote for a man like Sutter, who is drunk more than half of the time?" He added for Lienhard's benefit, although it was unnecessary, to persuade the convinced, "Once I saw two sailors, who were also drunk, place Sutter between them when he was in such a condition that he could scarcely stand on his own feet."

Only four days after his defeat at the polls, a Washington official revived Sutter's morale. Secretary of the Interior Thomas Ewing reappointed him Indian sub-agent for the Sacramento valley, asking Commissioner of Indian Affairs Orlando Brown to send Sutter his commission and instructions. This was done on November 24, Brown attaching a letter to the documents in which he asked Sutter to supply him with statistics and other information on California's tribes since they were largely unknown in Washington. The choice still seemed a logical one. Visitors to Hock Farm in 1850 noted that Sutter, for all his fall from grace and power, still exerted great influence over the Indians. Some were put off by what they took to be new "aristocratic" airs in Sutter, who asked them to make their business calls at the office of his agent-attorney, John S. Fowler, rather than directly at his quarters. Actually, Sutter had not lost his hospitality, only his health. He and his entire family and all the servants were down with fever, and it was the order of his physician which kept them from being disturbed by Hock Farm's incessant visitors. The *Placer Times* printed the correct story and the widely read San Francisco *Daily Alta California* picked up the item and ran it again on August 6, 1850, sympathizing, "His generous and hospitable disposition makes all welcome to his mansion . . . but he needs a respite."

Some time before March 1, 1850, the newly appointed Indian sub-agent for the San Joaquin Valley, Adam Johnston, visited Sutter for a conference. They agreed to start out on their respective tours of inspection as soon as the streams should drop and the trails dry up. Doubtless, Sutter believed that he would shake off his fever by then. Johnston placed high hopes in his colleague and tutor, writing the Indian commissioner on March 1, 1850, "I was glad to learn of his appointment, as he is known to almost all the Indians of this country and is perhaps better calculated for success with them than most of men." But Sutter was feeling his age, and his ill health. These factors, together with the ridiculously low salary of $750 a year in gold-booming, inflationary California led him to reconsider and to decline the appointment on May 23, 1850. It has been said that he found that he spent more than a year's salary in but one field trip.

But poor pay was not the only excuse which he gave in turning down the post. After tendering his sincere thanks for the honor of being appointed, he recommended that Johnston be given both districts and paid a salary fully commensurate with his responsibilities. In begging off, Sutter said, "My old age [forty-seven!] and the decline of life, together with the multiplicity of my private business, would render it impossible for me to discharge the duties of the office in such a manner as would be satisfactory to myself or acceptable to the government." He then proceeded to give Commissioner Brown some free advice. First, he suggested that more interpreters be hired than the one apiece allowed him and Johnston, at a time, at $300 a year each. This, because of the babble of tongues spoken in California's scattered *rancherías*. He also urged much larger sums for contingent expenses than the $300 (and two horses at $100 each) set by the Indian Bureau as a limitation on all sub-agents. "While I freely admit that had it been in my power to perform the duties of the office at this advanced age of life, I would not have interposed the pecuniary sacrifices necessarily consequent upon it as an objection to its acceptance, yet I can not pass the matter without calling the attention of your department to the fact that the Indians of this country are scattered over a very wide extent of country, made up of many small tribes, and treaties must be made with each of these, if treaties are to be made at all."

Johnston again visited Sutter at Hock Farm in the summer of 1850, and the Swiss turned over to him all his instructions and accounting forms. The gesture proved invaluable to Johnston, since his own papers were lost in transit to California.

Sutter swallowed his disappointment in the gubernatorial race with ease; it was only in later life that he felt it necessary to concoct excuses. Then he blamed his defeat on his late start and Burnett's victory on the fact that he had stumped the whole state in order to win. (Sutter would also boast of having received 10,000 votes in San Francisco alone, whereas his statewide total was only a little more than 2,000.) However, Sutter was never very good at bearing grudges, or crosses—at least not until after his removal from California. He was once more the interested spectator, not the jealous rival, as Burnett served briefly in office, then turned the governorship over to Lt. Gov. John McDougal. Sutter viewed the first California legislature—the fabled "Legislature of a Thousand Drinks"—with amused detachment, too. He told people that it was composed of one-third good men and two-thirds bad, most of whom wore guns and bowie knives in the legislative halls and drank, swore and rioted during debates.

Although Lienhard in 1850 believed that no one had the nerve to fight the arrogant, well-organized and powerful Sacramento Valley squatters, Sutter made a game try to oust these drifters, who clung leech-like to his property. Perhaps these strenuous efforts kept him from moping about the election results. On December 11, 1849, he had called on General Riley for help: "Their number is so great that in the event of an attempt on my part in connection with others who labor under similar grievances to protect our own rights, the worse consequences are to be expected." He asked Riley to station a company of soldiers in Sacramento City to aid enforcement of the law there and to force the squatters to submit to the law without bloodshed. He was optimistic, he wrote the general, that "there is honesty and strength in the well-disposed inhabitants of this country to arrest any set of men who shall impudently, wantonly, array themselves in opposition against the numerous title holders of Sacramento City, but I desire to effect this object by the most peaceful means." Adam Johnston was worried, too, about the squatters stealing Indian lands, and reinforced Sutter's view of the situation when he wrote the Indian Commissioner in 1850 to report "the most unjustifiable and wholesale land piracy, carried on here, that has ever developed itself in any country." The Army did not choose to gallop to Sutter's rescue. The Gettysburg for the squatters would come in that very summer of 1850, however, when they killed the mayor and sheriff in Sacramento, among others.

The pillaging of Sutter's properties was now epidemic. Squatters evaded his Indian *vaqueros* or backed them off at pistol point and stole and killed his stock by the hundreds. He estimated his loss from rustling alone to be $60,000. A whole herd of his horses was driven away from Hock Farm by rustlers and trailed to Oregon. During the great flood of the winter of 1849–50, his cattle had had to take refuge from the high waters by gathering on the knolls, hillocks, and new-born islands of the plain, extending all the way from Sutter Buttes to the mouth of the Feather River. There were too many such isolated knots of stock for his Indian cowboys to protect, and townspeople now joined squatters in descending on them by boat to kill and butcher the steers. Looting of John Sutter became big business around Marysville as well as Sacramento, and five men actually formed a partnership to imitate the free-lance, waterborne "hunters." They hired men to hunt, also secured boat crews, and established a virtual meat monopoly by slaughtering Sutter's beeves. He estimated that these market hunters divided $6,000 in profits that one spring of 1850, then left for the East Coast to return in time for the following winter's flood and "harvest" of Sutter's beef cattle.

When the *vaqueros* reported this mass butchery, Sutter sent for Sheriff J. Hopkins, late of New York. He was an old man and he demanded a very strong posse before he would dare to confront the butchers. This Sutter provided him. When he and Sutter's cowboys reached the rustlers, they became so frightened that they jumped into their boats without resistance. They disregarded the sheriff's shouted demand of "Surrender!" but when the Indians were about to shoot them, Hopkins forbade it. He would not tolerate even Sutter's civilized Indians killing white men, and he allowed the culprits to escape. All Sutter could do was to send out wagons for the fresh beef. He then tried to make the best of a bad situation by allowing a Missourian named Owens to kill and sell all his cattle which he found strayed beyond the Sutter Buttes, in return for half the profit on the beef. But when Owens began his operations by slaughtering a fine, $300 Durham cow within view of Hock Farm, Sutter drove him away with curses.

A bigger reason for Sutter's declining the Indian sub-agent's commission than his age, ill health, or the stage of near siege at Hock, was his changed—reverted, or resumed—marital status. As of January 21, 1850, Sutter was again a family man. On that day, the *Panama* reached San Francisco with Lienhard and Sutter's family. Their escort was happy to arrive; he was thoroughly tired of his querulous wards. He found them prestige- and money-hungry, conceited, quarrelsome, haughty and rude. In New York, where Mama Sutter, despite her deafness, had picked up rumors of Johann's candidacy for governor, their conceit had doubled, if that was possible. Frau Sutter had been deflated when her long-lost husband failed to win the key to the Executive Mansion. Lienhard rented rooms for them in the Graham House. He would have liked to move them right up to Hock Farm, to be rid of them, but was leery of wounding Captain Sutter's vanity. So, he decided to bring the Old Man down to greet him and to welcome them personally to the Land of Gold.

Lienhard booked passage on the steamboat *El Dorado,* which fought its way up the flooded Sacramento past drowned carcasses, lodged in trees and brush, at which coyotes and buzzards were tearing. Just as Sutter had predicted to him, the city of Sacramento was so far under water that winter that boats were entering the City Hotel via its second-floor windows. This was the building of which Sutter was so fond because its frame was nothing other than that of his old grist mill at Natoma, brought down to lumber-poor Sacramento after the mill was abandoned. Lienhard found Sutter there, dickering with six of his fellow Swiss over the sale to them of his one-time wheat field for only $7,000. The month before, Lienhard learned, he had sold fifty acres to A. P. Smith, to found Smith's Pomological and Floral Gardens, a kind of poor man's Kew whose lineage could be traced back to Sutter's, and Lienhard's, watermelon patch. That night, Sutter and Lienhard had to put up near the outlet of the lagoon, or Sutter's Lake, in the Swiss's old rat-infested zinc warehouse, which had been pressed into service as lodgings. When his courier, spoiled by European hotels and transatlantic packet cabins, began to complain, Sutter reminded him, as he had done so often during their acquaintance, "In a new land, we must take things as they are."

Next morning, Sutter accompanied Lienhard back to San Francisco, without notifying his son, August, of the family's arrival. An affectionate greeting at the hotel became a grand reunion after Lienhard got rid of a sharp speculator who had attached himself to the family while awaiting a crack at Sutter. But the warmth soon wore off. Sutter found Anna to be as quarrelsome as ever, hard of hearing, and prematurely aged. Emil was moody, somewhat deaf, too, and not a good-looking boy. Sutter was fond of Eliza, his only daughter, but his favorite, like Lienhard's, was young Alphonse. The boy proved to be more than a kindred spirit, he was a faithful replica of his adventuresome, soldier-of-fortune father. Sutter took the lad for long walks in San Francisco, and once, prowling the blackened ruins where a fire had swept, Alphonse told his father that he hoped some day to be an Army officer. Sutter swore that his wish would be fulfilled, saying, "I will be made Supreme General of California, and then you will have an opportunity to become an officer." This proved no idle boast.

Sutter refused to move his family upriver on the shabby little *Captain Sutter,* or the *Sacramento,* lying at Clark's Point, but waited, instead, for the luxury riverboat, the 4,500-ton *Senator,* the most beautiful boat on the river. Lienhard paid a steep fare for a wagon to carry the captain, Mrs. Sutter and Eliza to the *embarcadero* while he and the boys negotiated San Francisco's quagmiry streets on foot. The *Senator* made a fast and comfortable trip to Sacramento, where Sutter put his family up in a newly opened brick hotel. Next morning, he got them aboard the tiny *Linda* for the last leg of their long journey. At fifty-two and a half tons, *Linda* was too small for the busy Sacramento–Marysville traffic, and Sutter had to leave Lienhard and the luggage behind for a later trip. They arrived at Hock Farm on February 9, 1850, to be greeted by the firing of a salute from its cannon. After this royal reception, Sutter settled his family into the Great House, which was almost finished, although a few doors had still to be hung and equipped with hardware.

When Lienhard's boat arrived at the wharf fronting the fine country house next day, it was welcomed by a rough-looking stranger in buckskin pants, red flannel shirt, and brown hat. In a scabbard on the man's broad leather belt hung a big bowie knife. Lienhard paid little attention to him until he saw Sutter, cane in hand, come up and talk to the red-shirted fellow. When Sutter greeted Lienhard, the latter asked, "Where is August?" Sutter blinked, then pointed his stick at the redshirt. "My August? Why, there he is." But a gloomy son would not even offer Lienhard his hand. He just stared coldly and myopically at him, resentful because he had not told him of the family's arrival in San Francisco. Lienhard soon learned that the bespectacled young dude had changed in more than just external appearance. He found that August had developed quite a thirst for liquor, like his father.

About the time that Sutter settled his brood in the comfortable Hock Farm mansion, the developers who had bought his Mimal ranch, four miles upstream, laid out a town. To please Sutter, they named it Eliza City, after his daughter. She was described as a very bold and masculine girl who walked with a nasty shake of the elbows and too much wagging of the hips. In April 1850, Sutter sold his land at Vernon (now Verona), where the Feather joined the Sacramento at a Hawaiian fishing village, but retained a quarter interest. Sutter was less fortunate with his other ventures. He suggested to August that he go into business, promising to underwrite him with capital up to $30,000, which, of course, he did not have. August fell into the hands of sharpers who persuaded him to get Sutter's remaining lots in Sacramento and a half mile of land between Sacramento and Sutterville for two token payments of $1 each, on May 7, 1850. When August decided to sell out, Sam Brannan and others offered him $125,000 for the property, guaranteeing to pay all taxes, fight the squatters and absorb the expenses of any title suits. August then sold them 2,200 town lots in Sacramento, plus lots in such paper towns as Nicolaus, Plumas, and Eliza City. At the time, August was too ill to leave his bed but a kindly physician administered such a powerful drug that he got to the buyers' office and signed the papers. As might be expected in any dealings with the Sutters, the buyers apparently welshed on the deal, postponed payment and even conned August, ever the dupe, into lending them money! A disgusted August Sutter left San Francisco on July 1, 1850, for Mexico, for health and peace of mind. His second try at managing Sutter's dwindling fortune was a short cut to ruin.

He may, indeed, have been drugged and possibly unbalanced. He had tried to burn down the Hock *ranchería* shortly before sailing, possibly (guessed the newspaper *Alta*) because of some indignity which he had suffered from the Indians. In Mexico, John Sutter, Jr., recovered his health, married, and decided to come back for the not-forthcoming money owed him. Brannan and the others sat tight until August was desperate. Then they offered him $40,000, payment in full, for the last great slice of his father's land. Panicking, August took it, but still got no cash, only notes, after signing receipts for the full $100,000, which he never saw. Then Brannan & Co. threw lawsuits at him until he was happy to realize even $3,500. With nothing left to sell, August found himself still $339 in debt. Again a nervous wreck, he ran away to Mexico, fleeing accusations of having squandered his father's lands.

As yet oblivious to the magnitude of this disaster done him by his bungling son, Sutter maintained open house for all comers, just as in the old days at the fort. Lienhard liked to hang about the place, sponging on the man whom he maligned so much in his memoirs. There was never any lack of company; every day four steamers passed Hock Farm Landing, and they often stopped to disgorge the curious, anxious to see the "Pioneer of Pioneers." Although sometimes under a doctor's care, Sutter welcomed as a guest none other than Alexander Rotcheff, once of Fort Ross, in October 1851. The Russian, ex-director of a gold mine in Siberia, was on his way to the placers with a gold-washing machine. Richard Kern paid Sutter a call in December 1851. Sutter greeted him warmly, reminisced about Mexican War days with his brother, Ned, at Fort Sacramento, and told him, "I hope that your brother will come here, in a land where 1,000 of chances are for one in comparison with an old country."

To the house Sutter brought George David Engler, to help make a real gentleman of his son, Alphonse, by teaching him to play on what was likely the first piano in the Sacramento Valley. Engler played more on the affections of Eliza; so much so that

328

gossip reached Sutter's ears. Unwilling to let his daughter marry at her station or below it, Sutter forbade any marriage, ordered Engler off his property, and told him never to see Eliza again. Only young Emil, abandoning his garden puttering (Sutter described him as his "botanist, gardener, and vineyardist" to Richard Kern), saw the crushed piano teacher off at the landing. Eliza was so unhappy that she attempted to commit suicide by cutting her wrists. Instead of cooing over her, her father was in such a thundering rage that, according to Lienhard, he offered her a pistol, to make a good job of it!

After an equally unsuitable portraitist, William Shaw, painting the family pictures at Hock, fell in love with Eliza, Sutter made a desperate attempt to play marriage broker for his own flesh and blood. He suggested to his old friend, perennial bachelor John Bidwell, that he marry his daughter. But his match-making was no more successful than most of his endeavors. Bidwell wrote a magnificently diplomatic letter which had nothing ill to say of Eliza but which firmly declined Sutter's gracious offer. "I cannot persuade myself to marry," said Bidwell. Marry he did, and before too long; but not with Eliza. Sutter gave up. He forgot about his vicarious social climbing and wrote to Engler, saying that all was forgiven, and invited him back. The marriage took place on Sunday, March 21, 1852, with Judge Cushing of Marysville presiding. It was, in the words of the Marysville, Sacramento and San Francisco press, a "magnificent affair," but it was also the beginning of a failed marriage, as Sutter had feared. Eliza got a divorce in 1853, and later remarried. But on that spring day of 1852, hopes were high. Some 200 guests arrived from all over California, many of them on the special Sunday-morning run of the steamer *Camanche*. They enjoyed the ceremony, a sumptuous wedding banquet, galaxies of toasts in fine wines, some speeches, Indian dancers and fireworks over the Feather River.

CHAPTER XIX

THE PATRIARCH

ON one of Heinrich Lienhard's last visits before returning to Europe, he found Captain Sutter, unwittingly, selling to three Americans the same old wheat field which he had sold earlier to six Swiss. But such was the chaos of land speculation, and peculation, in 1850 that the buyers were quicker to turn a deaf ear to Lienhard's warning than was Sutter, the seller. But when Lienhard tried to buy some land from Sutter, offering the captain some notes of August's which he held, he refused, still angry at his son's mismanagement of his affairs. "I have done as much for my son as I can, at present," was all that he would say. Sutter had less and less land to sell now, the *Alta California* venturing in August of 1850 that he had sold all his Californian acreages for $6,000 in cash and an annuity derived from a one-sixth interest of the net proceeds of the sale or lease of the lands he ceded. The paper reported that Hock Farm was not involved because Sutter had already assigned that property to his wife.

In 1852, Rev. Joseph A. Benton reported that the New Helvetia flagpole had tumbled onto the ruined fort, occupied only by moles and bats and brightened only—and ironically—by the gold of the poppies which overran its yards. By 1853, the fort was largely razed of all buildings save Sutter's *Casa Grande* by lumber looters. In 1854, Episcopalian Bishop William I. Kip saw only melting adobe walls where once the pulsing heart of Sutter's empire had stood.

Although almost landless now, Sutter never lost his consuming interest in agriculture. He still believed what he had told Jacob Hess: "Gold digging is a lottery; among hundreds, maybe one or two get rich from it. Most people prefer a safe investment; farming is the best of all." He still raised and sold cattle, tended his peach orchard, and helped Emil with the truck garden. He liked to exchange seeds with other botany lovers, like Louisa Kunze of San Francisco. He offered vines for sale to Bidwell and others and he encouraged Jacob Hess, a childhood friend in Kandern now living in Ohio, to come and join him in his garden spot, Hock Farm.

Sutter's discomfort with his still "new" family sent him back to the saloons. Perhaps he found his Anna to be just as she was described, "a fretted-looking woman . . . deficient in common politeness." She and Eliza slammed the door on too many of his friends, told others that he was out, and feigned ignorance of the English language to still other visitors to the farm. This kind of conduct led Sutter inevitably to seek escape in the bottle, again. One day in 1850, Lienhard saw him being assisted by August, Alphonse and two other men from the tent of a "vulgar French woman" in Sacramento so that he would not miss the sailing of the *Governor Dana* from the *embarcadero* for Hock Farm. Sutter had to be almost carried bodily aboard after being marched down the street by the two strangers, one on each arm, in a bizarre parody of Sutter's escorting of Semple in the constitutional convention. August led the way and an embarrassed Alphonse brought up the rear, very conscious of the smirks and sly smiles of onlookers who enjoyed seeing the shipwreck of Captain Sutter's career.

That summer, Sutter defied Anna and played host to many

travelers. For a week or so in July, he entertained Prince Paul of Württemberg and his entourage of Germans and Hungarians, and on another occasion, Governor Peter Burnett. "Young" Gutiérrez and Dr. John Baird were seen staggering home at 1 A.M., "well lined with Old Sutter's champagne." Sutter introduced Theodore Cordua to Prince Paul; His Highness liked the bluntness of Yankees and greeted them with a hearty, plebeian handshake.

More exciting to northern Californians than Sutter's "Bacchanalias" were the squatter difficulties, culminating in the great Squatter Riot of August 14, 1850. Some forty squatters marched on the prison hulk, grounded at Sutter's *embarcadero* on the Sacramento River, to release two of their number held there on charges of rebellion. In their mass meetings, they argued that the California government was unlawfully interfering with their personal and property rights. When the mayor, sheriff, assessor and many citizens opposed them, firing broke out and a dozen men were shot, of whom five or six died. Another battle followed on the next day, in which the sheriff, among others, was killed. The governor called out a brigade of militia to quell the squatters' riots. Public indignation was aroused against them, too, and they were defeated, but in the Hock Farm area they were still swearing that they would not be ejected from Sutter's land except by due process of law. This took time, which they were counting on, for time worked against Sutter. As late as December 1853, Sutter was writing to Ned Kern, "The squatters are loose in my fields; all is squatted over. So long as it [his land claims] is not decided, I am in debt and cannot sell a foot of land at present. Our government did not act right with us Californians."

Ceremonies in which he participated always pleased Sutter and helped keep his mind off such nagging problems as squatters and debts. On October 28, 1852, he enjoyed a military fete which featured a visit from San Francisco's militia company, the Marion Rifles, to Sacramento. There, the newly formed Sutter Rifles, or Sutter Light Infantry, were the hosts. Captain Sutter presented a silk flag to the San Francisco contingent in the afternoon and then enjoyed a reception and ball at the Orleans House. He still adored showing off, and, some of his letters were shot through with the old bravado, such as the long one he wrote to his old friend, Jacob Hess: "When I arrived here there were only four houses in the village [San Francisco]. I built miles of the inner part of California, with a sword in my fist, and through my labors gold was discovered. . . . I commanded the 2d Division under General Micheltorena, was in many a hard battle and was once a prisoner of war and was to be shot but was rescued and often I had bloody battles with Indians. In short, it is a wonder that I am alive." For some reason, Sutter even thought it necessary to embroider the details of his Hawaii–Alaska–California passage, for he told Hess that he had sailed from Hawaii to Australia, thence to Asia, and only then to Sitka and San Francisco. He rambled on, possibly to substantiate his boast that "I can be a sea captain, as well; this, too, I learned," saying, "I have wandered, you see, far and wide. If you want to know more about me, just ask the Americans. I am so well known here that almost every child knows my name as well as many of my deeds. How many I have saved from starvation, and have helped many to their good luck." Even when he confessed to losing his wealth, he had to boast that a million francs—$200,000—had gone in eighteen months. "I thought my money was safe and, for that reason, I was deceived. Likewise, I lost through lawsuits and in many other ways very much." He added, optimistically, "But, of course, everything will come out all right again because my large territorial possessions are becoming worth a great deal. I still have the Russian possessions [Fort Ross] along the ocean coast, with a harbor, a fort, a fruit garden and a territory of 1,500 square *stunden*." (A *stunde* was one hour's walking, or about two and a half miles.) Then, overcome by modesty, Sutter added, "I still keep my title, Captain, because I am best known by it." Still as generous as ever, he offered a warm welcome to Hess: "Here, I shall, indeed, lend you a helping hand so that you can gain for yourself, in a few years, a respectable future which you

334

would never have attained during your whole life in Ohio. You will be pleased with the land and the climate because we have, as one says, no winter. We have vegetables and flowers the whole winter through in my garden. We have snow here only in the highest mountains."

Sutter's mercurial spirit was raised for the nth time on February 16, 1853, only a week after the Sutter Rifles presented him with Ticket Number One—sold for $1,200 at auction—to a recital in Sacramento by Kate Hayes. Sutter made a grand, escorted appearance to loud applause. On the sixteenth, the legislature made him, by concurrent resolution, major general commanding the California militia. This was just what he had predicted to Alphonse in 1850. He wrote Bidwell a day later, "I can assure you that I feel proud of it." Bishop William Kip was unimpressed: "The prey of sharpers who gradually stripped him of his possessions, the patriarch of California and the Pioneer—all she has given him is the empty title of major general of the militia, a cocked hat and a pair of epaulets." The bishop, however, was badly mistaken. The legislature gave back to Sutter something which he needed desperately—pride, prestige, "face." It was a happy gesture for Sutter. There was no salary, to be sure, but there were hardly any duties either, except for the highly pleasurable ones of uniforms, parades, reviews, banquets, drills and toasts. Sutter was able to appoint aides for his staff and even to issue military orders, such as the military convention he called for Sacramento on January 8, 1854. This meeting was for the purpose of organizing the militia and volunteer corps, but he scheduled it for a particular day and told Ned Kern why: "As it is the anniversary day of the Battle of New Orleans, we will have an excellent military ball."

A military career to Sutter was a life of reviews and military balls. He was playing soldier with real zest now. Alphonse was an aide to Governor Bigler as well as to his father, with the rank of a colonel of cavalry. But Sutter's ambitions for the boy were not entirely realized. He had written Ned Kern on January 10, 1852:

"He wishes very much to go to West Point and become an officer of cavalry. I have done all that I could. I wrote to many gentlemen to recommend him, about eighteen months ago, but no answer." Sutter never did get an answer, but he sent the boy back to Europe for more training at a polytechnical school, and Alphonse eventually joined filibusterer William Walker as one of his officers in Nicaragua. On July 4, 1853, Sutter, assisted by his staff, including Alphonse, celebrated Independence Day by reviewing the Sutter Rifles, Marion Rifles, National Lancers, First California Guard, San Francisco Blues and Eureka Light Horse Guard, as they drilled in the San Francisco Plaza, then marched to Russ's Gardens for presentation of the colors to them by the charming actress, Catherine Sinclair. Sutter responded gallantly, gave her his thanks in behalf of all the units and led his men to a banquet and theater party. On December 7 he sent Kern a description of the festive day, "You will see now that I have a very brilliant position, as chief commander. I am the first person in rank under the governor."

While the rather pathetic major general paraded in his new uniform—just as fine as Winfield Scott's—speculators were trimming away at his reduced empire, closing in on Hock Farm itself. In February 1853 he told Bidwell that he had sold most of it to John B. Steinberger at the urging of Mesick and other friends who had advised him that it was the thing to do. Sutter later unmasked Steinberger, revealing him as a liar and a cheat, entirely without funds. Instead of cultivating and sowing the land, he was stripping off all the timber, employing 100 woodcutters (or so Sutter claimed), in a frenzy to denude Sutter's riverbank before March 1, when the sale agreement would become null and void for nonpayment. Said Sutter, "He acts just as if he would be the richest man in the country and is commanding the whole day just as if they [the workers] would be Negroes." Sutter estimated that Steinberger owed his lumberjacks between $3,000 and $4,000. "All would leave if they could get the money. . . . He is a most disgusting man in every way and shape." Sutter told Bidwell that he had learned that Steinberger had been trying to snare him for years. "It seems to be, my whole life long, the victim of such people." But he promised, on March 1, "We will tell him to clear out from here and if he don't like to go, we will turn out this great renowned swindler and rascal by force."

Honors did not balance out with setbacks such as Steinberger's, but still they came to Sutter. In August of 1853 Col. A. Andrews, lately a captain of Ohio militia and now of California's, presented him with a fine sword in consideration of his early services to California. Andrews' tribute to the Swiss pioneer stressed his personal kindness and self-sacrifice for the good of California. "Accept this sword in proof of the fact that virtue in the distinguished citizen is not always unappreciated. . . . You are honored and esteemed by not only those who have known you but wherever your reputation has extended." Sutter thanked him profusely, then responded nobly and modestly: "I claim no credit whatever for any services I may have rendered in the early days of California. As one of its pioneers, I could not do less than use my best exertion to promote its prosperity and contribute to the comfort and enjoyment of those who followed me to its lovely valleys. To do so was a pleasure and that alone prompted me in everything I did. If in promoting my own pleasure, I have been so fortunate as to secure the esteem of my fellow-citizens, I am doubly paid." (Later, Sutter put Andrews in for a promotion to full colonel, in gratitude for the Ohioan's gesture.)

Even as vain a man as Sutter did not let his ego blind him to the glaring fact that a total vote of 2,223 votes in a statewide election meant that he was no longer a major force in California affairs. He turned to the salvage of his own fortune and those of his friends. Besides testifying himself and sending Bidwell before the U.S. Land Commission to protect his own grants, he also appeared as a witness in behalf of Reading and others. To his great relief, the commission approved his New Helvetia and Sobrante grants on May 15, 1855. Now he could look forward to the loosening of credit and to the appearance of buyers, since his title would not be in doubt. But, to his dismay, squatters on his land appealed the decision to the U.S. District Court for Northern California. The body, on January 14, 1857 confirmed his title but the case was again appealed. In 1858 the blow came. The U.S. Supreme Court confirmed his New Helvetia grant but denied his Sobrante claim because of the captious reasoning that Governor Micheltorena had "abandoned" his capital at the time he awarded the land to fellow-campaigner Sutter. This reduced Sutter's holdings from 230 to 75 miles. Since he had long ago sold off parcels of the Sobrante grant, he was obliged to reimburse the buyers. Eventually, he would estimate that it cost him nearly a third of a million dollars to establish legal ownership to lands given him in the Mexican period. Some of this money came from land he sold to keep his case going, from grapes, figs and peaches which he and Emil marketed in Marysville and Sacramento, and from the modest charity of a Sutter relief fund, based on the sale of lots.

Meanwhile, Alphonse had persuaded August to return, to try again to recover the money never paid him by Brannan, Wetzlar and others. Alphonse suggested to his older brother that he base his case on the fact that the doctor, in league with Wetzlar, had kept him drugged during the transactions. But August, ironically, decided to ground his case on the illegality of the original transfer of property from his father to himself, the act which had once saved Sutter's neck. William S. Mesick joined him in the battle against Brannan *et al.* Mesick filed suit to eject the settlers on the land although the Sacramento *Union* on September 30, 1856, stated that August Sutter was without honor if he was selling property twice over.

This attack stung Sutter, Sr., out of his torpor. On October 6 he wrote the paper that Brannan had swindled August of all but $12,000 to $13,000 of the promised $125,000. He related how August's lawyer had been bought by the opposition, how others refused to take the case because the Sutters were now poor, and how still others refused out of fear of Brannan. Only Mesick,

338

said Sutter, had had the nerve to fight alongside his son. Julius Wetzlar shot in a reply to the editor the following day, pooh-poohing Sutter's prediction that the world would be astonished when the truth about the transaction was revealed. He stated that August had been satisfied, completely, and that Sutter, Sr., had obviously been prevailed upon to sign his name to the charge of swindling and, since he always obligingly signed anything laid before him, the accusation meant nothing. Brannan won but Mesick appealed to the State Supreme Court, which found that Wetzlar had lied and that he and his associates had indeed swindled August. The court also ruled, however, that the titles of the innocent land-buyers were valid, and August Sutter's biographer, Allan R. Ottley, believes that he secured only a few hundred dollars in this hollow victory.

According to Brannan, August's erstwhile ally, Mesick, now took his turn at bilking him. Captain Sutter agreed. Writing Judge Orville Pratt on December 29, 1855, he said of August, "He don't come [here] more, and even if he would, he could no more come home now. Mr. Messick had him entirely in his power and persuaded him, under false representations, to consent." Sutter felt that Pratt, if he would become his agent, could save him half a million dollars while rewarding himself handsomely, too. Sutter was still a Diogenes, even though his lamp had blown out in the gales accompanying the Gold Rush.

August gave up and returned to Mexico. He would never see California again. From such a distance, Sutter was able to reconcile with him and watched his son's growing success in business and the United States consular service with pride. He wrote letters, got other prominent men to do likewise, and may have contributed to August's nomination to the post of United States consul in Acapulco.

Because of his vanity, Sutter loved to sit for portraits. He had done so for the artist Samuel Osgood in 1849 and for William Shaw, who had pursued Eliza. In 1853 he sat for Charles Fendrick, and then sat again in 1854 because this time he wore the resplendent uniform of a major general. Sutter had lithographs made of this portrait and sent them to friends like Ned Kern, but also to the French consul and even to Emperor Louis Napoleon, of whom he still bragged, "We were brothers in arms when he was a captain of artillery in our country." Next, artist William S. Jewett painted a portrait of Sutter which he wished to present to the legislature. It was to be a labor of love, but he got Sutter to write to Col. Philip L. Edwards that perhaps some remuneration was in order, for his supplies and for the frame, which alone, cost the artist $300. Wrote Sutter, "The artist undertook this great labor for love of his art and warm friendship for me, and certainly Mr. Jewett, who is a noble soul, would not ask for a remuneration but he can hardly afford to have such an outlay on his own shoulders and I am too poor, myself." Sutter asked Edwards to take the matter to the floor of the legislature. He did so, the bill went through, and Governor Bigler signed it, although he declared the "slight remuneration" for the artist— $2,500—a damned extravagance. Sutter's portrait now hangs in the Capitol.

For almost a decade, Sutter had his family with him to bolster him up and to nag him for his drinking and other weaknesses. He was henpecked unmercifully. A friend wrote, "It is not the old chap's fault. He is a right decent fellow, by all accounts, but is kept under by his wife and children. He likes to see visitors but they cannot bear the sight of him. He has given charge of the farm and stock over to the son, who is about seventeen years of age and a pretty-looking fellow to be the head of such an establishment. The old captain may sleep on as long as he has got his daughter and wife; they will manage for him. But the Sutters have lost their repute at Plumas." His drinking became so bad that Bidwell brought a celebrated temperance lecturer, Sarah Pellet, to Hock Farm to try to dry him out. It was a failure. Sutter wrote to Ned Kern at the time (November 23, 1855), "She is a very interesting lady but I told her that she could not convert me as I have so many acquaintances in the cities that I could not do otherwise [than drink] and, particularly, when I am with the citizenry-soldiery on great dinner parties."

By 1860, all of Sutter's children had left his side and only a few aging retainers remained at Hock with Anna and himself. These were dull, drab days of retirement, enlivened only by the visitors who never stopped coming. His vines and peach trees—with an assist in 1862 from the Society of California Pioneer's charity, the Sutter Pioneer Testimonial Fund (in which his nemesis, Brannan, was prominent)—made ends meet. In April 1864, the legislature took pity on the nearly impoverished pioneer and voted him $15,000, payable in monthly amounts of $250 for five years. Sutter swore that he would never be the object of charity, although he took the relief-fund money gladly. He accepted the state's money only because, he said, he considered it to be repayment of the taxes he had lavished on the Sobrante grant.

One side benefit of Sutter's straightened circumstances may have been a sobering-up in more than just business affairs. No longer could he afford the roaring drunks of an earlier decade when, according to Laufkotter, he had once spent $15,000 in a four-week Frisco binge, then borrowed $1,000 more, blew it, and offered a note for $10,000—due in two weeks!

Thieving and vandalism continued to hurt Sutter even in the 1860's, a more law-abiding decade in California than the prior one. Although he had little or no cash, Hock Farm was still a considerable property, even if he exaggerated in the 1850 census, claiming the value of his farm equipment to be $10,000 and his stock (1,000 horses, 25 mules, 950 cattle and oxen, 500 sheep and 60 swine), $46,250. He said he had 200 improved and 10,000 unimproved acres. He did not tell the census man but he did tell Richard Kern that he had sunk over $100,000 worth of improvements into what had become his model farm. His livestock and woodlots were always in jeopardy, but he was well able to survive robbery and embezzlement.

The crime which put Sutter out of business and drove him

forever from the land he had pioneered was a more serious one—arson. Still playing the role of a brother of St. Bernard to all pilgrims, Sutter let a vagrant ex-soldier loaf about Hock Farm in June 1865. When the fellow repaid his kindness by thieving, Sutter justifiably had him tied up and whipped. Once he was released, the ex-soldier took his revenge. He set fire to Hock Farm (the Great House was completely uninsured by a hard-pressed Sutter) and burned it to the ground. Major General Sutter and his wife were barely able to escape from what had been their lovely home and his militia headquarters. All his belongings—clothing, art works, documents, relics—were destroyed in the June 21, 1865, holocaust, except for a few treasured medals and portraits which Sutter rescued. Sutter's mind may have flashed back to August 1842 when, in puzzlement, he had written a friend: "I will bet that there are many people who are my enemies and I don't know why; people who are trying to hinder me and to do me harm, if they can."

His will finally broken, the pioneer of American California turned his back on the blackened ruin of all his hopes. Five months after he was burned out, he sailed for the East with his wife. He never saw the accursed Land of Gold again.

CHAPTER XX

THE VICTIM

AS early as 1850, Sutter had prepared a petition to the United States government for redress of the injuries inflicted upon him and his property by American immigrants. Congressman Edward Gilbert, who took it to Washington, did not present it to Congress after he learned that Sutter had disposed of all his property. But fifteen years later, Sutter determined to launch an all-out campaign for reimbursement. He was aided by his agent, Col. William H. Russell, who bombarded Washington with accusations that the imperfectly organized courts of 1848 and 1849 in California had been unable to render Sutter relief from trespassers and squatters whose number had been equaled only by their strength and audacity. Sutter and Anna descended on Washington in December 1865.

He brought with him, just as he had done when he invaded California in 1839, letters of introduction and recommendation, and he provided himself with new supplies of them from time to time. One of these was by J. Ross Browne, traveler, civil servant and very popular writer. Browne directed his letter to the Hon. Daniel Clark, chairman of the Committee on Claims of the Senate, on June 8. Wrote Browne: "In a legal point of view, I have no knowledge of the merits of his claim, or the grounds upon which he takes exception to the decision of the courts but I know that he has rendered eminent services to the citizens of California and to our government and is entitled to grateful consideration for his unselfish devotion to our interests." Then the skilled contributor to *Harper's Magazine* really warmed to his task: "With a noble scorn for self-aggrandizement and a patriotic love for our free institutions, General Sutter devoted himself enthusiastically to the interests of our government and it is but simple justice to say that, without his experience, courage and fidelity to our cause, the struggle would have been prolonged for years and the cost augmented by many millions of dollars. General Sutter was the founder of the state of California. To him is mainly due the wealth which has sprung from its vast mineral deposits and the commerce which has built up populous cities on its shores and rivers."

"And for all this," asked Browne, "what has been the reward of the generous, guileless and patriotic old soldier? He has been stripped of his possessions by a class of men against whom he was powerless to cope. He has been reduced to poverty in his declining years. He stands now, humbly, at your door, asking not a reward for his services, not a bounty for his hospitality, but justice—simple justice." Browne finished, "My only motive has been sympathy for his misfortune and a profound sense of gratitude to one whom I cannot but regard as a benefactor to my state and to my country."

Other fine letters came to Sutter, one of which he appended to the printed version of his petition, which was sent to the Senate Committee on Claims. It was a letter which California's governor, Frederick F. Low, wrote for him on October 6, 1866. It read, in part, "Major General Sutter was one of the early pioneers of this coast and by his industry, bravery and indomitable energy, did more to subdue the savage tribes and encourage settlement than any other man. His name and fame are world wide. . . . His kindness and generosity to the early immigrants who arrived here are proverbial. Although possessed of large grants ceded to him by the Mexican government . . . , the delays and expenses incident to the legal adjudication of these titles have stripped him of all his property, leaving him in his old age comparatively penniless. . . . I earnestly commend his claims to the favorable consideration of Congress."

Sutter seemed assured of a sympathetic hearing in Congress, and at first his hopes were high. His advisers had trimmed his request from $120,000 to an easier to secure $50,000—only a fragment of his loss, of course. The Senate Claims Committee, while ruling that the government was not responsible for the depredations of American settlers in California, recommended that Sutter be paid from the proceeds of the sale of the Sobrante grant. Sutter enjoyed the capital's high society, in which he now moved. But winter came, and another, and another, and another . . . winters that brought only aggravation of his rheumatism and confinement to bed.

When healthy, Sutter continued his buttonholing of legislators. Reinforcements of a sort arrived in February of 1868 when Mark Twain, Adolph Sutro and others joined the earlier Browne, Low and Gen. James W. Denver in petitioning Congress in his behalf. When Ulysses S. Grant was elected President that November, Major General Sutter presented his congratulations and was pleased when the Washington press linked him with five other generals. His optimism was titillated during the second term of the Forty-first Congress (1869–70) when "A Bill For the Relief of John A. Sutter" was introduced in the Senate. But the bill was reported on adversely in committee and went nowhere. Sutter fell back on the solace of another testimonial letter which he could now make public, where it counted. From Gen. William T. Sherman, it said, "Your hospitality was proverbial. It was the common belief that had it not been for your fort, and your herds of cattle, sheep, etc., the immigrants arriving in California during the years 1847, 8 and 9 would have suffered for food. It was owing to your efforts to develop the country, more especially in your building the grist mill and the sawmill at Coloma, that the world was indebted for the discovery of the gold mines."

By the time the 1870–71 session came to a fruitless (for him) end, Sutter was sick and tired of hotel and boarding-house living. Although Hubert H. Bancroft found it a "dismal Dutch town," the captain became fond of the village of Lititz, near Philadelphia. It was something of a health resort; considering his precarious health, living in a spa, of sorts, was preferable to Washington hotels. He placed his grandson and two granddaughters in Moravian schools there, after August and his Mexican wife separated, then moved Anna and himself to Lititz. He planned to make the little Moravian town his headquarters for his dogged, Grant-like campaign against the United States government. While he lay in bed for two months with painful rheumatism, his wife oversaw the construction of his fine brick home. In a letter to his wife's sister, he gave one reason for building the house— "We should not exactly care to die in a hotel."

Sutter's circumstances were comfortable, although he had to pose as a destitute petitioner in his memorials to Congress. He received his California pension of $250 a month for five years and was successful in getting two renewals, for a total of four years more, by writing to the Speaker of the California assembly. He may also have been receiving some annuities, such as those of $250 he received monthly during 1864 after giving financier Darius O. Mills his power of attorney. When the California pension finally ran out, August apparently came to his rescue.

Sutter never knew really grinding poverty. As he aged, he saddened from frustration and became something of a recluse between sessions, holed up at Lititz with his loyal Anna and his books. On sunny days, he liked to sit in the back garden, admiring the flowers and the peach trees which reminded him of Hock Farm. Early in 1870, with four inches of snow on the ground, he wrote to Mrs. John Bidwell, "We are so well content here but the cold winters make us rather homesick for California. . . ." Still the farmer, Sutter had to add, "Your raisins raised at Chico must be delicious. This will become a great article of exportation from California, as they are far superior to those imported from Greece and Spain and I think will pay better as [than] to make wine."

But the sometime recluse had not yet turned into a hermit. He reverted to his usual self in 1876 when he was asked to preside at the Swiss Day festivities at the centennial celebration in Philadelphia. That one hundredth anniversary year of American independence also brought historian Hubert H. Bancroft east. With great trepidation, Bancroft came to Lititz, having heard of Sutter's introversion and ill health. Certainly, Mrs. Sutter was not the very soul of courteous hospitality, but she admitted him to Captain Sutter's house.

Sutter surprised his guest with his firm step and military carriage although, at age seventy-three, he was often in pain and no longer carried his cane merely for show. Thought Bancroft, "In his younger days, he must have been a man of much endurance, with a remarkably fine physique." The historian was particularly impressed with the way the aged Swiss's deep, clear eyes met his, earnestly and truthfully, as they conversed. Bancroft explained his mission; he wanted to interview Sutter about his quarter of a century of pioneering in California. Sutter readily assented, beginning bitterly, "I have been robbed and ruined by lawyers and politicians. My men were crushed by the iron heel of civilization; my cattle were driven off by hungry gold-seekers; my fort and mills were deserted and left to decay; my lands were squatted on by overland immigrants; and, finally, I was cheated out of all my property. All Sacramento was once mine. . . ."

Tears came to Sutter's eyes when Bancroft responded, "You fill an important niche in the history of the western coast. Of certain events you are the embodiment—the living, walking, history of a certain time and locality. Often in my labors I have encountered your name, your deeds; and let me say that I have never yet heard the former mentioned but in kindness, nor the latter except in praise." Sutter fed Bancroft anecdotes and history for up to ten

347

hours a day, for five days. In his *History of California,* Bancroft would call Sutter a mere adventurer not entitled to either admiration or sympathy. Yet he could not help being moved by the pioneer's personality. In describing his visit to Lititz, he wrote, "No one could be in General Sutter's presence long without feeling that if not the shrewdest, he was an inborn gentleman. He had more the manners of a courtier than those of a backwoodsman; with this difference: his speech and bearing were the promptings of a kind heart, unaffected and sincere. . . ."

A full decade after his first attempt, Sutter, in 1876, was addressing another petition to Congress, a sixteen-page pamphlet titled *Memorial of John A. Sutter to the Senate and House of Representatives of the United States in Congress Assembled.* In this version, the "humble but earnest suitor for justice" could more honestly refer to his state of penury to make his plea more dramatic. The centennial year was the most hopeful of a largely mortifying decade for the self-lobbyist. General Sherman and several hundred old California comrades memorialized Congress on April 15 on Sutter's behalf. The Private Land Claims Committee in the House recommended passage of a bill which would grant him $50,000 in consideration of his many services to American immigrants as well as recognition of the losses he had incurred because of the lack of legal protection and the rejection of his Sobrante grant.

Although no bill passed, these other actions so revived Sutter's flagging spirits that he began to leave his Lititz refuge. Whenever his health permitted, he attended the annual reunions of the Associated Pioneers of the Territorial Days of California. He was their guest of honor during the 1877 meeting in Long Branch, New Jersey, and became so emotional that he could not reply when he was cheered at great length. All he could say was, "It is not possible . . ." The entire assembly rose, toasted him, and saluted him with three huge cheers which drowned out the band and rocked the walls of the Ocean Hotel. At the 1878 meeting, he was elected president of the Associated Pioneers and was presented with a gold-headed cane of California rosewood as a token of the Pioneers' esteem for "the friend of all Californians, who has illustrated by his life and by his signal benefactions the divine precept of charity." Sutter thanked them on March 2, 1878, adding, rather gloomily, "We are now hastening onward to our final resting place but the romance of our history as California pioneers, with its reverses and its successes, will tend, for ages, to stimulate the energy of our posterity."

Sutter enjoyed having the support of such men as Mark Twain and General Sherman. When someone garbled California history, he took time to correct them. He wrote the editor of the San José *Pioneer* to criticize its story of September 15, 1877, on a speech by the Hon. Lawrence A. Archer, who dismissed California's pre-1841 settlers as a few restless adventurers who had scarcely known how or why they had come west. Sutter's November 29 letter objected, "Some people came prior to 1841 to settle in California and I wrote letters to Missouri and other parts of the United States and encouraged the people to immigration. And I think I have done just like a missionary to tame and civilize the wild Indians."

By 1879, Sutter had almost abandoned hope of ever winning his fight. He had seen session after session, born in hope, die in despair. Bereft, at last, of optimism, he was forced by rheumatism and kidney trouble to decline attending the Associated Pioneers meeting in a telegram of January 20, 1879: "Sick in heart and body, in vain appealing to Congress to do me justice and to return only part of what was wrongly taken from me, and with little hope of success this session unless you, my friends, by your influence will aid me, I could not feel cheerful as your guest at table tonight and did not want to mar your pleasure by my presence. Remember old times without me."

The San Francisco *Daily Alta California* on May 12, 1879, ran an editorial which reviewed Sutter's struggle, praised him for his benevolence and damned the shysters and land grabbers for stripping him of his great domain. In supporting the Sutter relief bill, the *Alta* wrote, "Now let us see whether our government has any soul and sense of gratitude left in it." The paper should have known Washington; an ingrate, soul-less Congress once again ignored Sutter's plea for help.

Shocked by Sutter's despair, the Pioneers vowed to take action. They resolved to press Congress for quick action on Sutter's case, in order that his declining years might be as comfortable as possible. Their persuasion seemed to take effect; Sutter was heartened when the House Committee on Claims reported favorably on April 8, 1880, on a Sutter relief bill. On June 11, Senator Daniel W. Voorhees introduced a joint resolution to reward Sutter for his services and losses with a lump payment of $50,000. Sutter was confident that he had won at last. But 1880 was an election year and as the legislators hurried to a June 16 adjournment, one of the matters which they swept under the congressional rug was Sutter's bill.

Sutter gave up hope. He plunged so deeply into depression that his friend, Col. Frank Schaefer, fearful for him, urged Senator Voorhees to come to his hotel room to reassure him that he would see the bill through, first thing, in the next session. A conflict in his schedule made Voorhees postpone the breakfast meeting with the old pioneer by one day. After fourteen years of frustration and disappointment, it was just one day too many. When Voorhees called at Charles Mades' Pennsylvania Hotel on June 18, 1880, he found that the Father of California had died earlier that afternoon, of despair.

EPILOGUE

SINCE J. Ross Browne's time, John Sutter has been called the Father of California. If we mean American California, he deserves the title—much as we might prefer a less clay-footed founder for the Golden State. More than any other single person he developed California's mineral and agricultural wealth.

A very common man and, like John C. Frémont, often not a very likable one, Sutter was not of the stuff from which the truly heroic are made. His sole talent—and it was a great one—was for sheer survival. He also possessed vision and compassion, commodities rare in frontier California. Romantics have created a noble Sutter, robbing himself to give to the poor. This is no more false than the unfortunate image drawn by his detractors. Only the slapdash school of biographers have found him an easy subject; they simply forced him into a preconceived stereotype. But Sutter stubbornly resists easy categorizing. He was a man of paradox—at once opportunist and philanthropist; one year largely a conniver, the next, an open-hearted host. He was a soldier of fortune but a picaresque one, his adventuring modified by a prudence which some call a lack of common courage. If a scoundrel

351

at all, he was too lazy or busy to be a thorough-going one; that much is certain.

No one has yet satisfactorily explained how Sutter, placed in such a supremely advantageous position, bungled his opportunities during the Mexican War, the Gold Rush and the less spectacular but no less important Land Rush. The secret of failure is often harder to determine than that of success.

Why was he no longer able, after about 1845, to adapt to changes of environment and opportunity? Was it simply the aging process? Did he merely go soft after forty? It did not happen to Bidwell, or Caleb Greenwood, or to many others, though many were swept to defeat like Sutter. Was it alcohol? Possibly. Liquor became Sutter's anodyne, his crutch. Perhaps there is no single clear-cut answer, unless he lay under a tinker's curse—damned to failure and always at the eleventh hour.

I believe that a kind of erosion of his powers set in, with success and increasing age and overindulgence. Somehow, Sutter gradually lost the knack of coping with new situations, new challenges. This fatal indecisiveness began as a numbness—a numbness that soon became paralysis. Like many a man before him, he lacked the strength of character to support the strain of his individualism and optimism. The genial, expansive but unscrupulous Sutter of youth was transformed by relative prosperity and genuine prestige into a respectable and fairly honest man—and it proved his undoing. When he acquired scruples and lost the need to live by the sharpness of his wits, he also lost his toughness of character. It was as if he disarmed himself. Later, when he was surrounded by rough Americans of his own earlier stamp, he suddenly found himself ill equipped to deal with them. As a California *patrón* he could no longer descend to their level. Assailed by self-doubt, he sought escape in the bottle and became increasingly irresolute and powerless.

But, for all this, Sutter's story is not a tragedy. It is an irony. Hence the title of this book: *Fool's Gold*. Fool's gold is ironic, false gold—iron pyrites. The myth is that Sutter, the discoverer of gold (which he was not), was alone plunged into utter ruin. It happened to almost all his old comrades eventually. Nor was his ruin complete; he was never near starvation or even poverty. He lived in the finest house in his town and died in a Washington hotel.

Perhaps Sutter was schizophrenic. That would explain the two diametrically opposed pictures of the man provided by those who knew him as well as by those depending upon hearsay. Sutter's partisans make him out to be an idealized frontier hero. J. Wesley Jones' verdict is, "Captain Sutter is a man of enlarged views, indomitable energy, and a noble and generous heart." Jacob B. Landis, in "The Life and Work of General John A. Sutter" (*Papers Read Before the Lancaster [Penna.] Historical Society*, XVII, No. 10, 1913), insists that Sutter's intrepid military spirit, not opportunism, led him to the New World and eventually to the Sacramento. Mrs. James Gregson typifies a whole legion of Californians ready to vouch for Sutter's generosity. On October 18, 1845, when rumors came to New Helvetia that Governor Pico would order Sutter to oust all American immigrants from California, she heard him say: "By Joe! You stand by me; I stand by you, to the end!" After his death, she reminisced, "The old captain was very generous; to a fault. So large was his heart that he could not say no."

Others have been less impressed. Sutter's critics range from the mildly disparaging to those who view him as a pathological adventurer. Albert Ferdinand Morris, for example: "Captain Sutter is a vain man, fond of pomp and parade. He liked to sally forth with a mounted guard of his Indian troopers, elatedly crying out, 'Dis does remind me so of my own country; dis does remind me of old times!' " Hubert H. Bancroft is ambivalent. At first, he seems ready to forgive Sutter's weaknesses and compliments him on his gift for making friends of men of all races. He admits that Sutter, easily a match for Mexican-Californians, was the victim of rascals from the States who were more cunning than he was. But ultimately Bancroft regards him as a mere adventurer, worthy of no admiration or even sympathy and denies his greatness. Bancroft simply cannot accept the idea of a "mere" dreamer being of any worth to the California frontier. His verdict on Sutter is that of a hard-headed businessman-historian:

> He was great only in his wonderful personal magnetism and power of making friends, for a time, of all who could be useful to him; good only in the possession of kindly impulses. His energy was a phase of his visionary and reckless enthusiasm; his executive ability did not extend beyond the skillful control of Indians and the management of an isolated trading post. Of principle, of honor, or respect for the rights of others, we find but slight trace in him. There was no side of any controversy that he would not readily adopt at the call of interest; nationality, religion, friendship, obligation, consistency, counted for little or nothing. There were no classes of his associates, hardly an individual, with whom he did not quarrel or whom, in his anger, he did not roundly abuse.... He never hesitated to assume any obligation for the future without regard to his ability to meet it; he rarely, if ever, paid a debt when due; and a general, vague, and kindly purpose to fulfill all his promises in the brilliant future but imperfectly excuses his shortcomings.

Bancroft's statements are true enough, yet his evaluation of Sutter, on the whole, is unfair. Josiah Royce makes a more balanced estimate. He gives Sutter his due, and not one ounce more, in a succinct paragraph in his classic, *California,* published in Boston in 1866 and still in print (New York, Knopf, 1948). First, Royce insists, rightly, that Sutter was more picturesque than manly. Then he goes on: "In character, Sutter was an affable and hospitable visionary, of hazy ideas, with a great liking for popularity and with a mania for undertaking too much. A heroic figure he was not, although his romantic position as pioneer in the great valley made him seem so to many travelers and historians. When the gold-seekers later came, the ambitious Sutter utterly lost his head and threw away all his truly wonderful opportunities." Acknowledging that Sutter suffered from American rascality, Royce makes the extremely important point that "If he was often wronged, he was also often in the wrong; and his fate was the ordinary one of the persistent and unteachable dreamer."

This hard-boiled estimate of Sutter as a born loser is likely to be as sound an assay as we shall ever have. Still, Royce's view of the improvident colonizer with the great appetite for life needs to be tempered somewhat by the voice of humanity; in this case, the voice of author James Hutchings:

"The men who shared most largely in his princely hospitality and possessions were the first to take advantage of it by stealing away his possessions. . . . May God forgive us Californians."

From these sharply divergent views, a picture of Sutter gradually emerges. He appears as a failure, but a spectacular one—a dreamer in a day of fierce, no-holds-barred competition. Even if we choose to ignore his philanthropy and compassion, his work as a colonizer—work which dominated a whole decade of California history—is surely impressive. In his way, Sutter belongs to that class of loners who preceded the first wave of men into the wilderness, far in the van of the more orthodox—and more ruthless—builders of civilization.

Weaknesses Sutter had by the score. He was little or no more honest than most of his contemporaries, which is hardly high praise. But he was at least kindly and easy-going. And if he was less astute than some of his rivals, he was also less calculating. His own yearnings for self-aggrandizement were checked by his kindness, prodigality and compassion.

What is too often forgotten is Sutter's vision. He saw that gold would be a curse to most Californians, ruining far more than it saved. His faith in the gold of California grain over the glinting placers was well founded, but it would take California decades to recognize the fact. Even today, with polluted air and water, devastated redwood groves and gutted mines, we are paying for the victory of the get-rich-quick motto California adopted during the unprincipled scramble for gold and land.

The last two lines of Sam Walter Foss' famous poem seem written to describe Sutter, the visionary: "Men with empires in their purpose, And new eras in their brains."

BIBLIOGRAPHICAL REPRISE

Scholars, collectors, librarians and *aficionados* of Western Americana will have to be content with these few paragraphs in lieu of a heavily documented narrative, pocked with the stigmata of formalized scholarship—footnotes. I have done my homework but rather than waste precious space in proving it by citing innumerable references, I am going to review only the books, manuscripts and articles which were most useful—or most distressing—to me. Readers need go no further than these pages for suggestions for further study of Capt. John A. Sutter. Those who wish to read more widely and deeply in his period of California history are urged to see the reference librarian of their choice, for directions to either Robert E. Cowan's *Bibliography of the History of California* or the California Library Association's *California Local History*.

Far too much has been written about Sutter and far too little has been said. Few are the primary sources and most of the secondary works should really be called tertiary. Let us review, first, the full-length volumes commonly accepted as biographies of Sutter. Although Sutter's story looms large in Edward E. Dunbar's *The Romance of the Age* (New York, D. Appleton, 1867), it is really a survey of the Gold Rush, Mexican War, Mormons in California and much else. Therefore, Thomas J. Schoonover's *The Life and Times of General*

John A. Sutter (Sacramento, D. Johnston & Co., 1895) might be considered first.

This volume was issued in a revised and enlarged edition in 1907 (Sacramento, Bullock & Carpenter). It is written in ornate Victorian prose. Thus, where today one would say that Sutter left his boats to encamp near the confluence of the American and Sacramento rivers, Schoonover poetizes: "Remote from the music of enterprise, in a solitude seldom broken except by the notes of the wild fowl and the guttural tones of the Red-man, our adventurer, with but fifteen men to assist him, pitched his tent, mounted his guns, established sentinels and laid the foundation of an empire which, for the beneficial consequences it entailed, is peerless in the republic of colonies. Sutter now found himself legally established in a country unsurpassed in natural resources, extending its boundaries over every variety of soil and climate, watered by the tranquil Sacramento and its tributaries and everywhere canopied by the softest tints of azure." A little of this ornamented prose is amusing but 310 pages of it cloys, like an entire meal of maraschino cherries.

Schooner's first line reads, "In preparing this narrative, my aim has been to preserve fidelity to truth." But his aim is woefully wide of truth, much of the time, because he absorbed much of Sutter's wishful thinking and daydreaming. Sutter's imagination was always several Spanish leagues ahead of his situation, but Schoonover did not realize this.

The volume is also, like Dunbar's, a grab bag of subjects. The author leaves Sutter to engage in rambling digressions on everything from bull fights to the San Francisco vigilantes.

After these two museum pieces of Dunbar and Schoonover, there is a lack of full-length narratives on Sutter until the appearance in 1925 of Blaise Cendrars' *L'Or,* a work which is still available in French in the paperback *Livre du Poche* series. In its American edition, *Sutter's Gold* (New York, Harper & Brothers, 1926), it was very successful, inspiring a motion picture, starring Edward Arnold, which can still be seen from time to time on television's late late show. *Sutter's Gold* may be the worst book ever written about California. As biography or history it is about as dependable as the third-rate novel about Sutter and his California, Julio Nombela y Tabares' *La Fiebre de Riquezas* (*The Lust For Riches*), which was published serially in Madrid in 1871 and 1872. Horrifyingly, many catalogers have classed Cendrars' pastiche of garbled history, myth and fiction as biography. The book will amuse students of Western Americana, for it is one long series of bloopers. When Sutter tosses a coin to prompt a decision, it is a doubloon; the Oregon missionaries whom he meets are on their way to tend to the spiritual needs of the Crees in Oregon; he is warned that Apaches are on the warpath in the Cascades of the Pacific Northwest. Sutter's cattle are all pedigreed stock; his mud fort, the focus of great alleys of magnolias, orange trees and banana palms, is almost overgrown with climbing roses and bougain-villeas. Best of all, Sutter's wife—who shared his last thirty years and then survived him—is depicted as falling dead on the very stoop of Hock Farm (renamed the Hermitage by Cendrars, perhaps out of affection for Andy Jackson) when she arrives in California.

Cendrars' fantasy and corrupted history spread and infected the next two—supposed—nonfiction studies of Sutter. Both authors indulge in flights of fancy, although neither with the florid imagination of Blaise Cendrars. Julian Dana's popular volume, *Sutter of California* (New York, Press of the Pioneers, 1934), is not only overly eulogistic, turning the Swiss pioneer into a knight in shining broadcloth, but is marred by invented conversations and incidents. It is, in fact, historical fiction. Similar to Dana's work is Marguerite Eyer Wilbur's *John Sutter, Rascal and Adventurer* (New York, Liveright, 1949), except that she considers him a scoundrel. It is fictionalized biography, and is still in print.

Sandwiched, chronologically, between the books of Dana and Wilbur is a much more factual volume, *Sutter's Own Story* by Dr. Erwin G. Gudde (New York, Putnam's, 1936). This book is based largely on Sutter's manuscript reminiscences, dictated to H. H. Bancroft in 1876 and now in the Bancroft Library. In his Author's Note, Dr. Gudde states plainly that he has rewritten the entire story, yet careless scholars fail to realize that the words within quotation marks are often *not* those actually used by Sutter. I have used the original manuscript in order to have Sutter's own style and flavor, not the improvements of his editor.

The only recent adult book on Sutter, Oscar Lewis' *Sutter's Fort* (Englewood Cliffs, N.J., Prentice-Hall, 1966), is a general survey of the history of New Helvetia and its founder. It is well written and provides pleasant reading but does not probe even as deeply as the last biography I shall mention—which is also the best: James P. Zollinger's *Sutter, the Man and His Empire* (New York, Oxford Press, 1939), a good book which should never have been allowed to go out of print. Zollinger's work is sometimes referred to as the "definitive" book or *the* biography of Sutter. It is hardly that, any more than the book in hand is to remain the last word on the subject. Zollinger went overboard on a psychoanalytic appraisal of Sutter from too insecure a base. Much has been learned about Captain Sutter since 1939, too, so that a few correctives can now be applied to Zollinger's narrative. The author states that Sutter probably did not have any military service in Switzerland, even as a militiaman. My Swiss correspondent, Dr. Dora Grob, found records of Sutter's military service and promotions in the archives in Berne, as did another friend, Dr. John Hawgood of the University of Birmingham, England. Zollinger doubts that Sutter ever declared his intention to become an American citizen while in Missouri. I have found the document, along with property records of Sutter's, in the manuscripts of the Missouri Historical Society, St. Louis. Apparently, Zollinger did not make use of the manuscripts on Sutter in the Hudson's Bay Company's Beaver House in London, which throw light on his conflict with the company trappers in California and his efforts, through Peter Burnett and his son, August, to pay off his Honourable Company debts. Finally, John Hawgood's criticism of Zollinger, for making Sutter prematurely senile and for ignoring his thirty years' war with the United States government, is well taken.

I found the best sources, by far, to be the manuscripts of Sutter and those of his friends and enemies. Besides his dictation of 1876 to H. H. Bancroft, there are many of Sutter's letters to study in the California State Library and in the Bancroft Library, plus a few scattered elsewhere. Especially good are his letters to Pierson B. Reading in the State Library; they reveal the real Sutter more than most of his correspondence. (I must warn researchers, however, that the typescript copies of the originals in the State Library are not completely reliable either in transcription or translation. They should be used with much care.) Huntington Library's resources on the subject are considerable, too, and most fruitful are Edward Kern's Fort Sutter papers and William A. Leidesdorff's manuscripts.

Sutter's so-called *Diary* was published in the San Francisco *Argonaut* of June 26, February 2, 9 and 16, 1878, but it is less complete and less useful than the 1876 dictation. Edited by Douglas S. Watson, it was reprinted as a book titled *The Diary of Johann August Sutter* (San Francisco, Grabhorn Press, 1932). Far more important is the great record book of Sutter's Fort for the period between September 1845 and May 1848. From the original in the keeping of the Society of California Pioneers there was published the *New Helvetia Diary* (San Francisco, Grabhorn Press, 1939). It is of the greatest value in amending John Sutter's faults of memory and veracity. The greatest single collection of manuscripts backgrounding Sutter has been published. This is George P. Hammond's superb editing of *The Larkin Papers* (Berkeley, University of California, 1951–64). The ten volumes of papers themselves are of great value, and Dr. Hammond's prefatory syntheses, taken together, constitute a fine history, in brief, of early California and deserve to be reprinted on their own.

I must observe that no one, as yet, has collected all of John A. Sutter's papers, much less edited and published them, although Dr. John A. Hawgood is currently engaged in that task. Single letters and groups of letters on or by Sutter have been published in journals and as small books. An example would be *Pioneers of the Sacramento* (San Francisco, Book Club of California, 1953); another is *Six French Letters, Captain John A. Sutter to Jean Jacques Vioget, 1842–43* (Sacramento, Nugget Press, 1942). One published letter attributed to Sutter is a fraud. It purports to be from him to a brother, Andrew, dated February 10, 1847; and is found in *Pacific Unitarian,* XXVI, No. 10, September 1917.

For the European period of Sutter's life, Zollinger's biography is unexcelled. He also contributed an article to the *California Historical Society Quarterly* (XIV, No. I, 28–46, March 1935) titled "John Augustus Sutter's European Background."

In accounting for Sutter in Missouri and New Mexico, the best source is that of the bitter Johann Laufkotter, whose *John A. Sutter, Sr., and His Grants* (Sacramento, Russell and Winterburn, 1867) deserves far more use by historians. It must be used with care, of course, because of Laufkotter's jealousy and bias. For details of

Sutter's transcontinental trek, I am indebted to the volumes of my friend, Dr. Clifford M. Drury: *Elkanah and Mary Walker, Pioneers* . . . (Caldwell, Idaho, Caxton, 1940); *The Diaries and Letters of Henry H. Spalding* (Glendale, Calif., Arthur H. Clark, 1958); and *First White Women over the Rockies* (Glendale, Calif., Arthur H. Clark, 1963–66).

There is little to be found on Sutter's Hawaiian stay, even in the Honolulu press, but Doyce Nunis' editing of *The California Diary of Faxon D. Atherton* is helpful (San Francisco, California Historical Society, 1964).

For Sutter's earliest days in California, one should refer to Sir George Simpson's *Narrative of a Journey Round the World* (London, H. Colburn, 1847); Charles Wilkes' *Narrative of the United States Exploring Expedition* . . . (Philadelphia, C. Sherman, 1844); George Colvocoresses's *Four Years in a Government Exploring Expedition* (New York, Cornish, Lamport, 1852); and G. M. Waseurtz af Sandels' *A Sojourn in California* (San Francisco, Book Club of California, 1945).

Best of all sources on Sutter is probably Heinrich Lienhard's memoir. This was translated, edited, and published—*in part*—by Marguerite Eyer Wilbur as *A Pioneer at Sutter's Fort, 1846–1850* (Los Angeles, Calafia Society, 1941). This graphic, critical portrait of Sutter and his fortress should be translated, edited and published *in full*. Perhaps some scholar like Dr. Hawgood will do the job. It is of the highest priority. Essential to an understanding of Sutter's tangled familial relationships is Allan R. Ottley's editing and annotating of John A. Sutter, Jr.'s *Statement Regarding Early California Experiences* (Sacramento, Sacramento Book Collectors Club, 1943).

For the dramatic story of Marshall's discovery of the placers and the Gold Rush itself, Sutter's own account, "The Discovery of Gold in California" in *Hutching's California Magazine* (II, No. 5, 194–198, November 1857), and Marshall's, which immediately followed Sutter's on pages 199–202 of the same issue of the magazine, should be joined by two modern books. These are Erwin G. Gudde's edition of Henry W. Bigler's diary, titled *Bigler's Chronicle of the West* (Berkeley, University of California, 1962), and Rodman W. Paul's *The California Gold Discovery* (Georgetown, Calif., Talisman Press, 1966).

Of general works about early California, there is no end. Hubert H. Bancroft's seven-volume *History of California* (San Francisco, A. L. Bancroft, 1884–90) is still the starting point for all serious investigations of the state's early story. Works of closer focus on the subject at hand include John Bidwell's *Echoes of the Past* (Chicago, R. R. Donnelly & Sons, 1928), Peter H. Burnett's *Recollections and Opinions of an Old Pioneer* (New York, D. Appleton, 1880), Edwin Bryant's *What I Saw in California* (New York, D. Appleton, 1898), and William Heath Davis' *Seventy-five Years in California* (San Francisco, John Howell, 1929). Almost all such works as Bryant's or Joseph Warren Revere's *A Tour of Duty in California* (New York, C. S. Francis, 1849) yield honest information. Possibly the only exceptions are the works of Thomas J. Farnham, which should be avoided, and Henry Vizetelly's spurious *California: Four Months Among the Gold Finders of California* (Paris, A. and W. Galignani, 1849), in which Sutter sports a (nonexistent) saber scar from his Polytechnic days.

Masters theses and doctoral dissertations, such as that of Dr. Clarence John DuFour, are listed in Pamela A. Bleich's bibliography, *A Study of Graduate Research in California History . . .* which, in seven parts as of 1966, appears in the *California Historical Society Quarterly,* starting with XLIII, No. 3, for September 1964.

Newspapers such as the *Daily Alta California* and the *Sacramento Union* I found of considerable value, also the pioneering paper (now available as a reprint), *The California Star, 1847–48* (Berkeley, Howell-North, 1965). The best newspaper index in the world for Californiana is that housed in Allan R. Ottley's card files of the California Section, State Library, Sacramento. Periodical literature on Sutter is voluminous but is largely rehash and seldom useful. Two recent articles are exceptions—Doyce Nunis' "A Mysterious Chapter in the Life of John A. Sutter" in the *California Historical Society Quarterly* (XXXVIII, No. 4, December 1959, 321–29) and John A. Hawgood's "John Augustus Sutter, A Reappraisal" in *Arizona and the West* (IV, No. 4, Winter, 1962, 345-56.)

INDEX

INDEX

367

MAP
OF
UPPER CALIFORNIA
BY THE
U.S. Ex. Ex.
AND
BEST AUTHORITIES
1841.